T0283411

# Cloud Computing

# Cloud Computing

Edited by
Sam Revere

Cloud Computing
Edited by Sam Revere
ISBN: 978-1-63549-676-5 (Hardback)

Published by Larsen and Keller Education,
5 Penn Plaza,
19th Floor,
New York, NY 10001, USA

**Cataloging-in-Publication Data**

Cloud computing / edited by Sam Revere.
p. cm.
Includes bibliographical references and index.
ISBN 978-1-63549-676-5
1. Cloud computing. 2. Web services. I. Revere, Sam.
QA76.585 .C56 2018
004.678 2--dc23



For more information regarding Larsen and Keller Education and its products, please visit the publisher's website www.larsen-keller.com

# Table of Contents

**Preface** VII

Chapter 1 **An Introduction to Cloud Computing** 1
a. Cloud Computing 1
b. Cloud Computing Issues 25
c. Cloud Computing Security 35
d. Cloud Computing Architecture 41
e. Cloud Management 43
f. Cloudlet 46

Chapter 2 **Data Storage in Cloud Computing** 49
a. Cloud Storage 49
b. Object Storage 53
c. File Hosting Service 61
d. Cloud Storage Gateway 65
e. Cloud E-commerce 99
f. Cooperative Storage Cloud 102

Chapter 3 **Cloud Computing as Service** 105
a. Cloud Engineering 105
b. Platform as a Service 107
c. Serverless Computing 110
d. Security as a Service 114
e. Mobile Backend as a Service 117
f. Fabasoft Folio Cloud 125
g. Rackspace Cloud 127
h. Citrix Cloud 132
i. Sun Cloud 133

Chapter 4 **Various Software Applications of Cloud Computing** 137
a. Software as a Service 137
b. Adobe Marketing Cloud 162
c. Google Cloud Connect 163
d. Cloudike 164
e. CloudMe 167
f. ownCloud 168

Chapter 5 **Technologies used in Cloud Computing** 172
a. Cloud Database 172
b. Data Center 174
c. Distributed File System for Cloud 195

d. Virtual Appliance 208
e. Virtual Private Cloud 210
f. Cloud Communications 211

**Permissions**

**Index**

# Preface

Cloud computing is a modern technology which enables Internet based computing and provides on demand data to computers and other devices. Through this technology, any company or individual can access the same data on various devices by the use of Internet. The different types of clouds present are multicloud, community cloud, private cloud, hybrid cloud, distributed cloud, intercloud, etc. The textbook is a compilation of chapters that discuss the most vital concepts in the field of cloud computing. While understanding the long-term perspectives of the topics, the book makes an effort in highlighting their impact as a modern tool for the growth of this discipline. It will provide comprehensive knowledge to the readers.

A detailed account of the significant topics covered in this book is provided below:

Chapter 1- Cloud computing provides Internet based services to users that allow for easy sharing of data and information. It is an advanced computing process that gives access to databases, servers, and miscellaneous applications. This is an introductory chapter which will introduce briefly all the significant aspects of cloud computing.

Chapter 2- Data storage in cloud computing can be done through cloud storage, object storage, file hosting service and cloud storage gateway. Each hosting service uses a particular architecture to appeal to different needs. This chapter has been carefully written to provide an easy understanding of the varied facets of cloud computing.

Chapter 3- Commercially, cloud computing is used in providing various services such as Platform as a service (PaaS), cloud engineering, Security as a service (SECaaS), etc. Such services aid businesses and entrepreneurships. The aspects elucidated in this chapter are of vital importance, and provide a better understanding of cloud computing.

Chapter 4- Popular software are now hosted in clouds for easy access to users. They are often referred to as "on-demand software". Google Cloud Connect, Adobe Marketing Cloud, Cloudike and CloudMe are some of the software listed in this section. The chapter on cloud computing offers an insightful focus, keeping in mind the complex subject matter.

Chapter 5- Cloud computing uses various technologies such as data centers, distributed file system for cloud, virtual private cloud and virtual appliance. Data centers house computers and storage systems and telecommunication networks. Cloud computing is best understood in confluence with the major topics listed in the following chapter.

It gives me an immense pleasure to thank our entire team for their efforts. Finally in the end, I would like to thank my family and colleagues who have been a great source of inspiration and support.

**Editor**

# An Introduction to Cloud Computing

Cloud computing provides Internet based services to users that allow for easy sharing of data and information. It is an advanced computing process that gives access to databases, servers, and miscellaneous applications. This is an introductory chapter which will introduce briefly all the significant aspects of cloud computing.

## Cloud Computing

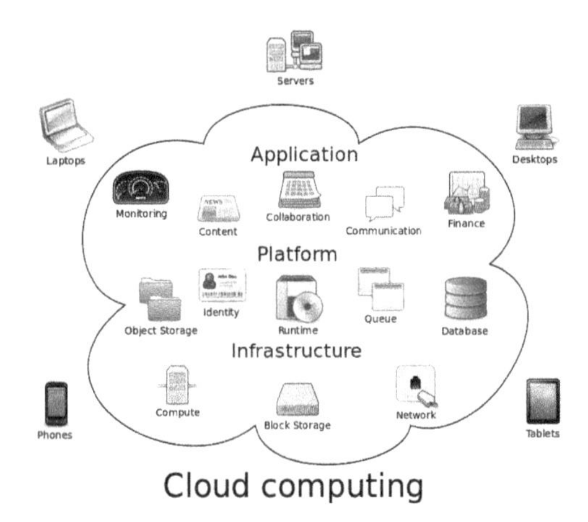


Cloud computing metaphor: For a user, the network elements representing the provider-rendered services are invisible, as if obscured by a cloud.

Cloud computing is a type of Internet-based computing that provides shared computer processing resources and data to computers and other devices on demand. It is a model for enabling ubiquitous, on-demand access to a shared pool of configurable computing resources (e.g., computer networks, servers, storage, applications and services), which can be rapidly provisioned and released with minimal management effort. Cloud computing and storage solutions provide users and enterprises with various capabilities to store and process their data in either privately owned, or third-party data centers that may be located far from the user–ranging in distance from across a city to across the world. Cloud computing relies on sharing of resources to achieve coherence and economy of scale, similar to a utility (like the electricity grid) over an electricity network.

Advocates claim that cloud computing allows companies to avoid up-front infrastructure costs (e.g., purchasing servers). As well, it enables organizations to focus on their core businesses instead of spending time and money on computer infrastructure. Proponents also claim that cloud computing allows enterprises to get their applications up and running faster, with improved manageability and less maintenance, and enables information technology (IT) teams to more rapidly adjust resources to meet fluctuating and unpredictable business demand. Cloud providers typically use a "pay as you go" model. This will lead to unexpectedly high charges if administrators do not adapt to the cloud pricing model.

In 2009, the availability of high-capacity networks, low-cost computers and storage devices as well as the widespread adoption of hardware virtualization, service-oriented architecture, and autonomic and utility computing led to a growth in cloud computing. Companies can scale up as computing needs increase and then scale down again as demands decrease. In 2013, it was reported that cloud computing had become a highly demanded service or utility due to the advantages of high computing power, cheap cost of services, high performance, scalability, accessibility as well as availability. Some cloud vendors are experiencing growth rates of 50% per year, but being still in a stage of infancy, it has pitfalls that need to be addressed to make cloud computing services more reliable and user friendly.

## History

The origin of the term *cloud computing* is unclear. The word "cloud" is commonly used in science to describe a large agglomeration of objects that visually appear from a distance as a cloud and describes any set of things whose details are not further inspected in a given context. Another explanation is that the old programs that drew network schematics surrounded the icons for servers with a circle, and a cluster of servers in a network diagram had several overlapping circles, which resembled a cloud. In analogy to the above usage, the word *cloud* was used as a metaphor for the Internet and a standardized cloud-like shape was used to denote a network on telephony schematics. Later it was used to depict the Internet in computer network diagrams. With this simplification, the implication is that the specifics of how the end points of a network are connected are not relevant for the purposes of understanding the diagram. The cloud symbol was used to represent networks of computing equipment in the original ARPANET by as early as 1977, and the CSNET by 1981—both predecessors to the Internet itself.

The term *cloud* has been used to refer to platforms for distributed computing. In *Wired's* April 1994 feature "Bill and Andy's Excellent Adventure II" on the Apple spin-off General Magic, Andy Hertzfeld commented on General Magic's distributed programming language Telescript that:

> "The beauty of Telescript ... is that now, instead of just having a device to program, we now have the entire Cloud out there, where a single program can go and travel to many different sources of information and create sort of a virtual service. No

one had conceived that before. The example Jim White [the designer of Telescript, X.400 and ASN.1] uses now is a date-arranging service where a software agent goes to the flower store and orders flowers and then goes to the ticket shop and gets the tickets for the show, and everything is communicated to both parties."

References to "cloud computing" in its modern sense appeared as early as 1996, with the earliest known mention in a Compaq internal document. The popularization of the term can be traced to 2006 when Amazon.com introduced its Elastic Compute Cloud.

### 1970s

During the 1960s, the initial concepts of time-sharing became popularized via RJE (Remote Job Entry); this terminology was mostly associated with large vendors such as IBM and DEC. Full time-sharing solutions were available by the early 1970s on such platforms as Multics (on GE hardware), Cambridge CTSS, and the earliest UNIX ports (on DEC hardware). Yet, the "data center" model where users submitted jobs to operators to run on IBM mainframes was overwhelmingly predominant.

### 1990s

In the 1990s, telecommunications companies, who previously offered primarily dedicated point-to-point data circuits, began offering virtual private network (VPN) services with comparable quality of service, but at a lower cost. By switching traffic as they saw fit to balance server use, they could use overall network bandwidth more effectively. They began to use the cloud symbol to denote the demarcation point between what the provider was responsible for and what users were responsible for. Cloud computing extended this boundary to cover all servers as well as the network infrastructure. As computers became more diffused, scientists and technologists explored ways to make large-scale computing power available to more users through time-sharing. They experimented with algorithms to optimize the infrastructure, platform, and applications to prioritize CPUs and increase efficiency for end users.

### 2000s

Since 2000, cloud computing has come into existence. In early 2008, NASA's OpenNebula, enhanced in the RESERVOIR European Commission-funded project, became the first open-source software for deploying private and hybrid clouds, and for the federation of clouds. In the same year, efforts were focused on providing quality of service guarantees (as required by real-time interactive applications) to cloud-based infrastructures, in the framework of the IRMOS European Commission-funded project, resulting in a real-time cloud environment. By mid-2008, Gartner saw an opportunity for cloud computing "to shape the relationship among consumers of IT services, those who use IT services and those who sell them" and observed that "organizations are switching from company-owned hardware and software assets to per-use service-based models" so that the "projected shift to computing ... will result in dramatic growth in IT products in some areas and significant reductions in other areas."

In August 2006 Amazon introduced its Elastic Compute Cloud. Microsoft Azure was announced as "Azure" in October 2008 and was released on 1 February 2010 as Windows Azure, before being renamed to Microsoft Azure on 25 March 2014. For a time, Azure was on the TOP500 supercomputer list, before it dropped off it. In July 2010, Rackspace Hosting and NASA jointly launched an open-source cloud-software initiative known as OpenStack. The OpenStack project intended to help organizations offering cloud-computing services running on standard hardware. The early code came from NASA's Nebula platform as well as from Rackspace's Cloud Files platform. As an open source offering and along with other open-source solutions such as CloudStack, Ganeti and OpenNebula, it has attracted attention by several key communities. Several studies aim at comparing these open sources offerings based on a set of criteria.

On March 1, 2011, IBM announced the IBM SmartCloud framework to support Smarter Planet. Among the various components of the Smarter Computing foundation, cloud computing is a critical part. On June 7, 2012, Oracle announced the Oracle Cloud. While aspects of the Oracle Cloud are still in development, this cloud offering is poised to be the first to provide users with access to an integrated set of IT solutions, including the Applications (SaaS), Platform (PaaS), and Infrastructure (IaaS) layers.

In April of 2008, Google released Google App Engine in beta. In May of 2012, Google Compute Engine was released in preview, before being rolled out into General Availability in December of 2013.

## Similar Concepts

Cloud computing is the result of the evolution and adoption of existing technologies and paradigms. The goal of cloud computing is to allow users to take benefit from all of these technologies, without the need for deep knowledge about or expertise with each one of them. The cloud aims to cut costs, and helps the users focus on their core business instead of being impeded by IT obstacles. The main enabling technology for cloud computing is virtualization. Virtualization software separates a physical computing device into one or more "virtual" devices, each of which can be easily used and managed to perform computing tasks. With operating system–level virtualization essentially creating a scalable system of multiple independent computing devices, idle computing resources can be allocated and used more efficiently. Virtualization provides the agility required to speed up IT operations, and reduces cost by increasing infrastructure utilization. Autonomic computing automates the process through which the user can provision resources on-demand. By minimizing user involvement, automation speeds up the process, reduces labor costs and reduces the possibility of human errors. Users routinely face difficult business problems. Cloud computing adopts concepts from

Service-oriented Architecture (SOA) that can help the user break these problems into services that can be integrated to provide a solution. Cloud computing provides all of its resources as services, and makes use of the well-established standards and best practices gained in the domain of SOA to allow global and easy access to cloud services in a standardized way.

Cloud computing also leverages concepts from utility computing to provide metrics for the services used. Such metrics are at the core of the public cloud pay-per-use models. In addition, measured services are an essential part of the feedback loop in autonomic computing, allowing services to scale on-demand and to perform automatic failure recovery. Cloud computing is a kind of grid computing; it has evolved by addressing the QoS (quality of service) and reliability problems. Cloud computing provides the tools and technologies to build data/compute intensive parallel applications with much more affordable prices compared to traditional parallel computing techniques.

Cloud computing shares characteristics with:

- Client–server model—*Client–server computing* refers broadly to any distributed application that distinguishes between service providers (servers) and service requestors (clients).
- Computer bureau—A service bureau providing computer services, particularly from the 1960s to 1980s.
- Grid computing—"A form of distributed and parallel computing, whereby a 'super and virtual computer' is composed of a cluster of networked, loosely coupled computers acting in concert to perform very large tasks."
- Fog computing—Distributed computing paradigm that provides data, compute, storage and application services closer to client or near-user edge devices, such as network routers. Furthermore, fog computing handles data at the network level, on smart devices and on the end-user client side (e.g. mobile devices), instead of sending data to a remote location for processing.
- Dew computing—In the existing computing hierarchy, the Dew computing is positioned as the ground level for the cloud and fog computing paradigms. Compared to fog computing, which supports emerging IoT applications that demand real-time and predictable latency and the dynamic network reconfigurability, Dew computing pushes the frontiers to computing applications, data, and low level services away from centralized virtual nodes to the end users.
- Mainframe computer—Powerful computers used mainly by large organizations for critical applications, typically bulk data processing such as: census; industry and consumer statistics; police and secret intelligence services; enterprise resource planning; and financial transaction processing.

- Utility computing—The "packaging of computing resources, such as computation and storage, as a metered service similar to a traditional public utility, such as electricity."
- Peer-to-peer—A distributed architecture without the need for central coordination. Participants are both suppliers and consumers of resources (in contrast to the traditional client–server model).
- Green computing
- Cloud sandbox—A live, isolated computer environment in which a program, code or file can run without affecting the application in which it runs.

## Characteristics

Cloud computing exhibits the following key characteristics:

- Agility for organizations may be improved, as cloud computing may increase users' flexibility with re-provisioning, adding, or expanding technological infrastructure resources.
- Cost reductions are claimed by cloud providers. A public-cloud delivery model converts capital expenditures (e.g., buying servers) to operational expenditure. This purportedly lowers barriers to entry, as infrastructure is typically provided by a third party and need not be purchased for one-time or infrequent intensive computing tasks. Pricing on a utility computing basis is "fine-grained", with usage-based billing options. As well, less in-house IT skills are required for implementation of projects that use cloud computing. The e-FISCAL project's state-of-the-art repository contains several articles looking into cost aspects in more detail, most of them concluding that costs savings depend on the type of activities supported and the type of infrastructure available in-house.
- Device and location independence enable users to access systems using a web browser regardless of their location or what device they use (e.g., PC, mobile phone). As infrastructure is off-site (typically provided by a third-party) and accessed via the Internet, users can connect to it from anywhere.
- Maintenance of cloud computing applications is easier, because they do not need to be installed on each user's computer and can be accessed from different places (e.g., different work locations, while travelling, etc.).
- Multitenancy enables sharing of resources and costs across a large pool of users thus allowing for:
    - centralization of infrastructure in locations with lower costs (such as real estate, electricity, etc.)

- peak-load capacity increases (users need not engineer and pay for the resources and equipment to meet their highest possible load-levels)
- utilisation and efficiency improvements for systems that are often only 10–20% utilised.

- Performance is monitored by IT experts from the service provider, and consistent and loosely coupled architectures are constructed using web services as the system interface.
- Productivity may be increased when multiple users can work on the same data simultaneously, rather than waiting for it to be saved and emailed. Time may be saved as information does not need to be re-entered when fields are matched, nor do users need to install application software upgrades to their computer.
- Reliability improves with the use of multiple redundant sites, which makes well-designed cloud computing suitable for business continuity and disaster recovery.
- Scalability and elasticity via dynamic ("on-demand") provisioning of resources on a fine-grained, self-service basis in near real-time (Note, the VM startup time varies by VM type, location, OS and cloud providers), without users having to engineer for peak loads. This gives the ability to scale up when the usage need increases or down if resources are not being used.
- Security can improve due to centralization of data, increased security-focused resources, etc., but concerns can persist about loss of control over certain sensitive data, and the lack of security for stored kernels. Security is often as good as or better than other traditional systems, in part because service providers are able to devote resources to solving security issues that many customers cannot afford to tackle or which they lack the technical skills to address. However, the complexity of security is greatly increased when data is distributed over a wider area or over a greater number of devices, as well as in multi-tenant systems shared by unrelated users. In addition, user access to security audit logs may be difficult or impossible. Private cloud installations are in part motivated by users' desire to retain control over the infrastructure and avoid losing control of information security.

The National Institute of Standards and Technology's definition of cloud computing identifies "five essential characteristics":

*On-demand self-service.* A consumer can unilaterally provision computing capabilities, such as server time and network storage, as needed automatically without requiring human interaction with each service provider.

*Broad network access.* Capabilities are available over the network and accessed through standard mechanisms that promote use by heterogeneous thin or thick client platforms (e.g., mobile phones, tablets, laptops, and workstations).

*Resource pooling.* The provider's computing resources are pooled to serve multiple consumers using a multi-tenant model, with different physical and virtual resources dynamically assigned and reassigned according to consumer demand.

*Rapid elasticity.* Capabilities can be elastically provisioned and released, in some cases automatically, to scale rapidly outward and inward commensurate with demand. To the consumer, the capabilities available for provisioning often appear unlimited and can be appropriated in any quantity at any time.

*Measured service.* Cloud systems automatically control and optimize resource use by leveraging a metering capability at some level of abstraction appropriate to the type of service (e.g., storage, processing, bandwidth, and active user accounts). Resource usage can be monitored, controlled, and reported, providing transparency for both the provider and consumer of the utilized service.

—*National Institute of Standards and Technology*

## Service Models

Though service-oriented architecture advocates "everything as a service" (with the acronyms EaaS or XaaS or simply aas), cloud-computing providers offer their "services" according to different models, of which the three standard models per NIST are Infrastructure as a Service (IaaS), Platform as a Service (PaaS), and Software as a Service (SaaS). These models offer increasing abstraction; they are thus often portrayed as a *layers* in a stack: infrastructure-, platform- and software-as-a-service, but these need not be related. For example, one can provide SaaS implemented on physical machines (bare metal), without using underlying PaaS or IaaS layers, and conversely one can run a program on IaaS and access it directly, without wrapping it as SaaS.

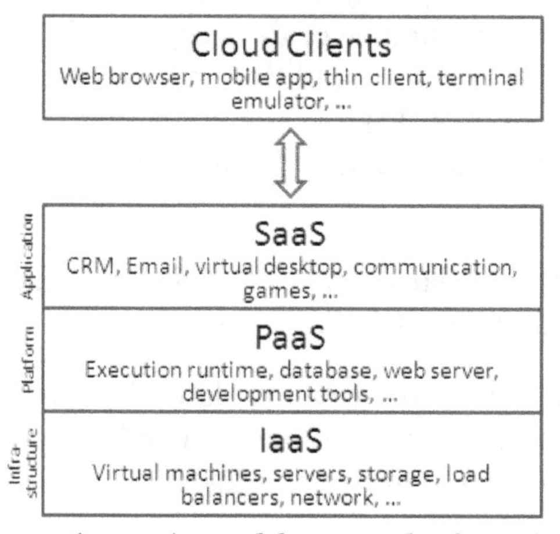


Cloud computing service models arranged as layers in a stack

The NIST's definition of cloud computing defines the service models as follows:

*Software as a Service (SaaS).* The capability provided to the consumer is to use the provider's applications running on a cloud infrastructure. The applications are accessible from various client devices through either a thin client interface, such as a web browser (e.g., web-based email), or a program interface. The consumer does not manage or control the underlying cloud infrastructure including network, servers, operating systems, storage, or even individual application capabilities, with the possible exception of limited user-specific application configuration settings.

*Platform as a Service (PaaS).* The capability provided to the consumer is to deploy onto the cloud infrastructure consumer-created or acquired applications created using programming languages, libraries, services, and tools supported by the provider. The consumer does not manage or control the underlying cloud infrastructure including network, servers, operating systems, or storage, but has control over the deployed applications and possibly configuration settings for the application-hosting environment.

*Infrastructure as a Service (IaaS).* The capability provided to the consumer is to provision processing, storage, networks, and other fundamental computing resources where the consumer is able to deploy and run arbitrary software, which can include operating systems and applications. The consumer does not manage or control the underlying cloud infrastructure but has control over operating systems, storage, and deployed applications; and possibly limited control of select networking components (e.g., host firewalls).

## Infrastructure as a Service (IaaS)

According to the Internet Engineering Task Force (IETF), the most basic cloud-service model is that of providers offering computing infrastructure – virtual machines and other resources – as a service to subscribers. Infrastructure as a service (IaaS) refers to online services that abstract the user from the details of infrastructure like physical computing resources, location, data partitioning, scaling, security, backup etc. A hypervisor, such as Xen, Oracle VirtualBox, Oracle VM, KVM, VMware ESX/ESXi, or Hyper-V, runs the virtual machines as guests. Pools of hypervisors within the cloud operational system can support large numbers of virtual machines and the ability to scale services up and down according to customers' varying requirements. Linux containers run in isolated partitions of a single Linux kernel running directly on the physical hardware. Linux cgroups and namespaces are the underlying Linux kernel technologies used to isolate, secure and manage the containers. Containerisation offers higher performance than virtualization, because there is no hypervisor overhead. Also, container capacity auto-scales dynamically with computing load, which eliminates the problem of over-provisioning and enables usage-based billing. IaaS clouds often offer additional resources such as a virtual-machine disk-image library, raw block storage, file or object storage, firewalls, load balancers, IP addresses, virtual local area networks (VLANs), and software bundles.

IaaS-cloud providers supply these resources on-demand from their large pools of equipment installed in data centers. For wide-area connectivity, customers can use either the Internet or carrier clouds (dedicated virtual private networks). To deploy their applications, cloud users install operating-system images and their application software on the cloud infrastructure. In this model, the cloud user patches and maintains the operating systems and the application software. Cloud providers typically bill IaaS services on a utility computing basis: cost reflects the amount of resources allocated and consumed.

## Platform as a Service (PaaS)

PaaS vendors offer a development environment to application developers. The provider typically develops toolkit and standards for development and channels for distribution and payment. In the PaaS models, cloud providers deliver a computing platform, typically including operating system, programming-language execution environment, database, and web server. Application developers can develop and run their software solutions on a cloud platform without the cost and complexity of buying and managing the underlying hardware and software layers. With some PaaS offers like Microsoft Azure and Google App Engine, the underlying computer and storage resources scale automatically to match application demand so that the cloud user does not have to allocate resources manually. The latter has also been proposed by an architecture aiming to facilitate real-time in cloud environments. Even more specific application types can be provided via PaaS, such as media encoding as provided by services like bitcodin.com or media.io.

Some integration and data management providers have also embraced specialized applications of PaaS as delivery models for data solutions. Examples include iPaaS (Integration Platform as a Service) and dPaaS (Data Platform as a Service). iPaaS enables customers to develop, execute and govern integration flows. Under the iPaaS integration model, customers drive the development and deployment of integrations without installing or managing any hardware or middleware. dPaaS delivers integration—and data-management—products as a fully managed service. Under the dPaaS model, the PaaS provider, not the customer, manages the development and execution of data solutions by building tailored data applications for the customer. dPaaS users retain transparency and control over data through data-visualization tools. Platform as a Service (PaaS) consumers do not manage or control the underlying cloud infrastructure including network, servers, operating systems, or storage, but have control over the deployed applications and possibly configuration settings for the application-hosting environment.

A recent specialized PaaS is the Blockchain as a Service (BaaS), that some vendors such as Microsoft Azure have already included in their PaaS offering.

## Software as a Service (SaaS)

In the software as a service (SaaS) model, users gain access to application software and databases. Cloud providers manage the infrastructure and platforms that run the applications. SaaS is sometimes referred to as "on-demand software" and is usually priced on a pay-per-use basis or using a subscription fee. In the SaaS model, cloud providers install and operate application software in the cloud and cloud users access the software from cloud clients. Cloud users do not manage the cloud infrastructure and platform where the application runs. This eliminates the need to install and run the application on the cloud user's own computers, which simplifies maintenance and support. Cloud applications differ from other applications in their scalability—which can be achieved by cloning tasks onto multiple virtual machines at run-time to meet changing work demand. Load balancers distribute the work over the set of virtual machines. This process is transparent to the cloud user, who sees only a single access-point. To accommodate a large number of cloud users, cloud applications can be *multitenant*, meaning that any machine may serve more than one cloud-user organization.

The pricing model for SaaS applications is typically a monthly or yearly flat fee per user, so prices become scalable and adjustable if users are added or removed at any point. Proponents claim that SaaS gives a business the potential to reduce IT operational costs by outsourcing hardware and software maintenance and support to the cloud provider. This enables the business to reallocate IT operations costs away from hardware/software spending and from personnel expenses, towards meeting other goals. In addition, with applications hosted centrally, updates can be released without the need for users to install new software. One drawback of SaaS comes with storing the users' data on the cloud provider's server. As a result, there could be unauthorized access to the data. For this reason, users are increasingly adopting intelligent third-party key-management systems to help secure their data.

### Security as a Service (SECaaS)

Security as a service (SECaaS) is a business model in which a large service provider integrates their security services into a corporate infrastructure on a subscription basis more cost effectively than most individuals or corporations can provide on their own, when total cost of ownership is considered. In this scenario, security is delivered as a service from the cloud, without requiring on-premises hardware avoiding substantial capital outlays. These security services often include authentication, anti-virus, anti-malware/spyware, intrusion detection, and security event management, among others.

### Mobile "Backend" as a Service (MBaaS)

In the mobile "backend" as a service (m) model, also known as backend as a service (BaaS), web app and mobile app developers are provided with a way to link their applications to cloud storage and cloud computing services with application programming interfaces (APIs) exposed to their applications and custom software development kits (SDKs). Services include user management, push notifications, integration with social networking services and more. This is a relatively recent model in cloud computing, with most BaaS startups dating from 2011 or later but trends indicate that these services are gaining significant mainstream traction with enterprise consumers.

## Serverless Computing

Serverless computing is a cloud computing code execution model in which the cloud provider fully manages starting and stopping virtual machines as necessary to serve requests, and requests are billed by an abstract measure of the resources required to satisfy the request, rather than per virtual machine, per hour. Despite the name, it does not actually involve running code without servers. Serverless computing is so named because the business or person that owns the system does not have to purchase, rent or provision servers or virtual machines for the back-end code to run on.

## Cloud Clients

Users access cloud computing using networked client devices, such as desktop computers, laptops, tablets and smartphones and any Ethernet enabled device such as Home Automation Gadgets. Some of these devices—*cloud clients*—rely on cloud computing for all or a majority of their applications so as to be essentially useless without it. Examples are thin clients and the browser-based Chromebook. Many cloud applications do not require specific software on the client and instead use a web browser to interact with the cloud application. With Ajax and HTML5 these Web user interfaces can achieve a similar, or even better, look and feel to native applications. Some cloud applications, however, support specific client software dedicated to these applications (e.g., virtual desktop clients and most email clients). Some legacy applications (line of business applications that until now have been prevalent in thin client computing) are delivered via a screen-sharing technology.

## Deployment Models

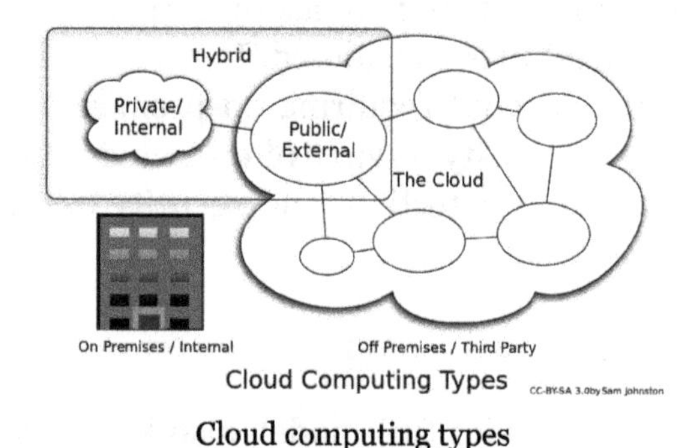


Cloud computing types

## Private Cloud

Private cloud is cloud infrastructure operated solely for a single organization, whether managed internally or by a third-party, and hosted either internally or externally. Undertaking a private cloud project requires a significant level and degree of engagement to virtualize the business environment, and requires the organization to reevaluate decisions about existing resources. When done right, it can improve business, but every step in the project raises security issues that must be addressed to prevent serious vulnerabilities. Self-run data centers are generally capital intensive. They have a significant physical footprint, requiring allocations of space, hardware, and environmental controls. These assets have to be refreshed periodically, resulting in additional capital expenditures. They have attracted criticism because users "still have to buy, build, and manage them" and thus do not benefit from less hands-on management, essentially "[lacking] the economic model that makes cloud computing such an intriguing concept".

### Public Cloud

A cloud is called a "public cloud" when the services are rendered over a network that is open for public use. Public cloud services may be free. Technically there may be little or no difference between public and private cloud architecture, however, security consideration may be substantially different for services (applications, storage, and other resources) that are made available by a service provider for a public audience and when communication is effected over a non-trusted network. Generally, public cloud service providers like Amazon Web Services (AWS), Microsoft and Google own and operate the infrastructure at their data center and access is generally via the Internet. AWS and Microsoft also offer direct connect services called "AWS Direct Connect" and "Azure ExpressRoute" respectively, such connections require customers to purchase or lease a private connection to a peering point offered by the cloud provider.

### Hybrid Cloud

Hybrid cloud is a composition of two or more clouds (private, community or public) that remain distinct entities but are bound together, offering the benefits of multiple deployment models. Hybrid cloud can also mean the ability to connect collocation, managed and/or dedicated services with cloud resources. Gartner, Inc. defines a hybrid cloud service as a cloud computing service that is composed of some combination of private, public and community cloud services, from different service providers. A hybrid cloud service crosses isolation and provider boundaries so that it can't be simply put in one category of private, public, or community cloud service. It allows one to extend either the capacity or the capability of a cloud service, by aggregation, integration or customization with another cloud service.

Varied use cases for hybrid cloud composition exist. For example, an organization may store sensitive client data in house on a private cloud application, but interconnect that application to a business intelligence application provided on a public cloud as a software service. This example of hybrid cloud extends the capabilities of the enterprise to deliver a specific business service through the addition of externally available public cloud services. Hybrid cloud adoption depends on a number of factors such as data security and compliance requirements, level of control needed over data, and the applications an organization uses.

Another example of hybrid cloud is one where IT organizations use public cloud computing resources to meet temporary capacity needs that can not be met by the private cloud. This capability enables hybrid clouds to employ cloud bursting for scaling across clouds. Cloud bursting is an application deployment model in which an application runs in a private cloud or data center and "bursts" to a public cloud when the demand for computing capacity increases. A primary advantage of cloud bursting and a hybrid cloud model is that an organization pays for extra compute resources only when they are needed. Cloud bursting enables data centers to create an in-house IT infrastructure that supports average workloads, and use cloud resources from public or private clouds, during spikes in processing demands. The specialized model of hybrid cloud, which is built atop heterogeneous hardware, is called "Cross-platform Hybrid Cloud". A cross-platform hybrid cloud is usually powered by different CPU architectures, for example, x86-64 and ARM, underneath. Users can transparently deploy and scale applications without knowledge of the cloud's hardware diversity. This kind of cloud emerges from the raise of ARM-based system-on-chip for server-class computing.

## Others

### Community Cloud

Community cloud shares infrastructure between several organizations from a specific community with common concerns (security, compliance, jurisdiction, etc.), whether managed internally or by a third-party, and either hosted internally or externally. The costs are spread over fewer users than a public cloud (but more than a private cloud), so only some of the cost savings potential of cloud computing are realized.

### Distributed Cloud

A cloud computing platform can be assembled from a distributed set of machines in different locations, connected to a single network or hub service. It is possible to distinguish between two types of distributed clouds: public-resource computing and volunteer cloud.

- Public-resource computing—This type of distributed cloud results from an expansive definition of cloud computing, because they are more akin to distributed computing than cloud computing. Nonetheless, it is considered a sub-class of cloud computing, and some examples include distributed computing platforms such as BOINC and Folding@Home.

- Volunteer cloud—Volunteer cloud computing is characterized as the intersection of public-resource computing and cloud computing, where a cloud computing infrastructure is built using volunteered resources. Many challenges arise from this type of infrastructure, because of the volatility of the resources used to built it and the dynamic environment it operates in. It can also be called peer-to-peer clouds, or ad-hoc clouds. An interesting effort in such direction is Cloud@Home, it aims to implement a cloud computing infrastructure using volunteered resources providing a business-model to incentivize contributions through financial restitution.

## Intercloud

The Intercloud is an interconnected global "cloud of clouds" and an extension of the Internet "network of networks" on which it is based. The focus is on direct interoperability between public cloud service providers, more so than between providers and consumers (as is the case for hybrid- and multi-cloud).

## Multicloud

Multicloud is the use of multiple cloud computing services in a single heterogeneous architecture to reduce reliance on single vendors, increase flexibility through choice, mitigate against disasters, etc. It differs from hybrid cloud in that it refers to multiple cloud services, rather than multiple deployment modes (public, private, legacy).

## Architecture

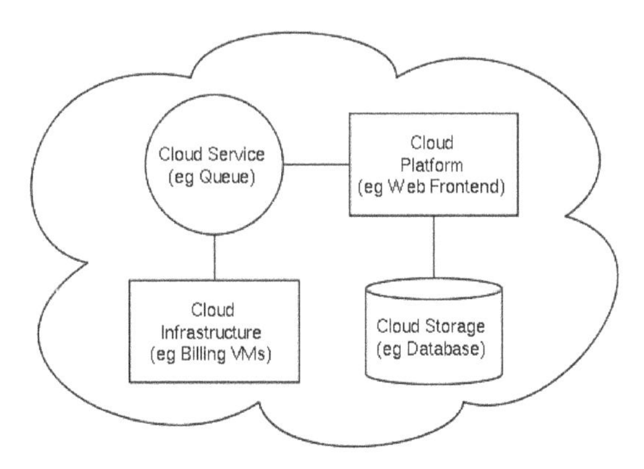


Cloud computing sample architecture

Cloud architecture, the systems architecture of the software systems involved in the delivery of cloud computing, typically involves multiple *cloud components* communicating with each other over a loose coupling mechanism such as a messaging queue. Elastic provision implies intelligence in the use of tight or loose coupling as applied to mechanisms such as these and others.

## Cloud Engineering

Cloud engineering is the application of engineering disciplines to cloud computing. It brings a systematic approach to the high-level concerns of commercialization, standardization, and governance in conceiving, developing, operating and maintaining cloud computing systems. It is a multidisciplinary method encompassing contributions from diverse areas such as systems, software, web, performance, information, security, platform, risk, and quality engineering.

## Security and Privacy

Cloud computing poses privacy concerns because the service provider can access the data that is in the cloud at any time. It could accidentally or deliberately alter or even delete information. Many cloud providers can share information with third parties if necessary for purposes of law and order even without a warrant. That is permitted in their privacy policies, which users must agree to before they start using cloud services. Solutions to privacy include policy and legislation as well as end users' choices for how data is stored. Users can encrypt data that is processed or stored within the cloud to prevent unauthorized access.

According to the Cloud Security Alliance, the top three threats in the cloud are *Insecure Interfaces and API's*, *Data Loss & Leakage*, and *Hardware Failure*—which accounted for 29%, 25% and 10% of all cloud security outages respectively. Together, these form shared technology vulnerabilities. In a cloud provider platform being shared by different users there may be a possibility that information belonging to different customers resides on same data server. Therefore, Information leakage may arise by mistake when information for one customer is given to other. Additionally, Eugene Schultz, chief technology officer at Emagined Security, said that hackers are spending substantial time and effort looking for ways to penetrate the cloud. "There are some real Achilles' heels in the cloud infrastructure that are making big holes for the bad guys to get into". Because data from hundreds or thousands of companies can be stored on large cloud servers, hackers can theoretically gain control of huge stores of information through a single attack—a process he called "hyperjacking". Some examples of this include the Dropbox security breach, and iCloud 2014 leak. Dropbox had been breached in October 2014, having over 7 million of its users passwords stolen by hackers in an effort to get monetary value from it by Bitcoins (BTC). By having these passwords, they are able to read private data as well as have this data be indexed by search engines (making the information public).

There is the problem of legal ownership of the data (If a user stores some data in the cloud, can the cloud provider profit from it?). Many Terms of Service agreements are silent on the question of ownership. Physical control of the computer equipment (private cloud) is more secure than having the equipment off site and under someone else's control (public cloud). This delivers great incentive to public cloud computing service providers to prioritize building and maintaining strong management of secure services. Some small businesses that don't have expertise in IT security could find that it's more secure for them to use a public cloud. There is the risk that end users do not understand the issues involved when signing on to a cloud service (persons sometimes don't read the many pages of the terms of service agreement, and just click "Accept" without reading). This is important now that cloud computing is becoming popular and required for some services to work, for example for an intelligent personal assistant (Apple's Siri or Google Now). Fundamentally, private cloud is seen as more secure with higher levels of control for the owner, however public cloud is seen to be more flexible and requires less time and money investment from the user.

## Limitations and Disadvantages

According to Bruce Schneier, "The downside is that you will have limited customization options. Cloud computing is cheaper because of economics of scale, and — like any outsourced task — you tend to get what you get. A restaurant with a limited menu is cheaper than a personal chef who can cook anything you want. Fewer options at a much cheaper price: it's a feature, not a bug." He also suggests that "the cloud provider might not meet your legal needs" and that businesses need to weigh the benefits of cloud computing against the risks. In cloud computing, the control of the back end infrastructure is limited to the cloud vendor only. Cloud providers often decide on the management policies, which moderates what the cloud users are able to do with their deployment. Cloud users are also limited to the control and management of their applications, data and services. This includes data caps, which are placed on cloud users by the cloud vendor allocating certain amount of bandwidth for each customer and are often shared among other cloud users.

Privacy and confidentiality are big concerns in some activities. For instance, sworn translators working under the stipulations of an NDA, might face problems regarding sensitive data that are not encrypted.

## Emerging Trends

Cloud computing is still a subject of research. A driving factor in the evolution of cloud computing has been Chief technology officers seeking to minimize risk of internal outages and mitigate the complexity of housing network and computing hardware in-house. Major cloud technology companies invest billions of dollars per year in cloud Research and Development. For example, in 2011 Microsoft committed 90 percent of its $9.6 billion R&D budget to its cloud. Research by investment bank Centaur Partners in late 2015 forecasted that SaaS revenue would grow from $13.5 billion in 2011 to $32.8 billion in 2016.

## Cloud Collaboration

Cloud collaboration is a way of sharing and co-authoring computer files through the use of cloud computing, whereby documents are uploaded to a central "cloud" for storage, where they can then be accessed by others. Cloud collaboration technologies allow users to upload, comment and collaborate on documents and even amend the document itself, evolving the document. Businesses in the last few years have increasingly been switching to use of cloud collaboration.

## Overview

Cloud computing is a marketing term for technologies that provide software, data access, and storage services that do not require end-user knowledge of the physical location and configuration of the system that delivers the services. A parallel to this concept can be drawn with the electricity grid, where end-users consume power without needing to understand the component devices or infrastructure required to utilize the technology.

Collaboration refers to the ability of workers to work together simultaneously on a particular task. Document collaboration can be completed face to face. However, collaboration has become more complex, with the need to work with people all over the world in real time on a variety of different types of documents, using different devices. Collaboration services include Google, Microsoft, WebEx, Jive Software, eXo Platform, Synaptop and Salesforce.com. A 2003 report mapped out five reasons why workers are reluctant to collaborate more. These are:

- People resist sharing their knowledge.
- Safety issues.
- Users are most comfortable using e-mail as their primary electronic collaboration tool.
- People do not have incentive to change their behaviour.
- Teams that want to or are selected to use the software do not have strong team leaders who push for more collaboration.
- Senior management is not actively involved in or does not support the team collaboration initiative.

As a result, many providers created cloud collaboration tools. These include the integration of email alerts into collaboration software and the ability to see who is viewing the document at any time. All the tools a team could need are put into one piece of software so workers no longer have to rely on email.

Before cloud file sharing and collaboration software, most collaboration was limited to more primitive and less effective methods such as email and FTP among others. These did not work particularly well.

Very early moves into cloud computing were made by Amazon Web Services who, in 2006, began offering IT infrastructure services to businesses in the form of web services. Cloud computing only began to come to prominence in 2007 when Google decided to move parts of its email service to a public cloud. It was not long before IBM and Microsoft followed suit with LotusLive and Business Productivity Online Standard Suite (BPOS) respectively. With an increase in cloud computing services, cloud collaboration was able to evolve. Since 2007, many firms entered the industry offering many features.

Many analysts explain the rise of cloud collaboration by pointing to the increasing use by workers of non-authorised websites and online tools to do their jobs. This includes the use of instant messaging and social networks. In a survey taken in early 2011, 22% of workers admitted to having used one or more of these external non-authorised websites. Cloud collaboration packages provide the ability to collaborate on documents together in real time, making the use of non-authorised instant messaging redundant. IT managers can now properly regulate internet based collaboration with a system tailor made for the office.

It has also been noted that cloud collaboration has become more and more necessary for IT departments as workforces have become more mobile and now need access to important documents wherever they are, whether this is through an internet browser, or through newer technologies such as smartphones and tablet devices.

The tech industry saw several large paradigm changes:

- The mainframe computing era enabled business growth to be untethered from the number of employees needed to process transactions manually.
- The personal computing era empowered business users to run their businesses based on individual data and applications on their PCs.
- A decade of network computing established an unprecedented level of transparency of information across multiple groups inside a company and an amazing rate of data exchange between enterprises.

Each of these revolutions brought with it new economies of scale. The cost-per-transaction, the cost of automating office and desktop processes, and finally the cost of network bandwidth fell quickly and enabled business users to apply ICT solutions more broadly to create business value. Most analysts (Forrester, Gartner, etc.) believe that cloud computing will help unleash the next wave of tech-enabled business innovation.

During the mainframe era, client/server was initially viewed as a "toy" technology, not viable as a mainframe replacement. Yet, over time the client/server technology found its way into the enterprise. Similarly, when virtualization technology was first proposed, application compatibility concerns and potential vendor lock-in were cited as barriers to adoption. Yet underlying economics of 20 to 30 percent savings compelled CIOs to overcome these concerns, and adoption quickly accelerated.

## Recent Developments

Early cloud collaboration tools were quite basic with limited features. Newer packages are much more document-centric in their approach to collaboration. More sophisticated tools allow users to "tag" specific areas of a document for comments which are delivered real time to those viewing the document. In some cases, the collaboration software can even be integrated into Microsoft Office, or allow users to set up video conferences.

Furthermore, the trend now is for firms to employ a single software tool to solve all their collaboration needs, rather than having to rely on multiple different techniques. Single cloud collaboration providers are now replacing a complicated tangle of instant messengers, email and FTP.

Cloud collaboration today is promoted as a tool for collaboration internally between different departments within a firm, but also externally as a means for sharing documents with end-clients as receiving feedback. This makes cloud computing a very versatile tool for firms with many different applications in a business environment.

The best cloud collaboration tools:

- Use real-time commenting and messaging features to enhance speed of project delivery
- Leverage presence indicators to identify when others are active on documents owned by another person
- Allow users to set permissions and manage other users' activity profiles
- Allow users to set personal activity feeds and email alert profiles to keep abreast of latest activities per file or user
- Allow users to collaborate and share files with users outside the company firewall
- Comply with company security and compliance framework
- Ensure full auditability of files and documents shared within and outside the organization
- Reduce workarounds for sharing and collaboration on large files

A 2011 report by Gartner outlines a five stage model on the maturity of firms when it comes to the uptake of cloud collaboration tools. A firm in the first stage is said to be "reactive", with only email as a collaboration platform and a culture which resists information sharing. A firm in the fifth stage is called "pervasive", and has universal access to a rich collaboration toolset and a strong collaborative culture. The article argues that most firms are in the second stage, but as cloud collaboration becomes more important, most analysts expect to see the majority of firms moving up in the model.

## Cloud Printing

Cloud printing is the technology that enables printers to be accessed over a network through cloud computing. There are, in essence, two kinds of cloud printing. On the one hand, consumer-based cloud printing connects any application to cloud-enabled home printers that people own or have access to. Using this technology, people can take digital media as their primary communications tool and create a printed page only when they need the content in a physical form.

On the other hand, professional cloud printing enables publishers, companies and content owners to print their digital publications by leveraging networks of production facilities through cloud computing technology. In short, professional cloud printing allows for the "ad-hoc transformation of digital information into physical forms in 2D or 3D."

### Benefits

For consumers, cloud ready printers eliminate the need for PC connections and print drivers, enabling them to print from mobile devices. As for publishers and content owners, cloud printing allows them to "avoid the cost and complexity of buying and managing the underlying hardware, software and processes" required for the production of professional print products.

Leveraging cloud print for print on demand also allows businesses to cut down on the costs associated with mass production. Moreover, cloud printing can be considered more eco-friendly, as it significantly reduces the amount of paper used and lowers carbon emissions from transportation.

### Providers

Only a handful of providers are currently working towards a professional cloud print solution. Most of these operate in their own niche or focus on mobile devices.

Significantly large steps have also been taken in the consumer market with Google Cloud Print. A few leading companies like Konica Minolta, Xerox and Ricoh followed in Google's footsteps with their mobile cloud solutions, while Hewlett-Packard implemented a similar mechanism with their ePrint solution.

Industry experts believe that as these services become more popular, users will no longer consider printers as necessary assets but rather as devices that they can access on demand when the need to generate a printed page presents itself.

While these cloud printing options do simplify the printing process, all the print data must travel through the public cloud as it makes its journey from device to printer.

## Cloud Manufacturing

Cloud manufacturing (CMfg) is a new manufacturing paradigm developed from existing advanced manufacturing models (e.g., ASP, AM, NM, MGrid) and enterprise information technologies under the support of cloud computing, Internet of Things (IoT), virtualization and service-oriented technologies, and advanced computing technologies. It transforms manufacturing resources and manufacturing capabilities into manufacturing services, which can be managed and operated in an intelligent and unified way to enable the full sharing and circulating of manufacturing resources and manufacturing capabilities. CMfg can provide safe and reliable, high quality, cheap and on-demand manufacturing services for the whole lifecycle of manufacturing. The concept of manufacturing here refers to big manufacturing that includes the whole lifecycle of a product (e.g. design, simulation, production,test,maintenance). The concept of Cloud manufacturing was initially proposed by the research group led by Prof. Bo Hu Li and Prof. Lin Zhang in China in 2009.

Related discussions and research were conducted hereafter. And some similar definitions (e.g. Cloud-Based Design and Manufacturing (CBDM). ) to cloud manufacturing were introduced.

Cloud manufacturing is a type of parallel, networked, and distributed system consisting of an integrated and inter-connected virtualized service pool (manufacturing cloud) of manufacturing resources and capabilities as well as capabilities of intelligent management and on-demand use of services to provide solutions for all kinds of users involved in the whole lifecycle of manufacturing.

## Types of Cloud Manufacturing Models

Cloud Manufacturing can be divided into two categories.

- The first category concerns deploying manufacturing software on the Cloud, i.e. a "manufacturing version" of Computing. CAx software can be supplied as a service on the Manufacturing Cloud (MCloud).

- The second category has a broader scope, cutting across production, management, design and engineering abilities in a manufacturing business. Unlike with computing and data storage, manufacturing involves physical equipment, monitors, materials and so on. In this kind of Cloud Manufacturing system, both material and non-material facilities are implemented on the Manufacturing Cloud to support the whole supply chain. Costly resources are shared on the network. This means that the utilisation rate of rarely used equipment rises and the cost of expensive equipment is reduced. According to the concept of Cloud technology, there will not be direct interaction between Cloud Users and Service Providers. The Cloud User should neither manage nor control the infrastructure and manufacturing applications. As a matter of fact, the former can be considered part of the latter.

In CMfg system, various manufacturing resources and abilities can be intelligently sensed and connected into wider Internet, and automatically managed and controlled using IoT technologies (e.g., RFID, wired and wireless sensor network, embedded system). Then the manufacturing resources and abilities are virtualized and encapsulated into different manufacturing cloud services (MCSs), that can be accessed, invoked, and deployed based on knowledge by using virtualization technologies, service-oriented technologies, and cloud computing technologies. The MCSs are classified and aggregated according to specific rules and algorithms, and different kinds of manufacturing clouds are constructed. Different users can search and invoke the qualified MCSs from related manufacturing cloud according to their needs, and assemble them to be a virtual manufacturing environment or solution to complete their manufacturing task involved in the whole life cycle of manufacturing processes under the support of cloud computing, service-oriented technologies, and advanced computing technologies.

Four types of cloud deployment modes (public, private, community and hybrid clouds) are ubiquitous as a single point of access.

- Private cloud refers to a centralized management effort in which manufacturing services are shared within one company or its subsidiaries. Enterprises' mission-critical and core-business applications are often kept in a private cloud.
- Community cloud is a collaborative effort in which manufacturing services are shared between several organizations from a specific community with common concerns.
- Public cloud realizes the key concept of sharing services with the general public in a multi-tenant environment.
- Hybrid cloud is a composition of two or more clouds (private, community or public) that remain distinct entities but are also bound together, offering the benefits of multiple deployment modes.

## Cloud Manufacturing Resources

From the resource's perspective, each kind of manufacturing capability requires support from the related manufacturing resource. For each type of manufacturing capability, its related manufacturing resource comes in two forms, soft resources and hard resources.

### Soft Resources

- Software: software applications throughout the product lifecycle including design, analysis, simulation, process planning, and etc.
- Knowledge: experience and know-how needed to complete a production task, i.e. engineering knowledge, product models, standards, evaluation procedures and results, customer feedback, and etc.
- Skill: expertise in performing a specific manufacturing task.
- Personnel: human resource engaged in the manufacturing process, i.e. designers, operators, managers, technicians, project teams, customer service, and etc.
- Experience: performance, quality, client evaluation and etc.
- Business Network: business relationships and business opportunity networks that exist in an enterprise.

### Hard Resources

- Manufacturing Equipment: facilities needed for completing a manufacturing task, e.g. machine tools, cutters, test and monitoring equipment and other fabrication tools.
- Monitoring/Control Resource: devices used to identify and control other manufacturing resource, for instance, RFID (Radio-Frequency IDentification), WSN (Wireless Sensor Network), virtual managers and remote controllers.
- Computational Resource: computing devices to support production process, e.g. servers, computers, storage media, control devices, and etc.
- Materials: inputs and outputs in a production system, e.g. raw material, product-in-progress, finished product, power, water, lubricants, and etc.
- Storage: automated storage and retrieval systems, logic controllers, location of warehouses, volume capacity and schedule/optimization methods.
- Transportation: movement of manufacturing inputs/outputs from one location to another. It includes the modes of transport, e.g. air, rail, road, water, cable, pipeline and space, and the related price, and time taken.

# Cloud Computing Issues

Cloud computing has become a social phenomenon used by most people every day. As with every important social phenomenon there are issues that limit its widespread adoption.

Most issues start from the fact that the user loses control of his or her data, because it is stored on a computer belonging to someone else (the cloud provider). This happens when the owner of the remote servers is a person or organization other than the user; as their interests may point in different directions (for example, the user may wish that his or her information is kept private, but the owner of the remote servers may want to take advantage of it for their own business).

Many issues relate to cloud computing, some of which are discussed here:

## Threats and Opportunities of the Cloud

GNU project initiator Richard Stallman has characterized cloud computing as raising cost and information-ownership concerns. Oracle founder Larry Ellison viewed the trend to "cloud computing" in terms of "fashion-driven [...] complete gibberish".

However, the concept of cloud computing appeared to gain steam, with 56% of the major European technology decision-makers seeing the cloud as a priority in 2013 and 2014, and the cloud budget may reach 30% of the overall IT budget.

According to the *TechInsights Report 2013: Cloud Succeeds* based on a survey, cloud implementations generally meet or exceed expectations across major service models, such as Infrastructure as a Service (IaaS), Platform as a service (PaaS) and Software as a service (SaaS).

Several deterrents to the widespread adoption of cloud computing remain. They include:

- reliability
- availability of services and data
- security
- complexity
- costs
- regulations and legal issues
- performance

- migration
- reversion
- the lack of standards
- limited customization
- issues of privacy

The cloud offers many strong points: infrastructure flexibility, faster deployment of applications and data, cost control, adaptation of cloud resources to real needs, improved productivity, etc. The cloud market of the early 2010s - especially for private clouds - was dominated by software and services in SaaS mode and IaaS (infrastructure). PaaS and the public cloud lag in comparison.

## Privacy

The increased use of cloud computing services such as Gmail and Google Docs has pressed the issue of privacy concerns of cloud computing services to the utmost importance. The provider of such services lie in a position such that with the greater use of cloud computing services has given access to a plethora of data. This access has the immense risk of data being disclosed either accidentally or deliberately. Privacy advocates have criticized the cloud model for giving hosting companies' greater ease to control—and thus, to monitor at will—communication between host company and end user, and access user data (with or without permission). Instances such as the secret NSA program, working with AT&T, and Verizon, which recorded over 10 million telephone calls between American citizens, causes uncertainty among privacy advocates, and the greater powers it gives to telecommunication companies to monitor user activity. A cloud service provider (CSP) can complicate data privacy because of the extent of virtualization (virtual machines) and cloud storage used to implement cloud service. CSP operations, customer or tenant data may not remain on the same system, or in the same data center or even within the same provider's cloud; this can lead to legal concerns over jurisdiction. While there have been efforts (such as US-EU Safe Harbor) to "harmonise" the legal environment, providers such as Amazon still cater to major markets (typically to the United States and the European Union) by deploying local infrastructure and allowing customers to select "regions and availability zones". Cloud computing poses privacy concerns because the service provider can access the data that is on the cloud at any time. It could accidentally or deliberately alter or even delete information. This becomes a major concern as these service providers employ administrators, which can leave room for potential unwanted disclosure of information on the cloud.

## Sharing Information without a Warrant

Many cloud providers can share information with third parties if necessary for purposes of law and order even without a warrant. That is permitted in their privacy policies which users have to agree to before they start using cloud services.

There are life-threatening situations in which there is no time to wait for the police to issue a warrant. Many cloud providers can share information immediately to the police in such situations.

## Example of a Privacy Policy that Allows this

The Dropbox Privacy policy states that

> We may share information as discussed below
>
> Law & Order. We may disclose your information to third parties if we determine that such disclosure is reasonably necessary to (a) comply with the law; (b) protect any person from death or serious bodily injury; (c) prevent fraud or abuse of Dropbox or our users; or (d) protect Dropbox's property rights.

## Previous Situation about this

The Sydney Morning Herald reported about the Mosman bomb hoax, which was a life-threatening situation, that:

> As to whether NSW Police needed a warrant to access the information it was likely to have, Byrne said it depended on the process taken. "Gmail does set out in their process in terms of their legal disclosure guidelines [that] it can be done by a search warrant ... but there are exceptions that can apply in different parts of the world and different service providers. For example, Facebook generally provides an exception for emergency life threatening situations that are signed off by law enforcement."
>
> Another computer forensic expert at iT4ensics, which works for large corporations dealing with matters like internal fraud, Scott Lasak, said that police "would just contact Google" and "being of a police or FBI background Google would assist them".
>
> "Whether or not they need to go through warrants or that sort of thing I'm not sure. But even for just an IP address they might not even need a warrant for something like that being of a police background.
>
> NSW Police would not comment on whether it had received help from Google. The search giant also declined to comment, instead offering a standard statement on how it cooperated with law enforcement.
>
> A spokesman for the online users' lobby group Electronic Frontiers Australia, Stephen Collins, said Google was likely to have handed over the need information on the basis of "probable cause or a warrant", which he said was "perfectly legitimate".

He also said "It happens with relative frequency. ... Such things are rarely used in Australia for trivial or malevolent purposes."

## Privacy Solutions

Solutions to privacy in cloud computing include policy and legislation as well as end users' choices for how data is stored. The cloud service provider needs to establish clear and relevant policies that describe how the data of each cloud user will be accessed and used. Cloud service users can encrypt data that is processed or stored within the cloud to prevent unauthorized access. Cryptographic encryption mechanisms are certainly the best options. In addition, authentication and integrity protection mechanisms ensure that data only goes where the customer wants it to go and it is not modified in transit.

Strong authentication is a mandatory requirement for any cloud deployment. User authentication is the primary basis for access control, and specially in the cloud environment, authentication and access control are more important than ever since the cloud and all of its data are publicly accessible. CloudID provides a privacy-preserving cloud-based and cross-enterprise biometric identification solutions for this problem. It links the confidential information of the users to their biometrics and stores it in an encrypted fashion. Making use of a searchable encryption technique, biometric identification is performed in encrypted domain to make sure that the cloud provider or potential attackers do not gain access to any sensitive data or even the contents of the individual queries.

## Compliance

To comply with regulations including FISMA, HIPAA, and SOX in the United States, the Data Protection Directive in the EU and the credit card industry's PCI DSS, users may have to adopt *community* or *hybrid* deployment modes that are typically more expensive and may offer restricted benefits. This is how Google is able to "manage and meet additional government policy requirements beyond FISMA" and Rackspace Cloud or QubeSpace are able to claim PCI compliance.

Many providers also obtain a SAS 70 Type II audit, but this has been criticised on the grounds that the hand-picked set of goals and standards determined by the auditor and the auditee are often not disclosed and can vary widely. Providers typically make this information available on request, under non-disclosure agreement.

Customers in the EU contracting with cloud providers outside the EU/EEA have to adhere to the EU regulations on export of personal data.

A multitude of laws and regulations have forced specific compliance requirements onto many companies that collect, generate or store data. These policies may dictate a wide array of data storage policies, such as how long information must be retained, the process used for deleting data, and even certain recovery plans. Below are some examples of compliance laws or regulations.

- United States, the Health Insurance Portability and Accountability Act (HIPAA) requires a contingency plan that includes, data backups, data recovery, and data access during emergencies.
- The privacy laws of Switzerland demand that private data, including emails, be physically stored in Switzerland.
- In the United Kingdom, the Civil Contingencies Act of 2004 sets forth guidance for a business contingency plan that includes policies for data storage.

In a virtualized cloud computing environment, customers may never know exactly where their data is stored. In fact, data may be stored across multiple data centers in an effort to improve reliability, increase performance, and provide redundancies. This geographic dispersion may make it more difficult to ascertain legal jurisdiction if disputes arise.

## FedRAMP

U.S. Federal Agencies have been directed by the Office of Management and Budget to use a process called FedRAMP (Federal Risk and Authorization Management Program) to assess and authorize cloud products and services. Federal CIO Steven VanRoekel issued a memorandum to federal agency Chief Information Officers on December 8, 2011 defining how federal agencies should use FedRAMP. FedRAMP consists of a subset of NIST Special Publication 800-53 security controls specifically selected to provide protection in cloud environments. A subset has been defined for the FIPS 199 low categorization and the FIPS 199 moderate categorization. The FedRAMP program has also established a Joint Accreditation Board (JAB) consisting of Chief Information Officers from DoD, DHS, and GSA. The JAB is responsible for establishing accreditation standards for 3rd party organizations who perform the assessments of cloud solutions. The JAB also reviews authorization packages, and may grant provisional authorization (to operate). The federal agency consuming the service still has final responsibility for final authority to operate.

## Legal

As with other changes in the landscape of computing, certain legal issues arise with cloud computing, including trademark infringement, security concerns and sharing of proprietary data resources.

The Electronic Frontier Foundation has criticized the United States government during the Megaupload seizure process for considering that people lose property rights by storing data on a cloud computing service.

One important but not often mentioned problem with cloud computing is the problem of who is in "possession" of the data. If a cloud company is the possessor of the data, the possessor has certain legal rights. If the cloud company is the "custodian" of the data, then a different set of rights would apply. The next problem in the legalities of cloud computing is the problem of legal ownership of the data. Many Terms of Service agreements are silent on the question of ownership.

These legal issues are not confined to the time period in which the cloud-based application is actively being used. There must also be consideration for what happens when the provider-customer relationship ends. In most cases, this event will be addressed before an application is deployed to the cloud. However, in the case of provider insolvencies or bankruptcy the state of the data may become blurred.

## Vendor Lock-in

Because cloud computing is still relatively new, standards are still being developed. Many cloud platforms and services are proprietary, meaning that they are built on the specific standards, tools and protocols developed by a particular vendor for its particular cloud offering. This can make migrating off a proprietary cloud platform prohibitively complicated and expensive.

Three types of vendor lock-in can occur with cloud computing:

- Platform lock-in: cloud services tend to be built on one of several possible virtualization platforms, for example VMWare or Xen. Migrating from a cloud provider using one platform to a cloud provider using a different platform could be very complicated.
- Data lock-in: since the cloud is still new, standards of ownership, i.e. who actually owns the data once it lives on a cloud platform, are not yet developed, which could make it complicated if cloud computing users ever decide to move data off of a cloud vendor's platform.
- Tools lock-in: if tools built to manage a cloud environment are not compatible with different kinds of both virtual and physical infrastructure, those tools will only be able to manage data or apps that live in the vendor's particular cloud environment.

Heterogeneous cloud computing is described as a type of cloud environment that prevents vendor lock-in, and aligns with enterprise data centers that are operating hybrid cloud models. The absence of vendor lock-in lets cloud administrators select his or her choice of hypervisors for specific tasks, or to deploy virtualized infrastructures to other enterprises without the need to consider the flavor of hypervisor in the other enterprise.

A heterogeneous cloud is considered one that includes on-premises private clouds, public clouds and software-as-a-service clouds. Heterogeneous clouds can work with environments that are not virtualized, such as traditional data centers. Heterogeneous clouds also allow for the use of piece parts, such as hypervisors, servers, and storage, from multiple vendors.

Cloud piece parts, such as cloud storage systems, offer APIs but they are often incompatible with each other. The result is complicated migration between backends, and makes it difficult to integrate data spread across various locations. This has been described as a problem of vendor lock-in. The solution to this is for clouds to adopt common standards.

Heterogeneous cloud computing differs from homogeneous clouds, which have been described as those using consistent building blocks supplied by a single vendor. Intel General Manager of high-density computing, Jason Waxman, is quoted as saying that a homogeneous system of 15,000 servers would cost $6 million more in capital expenditure and use 1 megawatt of power.

### Open Source

Open-source software has provided the foundation for many cloud computing implementations, prominent examples being the Hadoop framework and VMware's Cloud Foundry. In November 2007, the Free Software Foundation released the Affero General Public License, a version of GPLv3 intended to close a perceived legal loophole associated with free software designed to run over a network.

### Open Standards

Most cloud providers expose APIs that are typically well documented (often under a Creative Commons license) but also unique to their implementation and thus not interoperable. Some vendors have adopted others' APIs and there are a number of open standards under development, with a view to delivering interoperability and portability. As of November 2012, the Open Standard with broadest industry support is probably OpenStack, founded in 2010 by NASA and Rackspace, and now governed by the OpenStack Foundation. OpenStack supporters include AMD, Intel, Canonical, SUSE Linux, Red Hat, Cisco, Dell, HP, IBM, Yahoo, Huawei and now VMware.

### Security

Security is generally a desired state of being free from harm (anything that compromises the state of an entity's well being). As defined in information security, it is a condition in which an information asset is protected against its confidentiality (quality or state of being free from unauthorised or insecure disclosure contrary to the defined access rights as listed in the access control list and or matrix), integrity (a quality or state of being whole/ as complete as original and uncorrupted as functionally proven by the hash integrity values) and availability (a desired state of an information resource being accessible only by authorised parties (as listed in access control list and or matrix) in the desired state and at the right time. Security is an important domain in as far as cloud computing is concerned, there are a number of issues to be addressed if the cloud is to be perfectly secure (a condition i doubt will ever be achieved)(Martin Muduva, 2015).

As cloud computing is achieving increased popularity, concerns are being voiced about the security issues introduced through adoption of this new model. The effectiveness and efficiency of traditional protection mechanisms are being reconsidered as the characteristics of this innovative deployment model can differ widely from those of traditional architectures. An alternative perspective on the topic of cloud security is that this is but another, although quite broad, case of "applied security" and that similar security principles that apply in shared multi-user mainframe security models apply with cloud security.

The relative security of cloud computing services is a contentious issue that may be delaying its adoption. Physical control of the Private Cloud equipment is more secure than having the equipment off site and under someone else's control. Physical control and the ability to visually inspect data links and access ports is required in order to ensure data links are not compromised. Issues barring the adoption of cloud computing are due in large part to the private and public sectors' unease surrounding the external management of security-based services. It is the very nature of cloud computing-based services, private or public, that promote external management of provided services. This delivers great incentive to cloud computing service providers to prioritize building and maintaining strong management of secure services. Security issues have been categorised into sensitive data access, data segregation, privacy, bug exploitation, recovery, accountability, malicious insiders, management console security, account control, and multi-tenancy issues. Solutions to various cloud security issues vary, from cryptography, particularly public key infrastructure (PKI), to use of multiple cloud providers, standardisation of APIs, and improving virtual machine support and legal support.

Cloud computing offers many benefits, but is vulnerable to threats. As cloud computing uses increase, it is likely that more criminals find new ways to exploit system vulnerabilities. Many underlying challenges and risks in cloud computing increase the threat of data compromise. To mitigate the threat, cloud computing stakeholders should invest heavily in risk assessment to ensure that the system encrypts to protect data, establishes trusted foundation to secure the platform and infrastructure, and builds higher assurance into auditing to strengthen compliance. Security concerns must be addressed to maintain trust in cloud computing technology.

Data breach is a big concern in cloud computing. A compromised server could significantly harm the users as well as cloud providers. A variety of information could be stolen. These include credit card and social security numbers, addresses, and personal messages. The U.S. now requires cloud providers to notify customers of breaches. Once notified, customers now have to worry about identity theft and fraud, while providers have to deal with federal investigations, lawsuits and reputational damage. Customer lawsuits and settlements have resulted in over $1 billion in losses to cloud providers.

### Sustainability

Although cloud computing is often assumed to be a form of *green computing*, there is currently no way to measure how "green" computers are.

The primary environmental problem associated with the cloud is energy use. Phil Radford of Greenpeace said "we are concerned that this new explosion in electricity use could lock us into old, polluting energy sources instead of the clean energy available today." Greenpeace ranks the energy usage of the top ten big brands in cloud computing, and successfully urged several companies to switch to clean energy. On Thursday, December 15, 2011, Greenpeace and Facebook announced together that Facebook would shift to use clean and renewable energy to power its own operations. Soon thereafter, Apple agreed to make all of its data centers 'coal free' by the end of 2013 and doubled the amount of solar energy powering its Maiden, NC data center. Following suit, Salesforce agreed to shift to 100% clean energy by 2020.

Citing the servers' effects on the environmental effects of cloud computing, in areas where climate favors natural cooling and renewable electricity is readily available, the environmental effects will be more moderate. (The same holds true for "traditional" data centers.) Thus countries with favorable conditions, such as Finland, Sweden and Switzerland, are trying to attract cloud computing data centers. Energy efficiency in cloud computing can result from energy-aware scheduling and server consolidation. However, in the case of distributed clouds over data centers with different sources of energy including renewable energy, the use of energy efficiency reduction could result in a significant carbon footprint reduction.

### Abuse

As with privately purchased hardware, customers can purchase the services of cloud computing for nefarious purposes. This includes password cracking and launching attacks using the purchased services. In 2009, a banking trojan illegally used the popular Amazon service as a command and control channel that issued software updates and malicious instructions to PCs that were infected by the malware.

### IT Governance

The introduction of cloud computing requires an appropriate IT governance model to ensure a secured computing environment and to comply with all relevant organizational information technology policies. As such, organizations need a set of capabilities that are essential when effectively implementing and managing cloud services, including demand management, relationship management, data security management, application lifecycle management, risk and compliance management. A danger lies with the explosion of companies joining the growth in cloud computing by becoming providers. However, many of the infrastructural and logistical concerns regarding the operation of cloud computing businesses are still unknown. This over-saturation may have ramifications for the industry as a whole.

## Consumer End Storage

The increased use of cloud computing could lead to a reduction in demand for high storage capacity consumer end devices, due to cheaper low storage devices that stream all content via the cloud becoming more popular. In a Wired article, Jake Gardner explains that while unregulated usage is beneficial for IT and tech moguls like Amazon, the anonymous nature of the cost of consumption of cloud usage makes it difficult for business to evaluate and incorporate it into their business plans.

## Ambiguity of Terminology

Outside of the information technology and software industry, the term "cloud" can be found to reference a wide range of services, some of which fall under the category of cloud computing, while others do not. The cloud is often used to refer to a product or service that is discovered, accessed and paid for over the Internet, but is not necessarily a computing resource. Examples of service that are sometimes referred to as "the cloud" include, but are not limited to, crowd sourcing, cloud printing, crowd funding, cloud manufacturing.

## Performance Interference and Noisy Neighbors

Due to its multi-tenant nature and resource sharing, cloud computing must also deal with the "noisy neighbor" effect. This effect in essence indicates that in a shared infrastructure, the activity of a virtual machine on a neighboring core on the same physical host may lead to increased performance degradation of the VMs in the same physical host, due to issues such as e.g. cache contamination. Due to the fact that the neighboring VMs may be activated or deactivated at arbitrary... times, the result is an increased variation in the actual performance of cloud resources. This effect seems to be dependent on the nature of the applications that run inside the VMs but also other factors such as scheduling parameters and the careful selection may lead to optimized assignment in order to minimize the phenomenon. This has also led to difficulties in comparing various cloud providers on cost and performance using traditional benchmarks for service and application performance, as the time period and location in which the benchmark is performed can result in widely varied results. This observation has led in turn to research efforts to make cloud computing applications intrinsically aware of changes in the infrastructure so that the application can automatically adapt to avoid failure.

### Monopolies and Privatization of Cyberspace

Philosopher Slavoj Žižek points out that, although cloud computing enhances content accessibility, this access is "increasingly grounded in the virtually monopolistic privatization of the cloud which provides this access". According to him, this access, necessarily mediated through a handful of companies, ensures a progressive privatization of global cyberspace. Žižek criticizes the argument purported by supporters of cloud computing that this phenomenon is part of the "natural evolution" of the Internet, sustaining that the quasi-monopolies "set prices at will but also filter the software they provide to give its "universality" a particular twist depending on commercial and ideological interests."

## Cloud Computing Security

Cloud computing security or, more simply, cloud security refers to a broad set of policies, technologies, and controls deployed to protect data, applications, and the associated infrastructure of cloud computing. It is a sub-domain of computer security, network security, and, more broadly, information security.

### Security Issues Associated with the Cloud

Cloud computing and storage provides users with capabilities to store and process their data in third-party data centers. Organizations use the cloud in a variety of different service models (with acronyms such as SaaS, PaaS, and IaaS) and deployment models (private, public, hybrid, and community). Security concerns associated with cloud computing fall into two broad categories: security issues faced by cloud providers (organizations providing software-, platform-, or infrastructure-as-a-service via the cloud) and security issues faced by their customers (companies or organizations who host applications or store data on the cloud). The responsibility is shared, however. The provider must ensure that their infrastructure is secure and that their clients' data and applications are protected, while the user must take measures to fortify their application and use strong passwords and authentication measures.

When an organization elects to store data or host applications on the public cloud, it loses its ability to have physical access to the servers hosting its information. As a result, potentially sensitive data is at risk from insider attacks. According to a recent Cloud Security Alliance Report, insider attacks are the sixth biggest threat in cloud computing. Therefore, Cloud Service providers must ensure that thorough background checks are conducted for employees who have physical access to the servers in the data center. Additionally, data centers must be frequently monitored for suspicious activity.

In order to conserve resources, cut costs, and maintain efficiency, Cloud Service Providers often store more than one customer's data on the same server. As a result, there is a chance that one user's private data can be viewed by other users (possibly even competitors). To handle such sensitive situations, cloud service providers should ensure proper data isolation and logical storage segregation.

The extensive use of virtualization in implementing cloud infrastructure brings unique security concerns for customers or tenants of a public cloud service. Virtualization alters the relationship between the OS and underlying hardware - be it computing, storage or even networking. This introduces an additional layer - virtualization - that itself must be properly configured, managed and secured. Specific concerns include the potential to compromise the virtualization software, or "hypervisor". While these concerns are largely theoretical, they do exist. For example, a breach in the administrator workstation with the management software of the virtualization software can cause the whole datacenter to go down or be reconfigured to an attacker's liking.

## Cloud Security Controls

Cloud security architecture is effective only if the correct defensive implementations are in place. An efficient cloud security architecture should recognize the issues that will arise with security management. The security management addresses these issues with security controls. These controls are put in place to safeguard any weaknesses in the system and reduce the effect of an attack. While there are many types of controls behind a cloud security architecture, they can usually be found in one of the following categories:

### Deterrent Controls

These controls are intended to reduce attacks on a cloud system. Much like a warning sign on a fence or a property, deterrent controls typically reduce the threat level by informing potential attackers that there will be adverse consequences for them if they proceed. (Some consider them a subset of preventive controls.)

### Preventive Controls

Preventive controls strengthen the system against incidents, generally by reducing if not actually eliminating vulnerabilities. Strong authentication of cloud users, for instance, makes it less likely that unauthorized users can access cloud systems, and more likely that cloud users are positively identified.

### Detective Controls

Detective controls are intended to detect and react appropriately to any incidents that occur. In the event of an attack, a detective control will signal the preventative or corrective controls to address the issue. System and network security monitoring, including intrusion detection and prevention arrangements, are typically employed to detect attacks on cloud systems and the supporting communications infrastructure.

### Corrective Controls

Corrective controls reduce the consequences of an incident, normally by limiting the damage. They come into effect during or after an incident. Restoring system backups in order to rebuild a compromised system is an example of a corrective control.

## Dimensions of Cloud Security

It is generally recommended that information security controls be selected and implemented according and in proportion to the risks, typically by assessing the threats, vulnerabilities and impacts. Cloud security concerns can be grouped in various ways; Gartner named seven while the Cloud Security Alliance identified fourteen areas of concern. Cloud Application Security Brokers (CASB) are used to add additional security to cloud services.

## Security and Privacy

### Identity Management

Every enterprise will have its own identity management system to control access to information and computing resources. Cloud providers either integrate the customer's identity management system into their own infrastructure, using federation or SSO technology, or a biometric-based identification system, or provide an identity management system of their own. CloudID, for instance, provides privacy-preserving cloud-based and cross-enterprise biometric identification. It links the confidential information of the users to their biometrics and stores it in an encrypted fashion. Making use of a searchable encryption technique, biometric identification is performed in encrypted domain to make sure that the cloud provider or potential attackers do not gain access to any sensitive data or even the contents of the individual queries.

### Physical Security

Cloud service providers physically secure the IT hardware (servers, routers, cables etc.) against unauthorized access, interference, theft, fires, floods etc. and ensure that essential supplies (such as electricity) are sufficiently robust to minimize the possibility of disruption. This is normally achieved by serving cloud applications from 'world-class' (i.e. professionally specified, designed, constructed, managed, monitored and maintained) data centers.

### Personnel Security

Various information security concerns relating to the IT and other professionals associated with cloud services are typically handled through pre-, para- and post-employment activities such as security screening potential recruits, security awareness and training programs, proactive.

### Privacy

Providers ensure that all critical data (credit card numbers, for example) are masked or encrypted and that only authorized users have access to data in its entirety. Moreover, digital identities and credentials must be protected as should any data that the provider collects or produces about customer activity in the cloud.

### Data Security

A number of security threats are associated with cloud data services: not only traditional security threats, such as network eavesdropping, illegal invasion, and denial of service attacks, but also specific cloud computing threats, such as side channel attacks, virtualization vulnerabilities, and abuse of cloud services. The following security requirements limit the threats.

### Confidentiality

Data confidentiality is the property that data contents are not made available or disclosed to illegal users. Outsourced data is stored in a cloud and out of the owners' direct control. Only authorized users can access the sensitive data while others, including CSPs, should not gain any information of the data. Meanwhile, data owners expect to fully utilize cloud data services, e.g., data search, data computation, and data sharing, without the leakage of the data contents to CSPs or other adversaries.

### Access Controllability

Access controllability means that a data owner can perform the selective restriction of access to his data outsourced to cloud. Legal users can be authorized by the owner to access the data, while others can not access it without permissions. Further, it is desirable to enforce fine-grained access control to the outsourced data, i.e., different users should be granted different access privileges with regard to different data pieces. The access authorization must be controlled only by the owner in untrusted cloud environments.

## Integrity

Data integrity demands maintaining and assuring the accuracy and completeness of data. A data owner always expects that his data in a cloud can be stored correctly and trustworthily. It means that the data should not be illegally tampered, improperly modified, deliberately deleted, or maliciously fabricated. If any undesirable operations corrupt or delete the data, the owner should be able to detect the corruption or loss. Further, when a portion of the outsourced data is corrupted or lost, it can still be retrieved by the data users.

## Effective Encryption

Some advanced encryption algorithms which have been applied into the cloud computing increase the protection of privacy. In a practice called crypto-shredding, the keys can simply be deleted when there is no more use of the data.

## Attribute-based Encryption Algorithm

### Ciphertext-policy ABE (CP-ABE)

In the CP-ABE, the encryptor controls access strategy, as the strategy gets more complex, the design of system public key becomes more complex, and the security of the system is proved to be more difficult. The main research work of CP-ABE is focused on the design of the access structure.

### Key-policy ABE (KP-ABE)

In the KP-ABE, attribute sets are used to explain the encrypted texts and the private keys with the specified encrypted texts that users will have the left to decrypt.

## Fully Homomorphic Encryption (FHE)

Fully Homomorphic encryption allows straightforward computations on encrypted information, and also allows computing sum and product for the encrypted data without decryption.

## Searchable Encryption (SE)

Searchable Encryption is a cryptographic primitive which offers secure search functions over encrypted data. In order to improve search efficiency, SE generally builds keyword indexes to securely perform user queries. SE schemes can be classified into two categories: SE based on secret-key cryptography and SE based on public-key cryptography.

## Compliance

Numerous laws and regulations pertain to the storage and use of data. In the US these include privacy or data protection laws, Payment Card Industry Data Security Standard (PCI DSS), the Health Insurance Portability and Accountability Act (HIPAA), the Sarbanes-Oxley Act, the Federal Information Security Management Act of 2002 (FISMA), and Children's Online Privacy Protection Act of 1998, among others.

Similar laws may apply in different legal jurisdictions and may differ quite markedly from those enforced in the US. Cloud service users may often need to be aware of the legal and regulatory differences between the jurisdictions. For example, data stored by a Cloud Service Provider may be located in, say, Singapore and mirrored in the US.

Many of these regulations mandate particular controls (such as strong access controls and audit trails) and require regular reporting. Cloud customers must ensure that their cloud providers adequately fulfil such requirements as appropriate, enabling them to comply with their obligations since, to a large extent, they remain accountable.

### Business Continuity and Data Recovery

Cloud providers have business continuity and data recovery plans in place to ensure that service can be maintained in case of a disaster or an emergency and that any data loss will be recovered. These plans may be shared with and reviewed by their customers, ideally dovetailing with the customers' own continuity arrangements. Joint continuity exercises may be appropriate, simulating a major Internet or electricity supply failure for instance.

### Logs and Audit Trails

In addition to producing logs and audit trails, cloud providers work with their customers to ensure that these logs and audit trails are properly secured, maintained for as long as the customer requires, and are accessible for the purposes of forensic investigation (e.g., eDiscovery).

### Unique Compliance Requirements

In addition to the requirements to which customers are subject, the data centers used by cloud providers may also be subject to compliance requirements. Using a cloud service provider (CSP) can lead to additional security concerns around data jurisdiction since customer or tenant data may not remain on the same system, or in the same data center or even within the same provider's cloud.

## Legal and Contractual Issues

Aside from the security and compliance issues enumerated above, cloud providers and their customers will negotiate terms around liability (stipulating how incidents involving data loss or compromise will be resolved, for example), intellectual property, and end-of-service (when data and applications are ultimately returned to the customer). In addition, there are considerations for acquiring data from the cloud that may be involved in litigation. These issues are discussed in Service-Level Agreements (SLA).

### Public Records

Legal issues may also include records-keeping requirements in the public sector, where many agencies are required by law to retain and make available electronic records in a specific fashion. This may be determined by legislation, or law may require agencies to conform to the rules and practices set by a records-keeping agency. Public agencies using cloud computing and storage must take these concerns into account.

## Cloud Computing Architecture

Cloud computing architecture refers to the components and subcomponents required for cloud computing. These components typically consist of a front end platform (fat client, thin client, mobile device), back end platforms (servers, storage), a cloud based delivery, and a network (Internet, Intranet, Intercloud). Combined, these components make up cloud computing architecture.

### Cloud Client Platforms

Cloud computing architectures consist of front-end platforms called clients or cloud clients. These clients are servers, fat (or thick) clients, thin clients, zero clients, tablets and mobile devices. These client platforms interact with the cloud data storage via an application (middleware), via a web browser, or through a virtual session.

### The Zero Client

The zero or ultra-thin client initializes the network to gather required configuration files that then tell it where its OS binaries are stored. The entire zero client device runs via the network. This creates a single point of failure, in that, if the network goes down, the device is rendered useless.

### Cloud Storage

An online network storage where data is stored and accessible to multiple clients. Cloud storage is generally deployed in the following configurations: public cloud, private cloud, community cloud, or some combination of the three also known as hybrid cloud.

In order to be effective, the cloud storage needs to be agile, flexible, scalable, multi-tenancy, and secure.

## Cloud based Delivery

### Software as a Service (SaaS)

The software-as-a-service (SaaS) service-model involves the cloud provider installing and maintaining software in the cloud and users running the software from their cloud clients over the Internet (or Intranet). The users' client machines require no installation of any application-specific software - cloud applications run on the server (in the cloud). SaaS is scalable, and system administrators may load the applications on several servers. In the past, each customer would purchase and load their own copy of the application to each of their own servers, but with the SaaS the customer can access the application without installing the software locally. SaaS typically involves a monthly or annual fee.

Software as a service provides the equivalent of installed applications in the traditional (non-cloud computing) delivery of applications.

Software as a service has four common approaches:

1. single instance
2. multi instance
3. multi-tenant
4. flex tenancy

### Development as a Service (DaaS)

Development as a service is web based, community shared development tools. This is the equivalent to locally installed development tools in the traditional (non-cloud computing) delivery of development tools.

### Data as a Service (DaaS)

Data as a service is web based design construct where by cloud data is accessed through some defined API layer. DaaS services are often considered as a specialized subset of a Software as a service offering.

### Platform as a Service (Paas)

Platform as a service is cloud computing service which provides the users with application platforms and databases as a service. This is equivalent to middleware in the traditional (non-cloud computing) delivery of application platforms and databases. We can take on example for this as Microsoft Azure provides platform as services for multilple language,if we use .net platform then we can build products using .net framework which will be provided by Microsoft Azure.

### Infrastructure as a Service (IaaS)

Infrastructure as a service is taking the physical hardware and going completely virtual (e.g. all servers, networks, storage, and system management all existing in the cloud). This is the equivalent to infrastructure and hardware in the traditional (non-cloud computing) method running in the cloud. In other words, businesses pay a fee (monthly or annually) to run virtual servers, networks, storage from the cloud. This will mitigate the need for a data center, heating, cooling, and maintaining hardware at the local level.

### Cloud networking

Generally, the cloud network layer should offer:

- High bandwidth (low latency)

  Allowing users to have uninterrupted access to their data and applications.

- Agile network

  On-demand access to resources requires the ability to move quickly and efficiently between servers and possibly even clouds.

- Network security

  Security is always important, but when you are dealing with multi-tenancy, it becomes much more important because you're dealing with segregating multiple customers.

## Cloud Management

Cloud management is the management of cloud computing products and services.

Public clouds are managed by public cloud service providers, which include the public cloud environment's servers, storage, networking and data center operations. Users of public cloud services can generally select from three basic categories:

- User self-provisioning: Customers purchase cloud services directly from the provider, typically through a web form or console interface. The customer pays on a per-transaction basis.
- Advance provisioning: Customers contract in advance a predetermined amount of resources, which are prepared in advance of service. The customer pays a flat fee or a monthly fee.
- Dynamic provisioning: The provider allocates resources when the customer

needs them, then decommissions them when they are no longer needed. The customer is charged on a pay-per-use basis.

Managing a private cloud requires software tools to help create a virtualized pool of compute resources, provide a self-service portal for end users and handle security, resource allocation, tracking and billing. Management tools for private clouds tend to be service driven, as opposed to resource driven, because cloud environments are typically highly virtualized and organized in terms of portable workloads.

In hybrid cloud environments, compute, network and storage resources must be managed across multiple domains, so a good management strategy should start by defining what needs to be managed, and where and how to do it. Policies to help govern these domains should include configuration and installation of images, access control, and budgeting and reporting. Access control often includes the use of Single sign-on (SSO), in which a user logs in once and gains access to all systems without being prompted to log in again at each of them.

## Aspects of Cloud Management Systems

A cloud management system combines software and technologies in a design for managing cloud environments. Software developers have responded to the management challenges of cloud computing with cloud management systems.

At a minimum, a cloud-management system should have the ability to:

- manage a pool of heterogeneous compute-resources
- provide access to end users
- monitor security
- manage resource allocation
- manage tracking

For composite applications, cloud management systems also encompass frameworks for workflow-mapping and -management.

Enterprises with large-scale cloud implementations may require more robust cloud management tools which include specific characteristics, such as the ability to manage multiple platforms from a single point of reference, or intelligent analytics to automate processes like application lifecycle management. High-end cloud management tools should also have the ability to handle system failures automatically with capabilities such as self-monitoring, an explicit notification mechanism, and include failover and self-healing capabilities. Cisco recently launched its InterCloud solution to provide flexibility to dynamically manage workloads across public and private cloud environments.

The concept of a Cloud Management Platform (CMP) has emerged.

## Second Section from Cloud Computing

Legacy management infrastructures, which are based on the concept of dedicated system relationships and architecture constructs, are not well suited to cloud environments where instances are continually launched and decommissioned. Instead, the dynamic nature of cloud computing requires monitoring and management tools that are adaptable, extensible and customizable.

## Cloud Management Challenges

Cloud computing presents a number of management challenges. Companies using public clouds do not have ownership of the equipment hosting the cloud environment, and because the environment is not contained within their own networks, public cloud customers do not have full visibility or control. Users of public cloud services must also integrate with an architecture defined by the cloud provider, using its specific parameters for working with cloud components. Integration includes tying into the cloud APIs for configuring IP addresses, subnets, firewalls and data service functions for storage. Because control of these functions is based on the cloud provider's infrastructure and services, public cloud users must integrate with the cloud infrastructure management.

Capacity management is a challenge for both public and private cloud environments because end users have the ability to deploy applications using self-service portals. Applications of all sizes may appear in the environment, consume an unpredictable amount of resources, then disappear at any time. A possible solution is profiling the applications impact on computational resources. As result, the performance models allow the prediction of how resource utilization changes according to application patterns. Thus, resources can be dynamically scaled to meet the expected demand. This is critical to cloud providers that need to provision resources quickly to meet a growing demand by their applications.

Chargeback—or, pricing resource use on a granular basis—is a challenge for both public and private cloud environments. Chargeback is a challenge for public cloud service providers because they must price their services competitively while still creating profit. Users of public cloud services may find chargeback challenging because it is difficult for IT groups to assess actual resource costs on a granular basis due to overlapping resources within an organization that may be paid for by an individual business unit, such as electrical power. For private cloud operators, chargeback is fairly straightforward, but the challenge lies in guessing how to allocate resources as closely as possible to actual resource usage to achieve the greatest operational efficiency. Exceeding budgets can be a risk.

Hybrid cloud environments, which combine public and private cloud services, sometimes with traditional infrastructure elements, present their own set of management challenges. These include security concerns if sensitive data lands on public cloud servers, budget concerns around overuse of storage or bandwidth and proliferation of mismanaged images. Managing the information flow in a hybrid cloud environment is also a significant challenge. On-premises clouds must share information with applications hosted off-premises by public cloud providers, and this information may change constantly. Hybrid cloud environments also typically include a complex mix of policies, permissions and limits that must be managed consistently across both public and private clouds.

### Cloud Services Brokerages

Like any other brokerage firm, a Cloud Services Brokerage (CSB) manages cloud services for clients. Gartner explains that CSBs play an intermediary role in the cloud computing management process. Cloud services brokerages consolidate cloud services from one or more sources and allow customers to access these services through one portal.

## Cloudlet

A cloudlet is a mobility-enhanced small-scale cloud datacenter that is located at the edge of the Internet. The main purpose of the cloudlet is supporting resource-intensive and interactive mobile applications by providing powerful computing resources to mobile devices with lower latency. It is a new architectural element that extends today's cloud computing infrastructure. It represents the middle tier of a 3-tier hierarchy: mobile *device - cloudlet - cloud*. A cloudlet can be viewed as a *data center in a box* whose goal is to *bring the cloud closer*. The cloudlet term was first coined by M. Satyanarayanan, Victor Bahl, Ramón Cáceres, and Nigel Davies, and a prototype implementation is developed by Carnegie Mellon University as a research project. The concept of cloudlet is also known as follow me cloud, and mobile micro-cloud.

### Motivation

Many mobile services split the application into a front-end client program and a back-end server program following the traditional client-server model. The front-end mobile application offloads its functionality to the back-end servers for various reasons such as speeding up processing. With the advent of cloud computing, the back-end server is typically hosted at the cloud datacenter. Though the use of a cloud datacenter offers various benefits such as scalability and elasticity, its consolidation and centralizion lead to a large separation between a mobile device and its associated datacenter. End-to-end communication then involves many network hops and results in high latencies and low bandwidth.

For the reasons of latency, some emerging mobile applications require cloud offload infrastructure to be close to the mobile device to achieve low response time. In the ideal case, it is just one wireless hop away. For example, the offload infrastructure could be located in a cellular base station or it could be LAN-connected to a set of Wi-Fi base stations. The individual elements of this offload infrastructure are referred to as cloudlets.

## Applications

Cloudlets aim to support mobile applications that are both resource-intensive and interactive. Augmented reality applications that use head-tracked systems require end-to-end latencies of less than 16 ms. Cloud games with remote rendering also require low latencies and high bandwidth. Wearable cognitive assistance system combines a device like Google Glass with cloud-based processing to guide a user through a complex task. This futuristic genre of applications is characterized as "astonishingly transformative" by the report of the 2013 NSF Workshop on Future Directions in Wireless Networking. These applications use cloud resources in the critical path of real-time user interaction. Consequently, they cannot tolerate end-to-end operation latencies of more than a few tens of milliseconds. Apple Siri and Google Now which perform compute-intensive speech recognition in the cloud, are further examples in this emerging space.

## Cloudlet vs Cloud

There is significant overlap in the requirements for cloud and cloudlet. At both levels, there is the need for: (a) strong isolation between untrusted user-level computations; (b) mechanisms for authentication, access control, and metering; (c) dynamic resource allocation for user-level computations; and, (d) the ability to support a very wide range of user-level computations, with minimal restrictions on their process structure, programming languages or operating systems. At a cloud datacenter, these requirements are met today using the virtual machine (VM) abstraction. For the same reasons they are used in cloud computing today, VMs are used as an abstraction for cloudlets. Meanwhile, there are a few but important differentiators between cloud and cloudlet.

## Rapid Provisioning

Different from cloud data centers that are optimized for launching existing VM images in their storage tier, cloudlets need to be much agiler in their provisioning. Their association with mobile devices is highly dynamic, with considerable churn due to user mobility. A user from far away may unexpectedly show up at a cloudlet (e.g., if he just got off an international flight) and try to use it for an application such as a personalized language translator. For that user, the provisioning delay before he is able to use the application impacts usability.

## VM Handoff Across Cloudlets

If a mobile device user moves away from the cloudlet he is currently using, the interactive response will degrade as the logical network distance increases. To address this effect of user mobility, the offloaded services on the first cloudlet need to be transferred to the second cloudlet maintaining end-to-end network quality. This resembles live migration in cloud computing but differs considerably in a sense that the VM handoff happens in Wide Area Network (WAN).

## OpenStack++

Since the cloudlet model requires reconfiguration or additional deployment of hardware/software, it is important to provide a systematic way to incentivise the deployment. However, it can face a classic bootstrapping problem. Cloudlets need practical applications to incentivize cloudlet deployment. However, developers cannot heavily rely on cloudlet infrastructure until it is widely deployed. To break this deadlock and bootstrap the cloudlet deployment, researchers at Carnegie Mellon University proposed OpenStack++ that extends OpenStack to leverage its open ecosystem. OpenStack++ provides a set of cloudlet-specific API as OpenStack extensions.

## References


- Y., Lu; X. Xu; J. Xu (2014). "Development of a Hybrid Manufacturing Cloud". Journal of Manufacturing Systems. doi:10.1016/j.jmsy.2014.05.003
- Winkler, Vic (2011). Securing the Cloud: Cloud Computer Security Techniques and Tactics. Waltham, Massachusetts: Elsevier. p. 60. ISBN 978-1-59749-592-9
- Chambers, Don (July 2010). "Windows Azure: Using Windows Azure's Service Bus to Solve Data Security Issues" (PDF). Rebus Technologies. Retrieved 2012-12-14
- Xu, X (2012). "From cloud computing to cloud manufacturing". Robotics and Computer-Integrated Manufacturing. doi:10.1016/j.rcim.2011.07.002
- Winkler, Vic (2011). Securing the Cloud: Cloud Computer Security Techniques and Tactics. Waltham, MA USA: Syngress. pp. 187, 189. ISBN 978-1-59749-592-9
- Cohn, Cindy; Samuels, Julie (31 October 2012). "Megaupload and the Government's Attack on Cloud Computing". Electronic Frontier Foundation. Retrieved 2012-12-14
- SU, Jin-Shu; CAO, Dan; WANG, Xiao-Feng; SUN, Yi-Pin; HU, Qiao-Lin. "Attribute-Based Encryption Schemes". Journal of Software. 22 (6): 1299–1315. doi:10.3724/sp.j.1001.2011.03993
- Winkler, Vic (2011). Securing the Cloud: Cloud Computer Security Techniques and Tactics. Waltham, MA USA: Elsevier. p. 59. ISBN 978-1-59749-592-9
- Vincent Wang, Xi; Xu, Xun W. (2013-08-01). "An interoperable solution for Cloud manufacturing". Robotics and Computer-Integrated Manufacturing. 29 (4): 232–247. doi:10.1016/j.rcim.2013.01.005
- Jon Brodkin (July 28, 2008). "Open source fuels growth of cloud computing, software-as-a-service". Network World. Retrieved 2012-12-14
- S.Hemalatha, Raguram (2014). "Performance of Ring Based Fully Homomorphic Encryption for securing data in Cloud Computing" (PDF). International Journal of Advanced Research in Computer and Communication Engineering
- Winkler, Vic (2011). Securing the Cloud: Cloud Computer Security Techniques and Tactics. Waltham, MA USA: Elsevier. pp. 65, 68, 72, 81, 218–219, 231, 240. ISBN 978-1-59749-592-9
- Armbrust, M; Fox, A.; Griffith, R.; Joseph, A.; Katz, R.; Konwinski, A.; Lee, G.; Patterson, D.; Rabkin, A.; Zaharia, M. (2010). "A view of cloud computing". Communication of the ACM. 53 (4): 50–58. doi:10.1145/1721654.1721672

2

# Data Storage in Cloud Computing

Data storage in cloud computing can be done through cloud storage, object storage, file hosting service and cloud storage gateway. Each hosting service uses a particular architecture to appeal to different needs. This chapter has been carefully written to provide an easy understanding of the varied facets of cloud computing.

## Cloud Storage

Cloud storage is a model of data storage in which the digital data is stored in logical pools, the physical storage spans multiple servers (and often locations), and the physical environment is typically owned and managed by a hosting company. These cloud storage providers are responsible for keeping the data available and accessible, and the physical environment protected and running. People and organizations buy or lease storage capacity from the providers to store user, organization, or application data.

Cloud storage services may be accessed through a co-located cloud computer service, a web service application programming interface (API) or by applications that utilize the API, such as cloud desktop storage, a cloud storage gateway or Web-based content management systems.

### History

Cloud computing is believed to have been invented by Joseph Carl Robnett Licklider in the 1960s with his work on ARPANET to connect people and data from anywhere at any time.

In 1983, CompuServe offered its consumer users a small amount of disk space that could be used to store any files they chose to upload.

In 1994, AT&T launched PersonaLink Services, an online platform for personal and business communication and entrepreneurship. The storage was one of the first to be all web-based, and referenced in their commercials as, "you can think of our electronic meeting place as the cloud." Amazon Web Services introduced their cloud storage service AWS S3 in 2006, and has gained widespread recognition and adoption as the storage supplier to popular services such as Smugmug, Dropbox, Synaptop and Pinterest. In 2005, Box announced an online file sharing and personal cloud content management service for businesses.

## Architecture

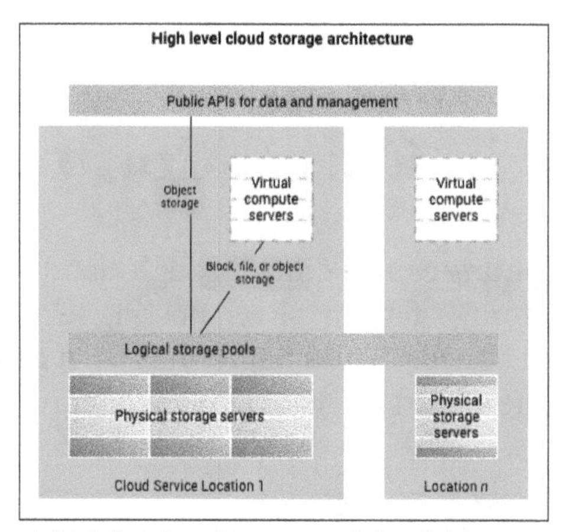


A high level architecture of cloud storage.

Cloud storage is based on highly virtualized infrastructure and is like broader cloud computing in terms of accessible interfaces, near-instant elasticity and scalability, multi-tenancy, and metered resources. Cloud storage services can be utilized from an off-premises service (Amazon S3) or deployed on-premises (ViON Capacity Services).

Cloud storage typically refers to a hosted object storage service, but the term has broadened to include other types of data storage that are now available as a service, like block storage.

Object storage services like Amazon S3 and Microsoft Azure Storage, object storage software like Openstack Swift, object storage systems like EMC Atmos, EMC ECS and Hitachi Content Platform, and distributed storage research projects like OceanStore and VISION Cloud are all examples of storage that can be hosted and deployed with cloud storage characteristics.

Cloud storage is:

- Made up of many distributed resources, but still acts as one, either in a federated or a cooperative storage cloud architecture
- Highly fault tolerant through redundancy and distribution of data
- Highly durable through the creation of versioned copies
- Typically eventually consistent with regard to data replicas

## Advantages

- Companies need only pay for the storage they actually use, typically an average of consumption during a month. This does not mean that cloud storage is less expensive, only that it incurs operating expenses rather than capital expenses.

- Businesses using cloud storage can cut their energy consumption by up to 70% making them a more green business. Also at the vendor level they are dealing with higher levels of energy so they will be more equipped with managing it in order to keep their own costs down as well.
- Organizations can choose between off-premises and on-premises cloud storage options, or a mixture of the two options, depending on relevant decision criteria that is complementary to initial direct cost savings potential; for instance, continuity of operations (COOP), disaster recovery (DR), security (PII, HIPAA, SARBOX, IA/CND), and records retention laws, regulations, and policies.
- Storage availability and data protection is intrinsic to object storage architecture, so depending on the application, the additional technology, effort and cost to add availability and protection can be eliminated.
- Storage maintenance tasks, such as purchasing additional storage capacity, are offloaded to the responsibility of a service provider.
- Cloud storage provides users with immediate access to a broad range of resources and applications hosted in the infrastructure of another organization via a web service interface.
- Cloud storage can be used for copying virtual machine images from the cloud to on-premises locations or to import a virtual machine image from an on-premises location to the cloud image library. In addition, cloud storage can be used to move virtual machine images between user accounts or between data centers.
- Cloud storage can be used as natural disaster proof backup, as normally there are 2 or 3 different backup servers located in different places around the globe.

## Potential Concerns

### Attack Surface Area

Outsourcing data storage increases the attack surface area.

1. When data has been distributed it is stored at more locations increasing the risk of unauthorized physical access to the data. For example, in cloud based architecture, data is replicated and moved frequently so the risk of unauthorized data recovery increases dramatically. Such as in the case of disposal of old equipment, reuse of drives, reallocation of storage space. The manner that data is replicated depends on the service level a customer chooses and on the service provided. When encryption is in place it can ensure confidentiality. Crypto-shredding can be used when disposing of data (on a disk).
2. The number of people with access to the data who could be compromised (i.e. bribed, or coerced) increases dramatically. A single company might have a small

team of administrators, network engineers and technicians, but a cloud storage company will have many customers and thousands of servers and therefore a much larger team of technical staff with physical and electronic access to almost all of the data at the entire facility or perhaps the entire company. Encryption keys that are kept by the service user, as opposed to the service provider limit the access to data by service provider employees. As for sharing the multiple data with multiple users in cloud, a large number of keys has to be distributed to users via secure channels for decryption, also it has to be securely stored and managed by the users in their devices. And storing these keys requires rather expensive secure storage. To overcome that Key-aggregate cryptosystem can be used.

3. It increases the number of networks over which the data travels. Instead of just a local area network (LAN) or storage area network (SAN), data stored on a cloud requires a WAN (wide area network) to connect them both.

4. By sharing storage and networks with many other users/customers it is possible for other customers to access your data. Sometimes because of erroneous actions, faulty equipment, a bug and sometimes because of criminal intent. This risk applies to all types of storage and not only cloud storage. The risk of having data read during transmission can be mitigated through encryption technology. Encryption in transit protects data as it is being transmitted to and from the cloud service. Encryption at rest protects data that is stored at the service provider. Encrypting data in an on-premises cloud service on-ramp system can provide both kinds of encryption protection.

### Supplier Stability

Companies are not permanent and the services and products they provide can change. Outsourcing data storage to another company needs careful investigation and nothing is ever certain. Contracts set in stone can be worthless when a company ceases to exist or its circumstances change. Companies can:

1. Go bankrupt.
2. Expand and change their focus.
3. Be purchased by other larger companies.
4. Be purchased by a company headquartered in or move to a country that negates compliance with export restrictions and thus necessitates a move.
5. Suffer an irrecoverable disaster.

### Accessibility

- Performance for outsourced storage is likely to be lower than local storage, depending on how much a customer is willing to spend for WAN bandwidth

- Reliability and availability depends on wide area network availability and on the level of precautions taken by the service provider. Reliability should be based on hardware as well as various algorithms used.
- Its a given a multiplicity of data storage.

### Other Concerns

- Security of stored data and data in transit may be a concern when storing sensitive data at a cloud storage provider
- Users with specific records-keeping requirements, such as public agencies that must retain electronic records according to statute, may encounter complications with using cloud computing and storage. For instance, the U.S. Department of Defense designated the Defense Information Systems Agency (DISA) to maintain a list of records management products that meet all of the records retention, personally identifiable information (PII), and security (Information Assurance; IA) requirements
- Cloud storage is a rich resource for both hackers and national security agencies. Because the cloud holds data from many different users and organizations, hackers see it as a very valuable target.
- Piracy and copyright infringement may be enabled by sites that permit filesharing. For example, the CodexCloud ebook storage site has faced litigation from the owners of the intellectual property uploaded and shared there, as have the GrooveShark and YouTube sites it has been compared to.
- The legal aspect, from a regulatory compliance standpoint, is of concern when storing files domestically and especially internationally.

## Object Storage

Object storage (also known as object-based storage) is a computer data storage architecture that manages data as objects, as opposed to other storage architectures like file systems which manage data as a file hierarchy and block storage which manages data as blocks within sectors and tracks. Each object typically includes the data itself, a variable amount of metadata, and a globally unique identifier. Object storage can be implemented at multiple levels, including the device level (object storage device), the system level, and the interface level. In each case, object storage seeks to enable capabilities not addressed by other storage architectures, like interfaces that can be directly programmable by the application, a namespace that can span multiple instances of physical hardware, and data management functions like data replication and data distribution at object-level granularity.

Object storage systems allow retention of massive amounts of unstructured data. Object storage is used for purposes such as storing photos on Facebook, songs on Spotify, or files in online collaboration services, such as Dropbox.

## History

In 1995, research led by Garth Gibson on Network Attached Secure Disks first promoted the concept of splitting less common operations, like namespace manipulations, from common operations, like reads and writes, to optimize the performance and scale of both. In the same year, 1995, a Belgium company - FilePool - was established to build the basis for archiving functions. Object storage was proposed at Gibson's Carnegie Mellon University lab as a research project in 1996 . Another key concept was abstracting the writes and reads of data to more flexible data containers (objects). Fine grained access control through object storage architecture was further described by one of the NASD team, Howard Gobioff, who later was one of the inventors of the Google File System. Other related work includes the Coda filesystem project at Carnegie Mellon, which started in 1987, and spawned the Lustre file system. There is also the OceanStore project at UC Berkeley, which started in 1999.

Centera, debuted in 2002. The technology. called content-addressable storage, was developed at Filepool, acquired by EMC Corporation in 2001.

## Development

From 1999 to 2013, at least $300 million of venture financing was related to object storage, including vendors like Amplidata, Bycast, Cleversafe, Cloudian, Nirvanix, and Scality. This does not include engineering from systems vendors like DataDirect Networks (WOS), Dell EMC Elastic Cloud Storage, Centera, Atmos, HDS (HCP), IBM, NetApp (StorageGRID), Redhat GlusterFS, cloud services vendors like Amazon (AWS S3), Microsoft (Microsoft Azure) and Google (Google Cloud Storage), or open source development at Lustre, OpenStack (Swift), MogileFS, Ceph and OpenIO. An article written illustrating products' timeline was published in July 2016.

## Architecture

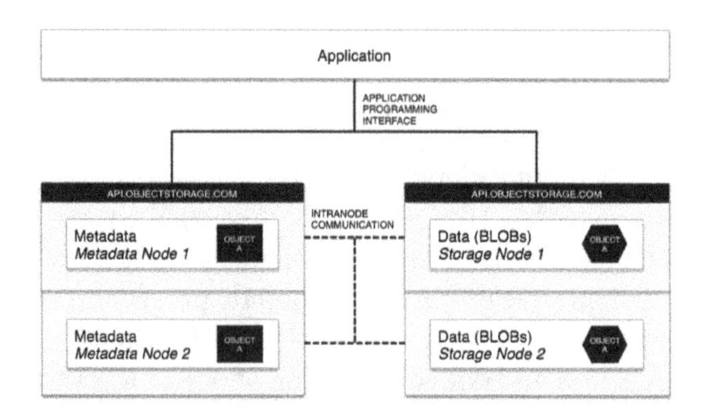

## Abstraction of Storage

One of the design principles of object storage is to abstract some of the lower layers of storage away from the administrators and applications. Thus, data is exposed and managed as objects instead of files or blocks. Objects contain additional descriptive properties which can be used for better indexing or management. Administrators do not have to perform lower level storage functions like constructing and managing logical volumes to utilize disk capacity or setting RAID levels to deal with disk failure.

Object storage also allows the addressing and identification of individual objects by more than just file name and file path. Object storage adds a unique identifier within a bucket, or across the entire system, to support much larger namespaces and eliminate name collisions.

## Inclusion of Rich Custom Metadata within the Object

Object storage explicitly separates file metadata from data to support additional capabilities: As opposed to fixed metadata in file systems (filename, creation date, type, etc.), object storage provides for full function, custom, object-level metadata in order to:

- Capture application-specific or user-specific information for better indexing purposes
- Support data management policies (e.g. a policy to drive object movement from one storage tier to another)
- Centralize management of storage across many individual nodes and clusters
- Optimize metadata storage (e.g. encapsulated, database or key value storage) and caching/indexing (when authoritative metadata is encapsulated with the metadata inside the object) independently from the data storage (e.g. unstructured binary storage)

Additionally, in some object-based file system implementations:

- The file system clients only contact metadata servers once when the file is opened and then get content directly via object storage servers (vs. block-based file systems which would require constant metadata access)
- Data objects can be configured on a per-file basis to allow adaptive stripe width, even across multiple object storage servers, supporting optimizations in bandwidth and I/O

Object-based storage devices (OSD) as well as some software implementations (e.g., Caringo Swarm) manage metadata and data at the storage device level:

- Instead of providing a block-oriented interface that reads and writes fixed sized blocks of data, data is organized into flexible-sized data containers, called objects
- Each object has both data (an uninterpreted sequence of bytes) and metadata (an extensible set of attributes describing the object); physically encapsulating both together benefits recoverability.
- The command interface includes commands to create and delete objects, write bytes and read bytes to and from individual objects, and to set and get attributes on objects
- Security mechanisms provide per-object and per-command access control

### Programmatic Data Management

Object storage provides programmatic interfaces to allow applications to manipulate data. At the base level, this includes CRUD functions for basic read, write and delete operations. Some object storage implementations go further, supporting additional functionality like object versioning, object replication, and movement of objects between different tiers and types of storage. Most API implementations are ReST-based, allowing the use of many standard HTTP calls.

### Implementation

### Object-based Storage Devices

Object storage at the protocol and device layer was proposed 20 years ago and approved for the SCSI command set nearly 10 years ago as "Object-based Storage Device Commands" (OSD), but has not been productized until the development of the Seagate Kinetic Open Storage platform. The SCSI command set for Object Storage Devices was developed by a working group of the Storage Networking Industry Association (SNIA) for the T10 committee of the International Committee for Information Technology Standards (INCITS). T10 is responsible for all SCSI standards.

### Object-based File Systems

Some distributed file systems use an object-based architecture, where file metadata is stored in metadata servers and file data is stored in object storage servers. File system client software interacts with the distinct servers, and abstracts them to present a full file system to users and applications. IBM Spectrum Scale (also known as GPFS), Dell EMC Elastic Cloud Storage, Ceph, XtreemFS, and Lustre are examples of this type of object storage.

### Archive Storage

Some early incarnations of object storage were used for archiving, as implementations were optimized for data services like immutability, not performance. EMC Centera and Hitachi HCP (formerly known as HCAP) are two commonly cited object storage products for archiving. Another example is Quantum Lattus Object Storage Platform.

### Cloud Storage

The vast majority of cloud storage available in the market leverages an object storage architecture. Two notable examples are Amazon Web Services S3, which debuted in 2005, and Rackspace Files (whose code was released as OpenStack Swift).

### "Captive" Object Storage

Some large internet companies developed their own software when object storage products were not commercially available or use cases were very specific. Facebook famously invented their own object storage software, code-named Haystack, to address their particular massive scale photo management needs efficiently.

### Hybrid Storage

A few object storage systems, such as Ceph, GlusterFS, Cloudian, IBM Spectrum Scale, and Scality support Unified File and Object (UFO) storage, allowing some clients to store objects on a storage system while simultaneously other clients store files on the same storage system. While "hybrid storage" is not a widely accepted term for this concept, interoperable interfaces to the same set of data is becoming available in some object storage products.

### Virtual Object Storage

In addition to object storage systems that own the managed files, some systems provide an object abstraction on top of one or more traditional filesystem based solutions. These solutions do not own the underlaying raw storage, but instead actively mirror the filesystem changes and replicate them in their own object catalog, alongside any metadata that can be automatically extracted from the files. Users can then contribute additional metadata through the virtual object storage APIs. A global namespace and replication capabilities both inside and across filesystems are typically supported.

Notable examples in this category are Nirvana, and its open-source cousin iRODS.

Most products in this category have recently extended their capabilities to support other Object Store solutions as well.

### Object Storage Systems

More general purpose object storage systems came to market around 2008. Lured by the incredible growth of "captive" storage systems within web applications like Yahoo

Mail and the early success of cloud storage, object storage systems promised the scale and capabilities of cloud storage, with the ability to deploy the system within an enterprise, or at an aspiring cloud storage service provider. Notable examples of object storage systems include NetApp StorageGRID, EMC Atmos, OpenStack Swift, Scality RING, Caringo Swarm (formerly CAStor), Cloudian, OpenIO, and Minio.

## Market Adoption

The Titan supercomputer at Oak Ridge National Laboratory

One of the first object storage products, Lustre, is used in 70% of the Top 100 supercomputers and ~50% of the Top 500. As of June 16, 2013, this includes 7 of the top 10, including the current fastest system on the list - China's Tianhe-2 and the second fastest, the Titan supercomputer at Oak Ridge National Laboratory (pictured on the right).

Object storage systems had good adoption in the early 2000s as an archive platform, particularly in the wake of compliance laws like Sarbanes-Oxley. After five years in the market, EMC's Centera product claimed over 3,500 customers and 150 petabytes shipped by 2007. Hitachi's HCP product also claims many petabyte-scale customers. Newer object storage systems have also gotten some traction, particularly around very large custom applications like eBay's auction site, where EMC Atmos is used to manage over 500 million objects a day. As of March 3, 2014, EMC claims to have sold over 1.5 exabytes of Atmos storage. On July 1, 2014, Los Alamos National Lab chose the Scality RING as the basis for a 500 petabyte storage environment, which would be among the largest ever.

"Captive" object storage systems like Facebook's Haystack have scaled impressively. In April 2009, Haystack was managing 60 billion photos and 1.5 petabytes of storage, adding 220 million photos and 25 terabytes a week. Facebook more recently stated that they were adding 350 million photos a day and were storing 240 billion photos. This could equal as much as 357 petabytes.

Cloud storage has become pervasive as many new web and mobile applications choose it as a common way to store binary data. As the storage backend to many popular applications like Smugmug and Dropbox, AWS S3 has grown to massive scale, citing over 2 trillion objects stored in April 2013. Two months later, Microsoft claimed that they stored even more objects in Azure at 8.5 trillion. By April 2014, Azure claimed over 20 trillion objects stored. Windows Azure Storage manages Blobs (user files), Tables (structured storage), and Queues (message delivery) and counts them all as objects.

## Market Analysis

IDC has begun to assess the object-based storage market annually using its MarketScape methodology. IDC describes the MarketScape as: "...a quantitative and qualitative assessment of the characteristics that assess a vendor's current and future success in the said market or market segment and provide a measure of their ascendancy to become a Leader or maintain a leadership. IDC MarketScape assessments are particularly helpful in emerging markets that are often fragmented, have several players, and lack clear leaders."

In 2013, IDC rated Cleversafe, Scality, DataDirect Networks, Amplidata, and EMC as leaders. In 2014, it rated Scality, Cleversafe, DataDirect Networks, Hitachi Data Systems, Amplidata, EMC, and Cloudian as leaders.

## Object-based Storage Device Standards

### OSD Version 1

In the first version of the OSD standard, objects are specified with a 64-bit partition ID and a 64-bit object ID. Partitions are created and deleted within an OSD, and objects are created and deleted within partitions. There are no fixed sizes associated with partitions or objects; they are allowed to grow subject to physical size limitations of the device or logical quota constraints on a partition.

An extensible set of attributes describe objects. Some attributes are implemented directly by the OSD, such as the number of bytes in an object and the modify time of an object. There is a special policy tag attribute that is part of the security mechanism. Other attributes are uninterpreted by the OSD. These are set on objects by the higher-level storage systems that use the OSD for persistent storage. For example, attributes might be used to classify objects, or to capture relationships among different objects stored on different OSDs.

A list command returns a list of identifiers for objects within a partition, optionally filtered by matches against their attribute values. A list command can also return selected attributes of the listed objects.

Read and write commands can be combined, or piggy-backed, with commands to get and set attributes. This ability reduces the number of times a high-level storage system has to cross the interface to the OSD, which can improve overall efficiency.

### OSD Version 2

A second generation of the SCSI command set, "Object-Based Storage Devices - 2" (OSD-2) added support for snapshots, collections of objects, and improved error handling.

A snapshot is a point in time copy of all the objects in a partition into a new partition.

The OSD can implement a space-efficient copy using copy-on-write techniques so that the two partitions share objects that are unchanged between the snapshots, or the OSD might physically copy the data to the new partition. The standard defines clones, which are writeable, and snapshots, which are read-only.

A collection is a special kind of object that contains the identifiers of other objects. There are operations to add and delete from collections, and there are operations to get or set attributes for all the objects in a collection. Collections are also used for error reporting. If an object becomes damaged by the occurrence of a media defect (i.e., a bad spot on the disk) or by a software error within the OSD implementation, its identifier is put into a special error collection. The higher-level storage system that uses the OSD can query this collection and take corrective action as necessary.

## Differences between Key-Value and Object Stores

A traditional block storage interface uses a series of fixed size blocks which are numbered starting at 0. Data must be that exact fixed size and can be stored in a particular block which is identified by its logical block number (LBN). Later, one can retrieve that block of data by specifying its unique LBN.

With a key/value store, data is identified by a key rather than a LBN. A key might be "cat" or "olive" or "42". It can be an arbitrary sequence of bytes of arbitrary length. Data (called a value in this parlance) does not need to be a fixed size and also can be an arbitrary sequence of bytes of arbitrary length. One stores data by presenting the key and data (value) to the data store and can later retrieve the data by presenting the key. This concept is seen in programming languages. Python calls them dictionaries, Perl calls them hashes, Java and C++ call them maps, etc. Several data stores also implement key/value stores such as Memcached, Redis and CouchDB.

Object stores are similar to key/value stores in two respects. First, the object identifier or URL (the equivalent of the key) can be an arbitrary string. Second, data is may be of an arbitrary size.

There are, however, a few key differences between key/value stores and object stores. First, object stores also allow one to associate a limited set of attributes (metadata) with each piece of data. The key, value and set of attributes is referred to as an object. Second, object stores are optimized for large amount of data (hundreds of megabytes or even gigabytes), whereas for key/value stores the value is expected to be relatively small (kilobytes). Finally, object stores usually offer weaker consistency guarantees such as eventual consistency, whereas key/value stores offer strong consistency.

Unfortunately, the border between an object store and a key/value store is blurred, with key/value stores being sometimes loosely referred to as object stores.

# File Hosting Service

A file hosting service, cloud storage service, online file storage provider, or cyberlocker is an Internet hosting service specifically designed to host user files. It allows users to upload files that could then be accessed over the internet from a different computer, tablet, smart phone or other networked device, by the same user or possibly by other users, after a password or other authentication is provided. Typically, the services allow HTTP access, and sometimes FTP access. Related services are content-displaying hosting services (i.e. video and image), virtual storage, and remote backup.

## Uses

### Personal File Storage

Personal file storage services are aimed at private individuals, offering a sort of "network storage" for personal backup, file access, or file distribution. Users can upload their files and share them publicly or keep them password-protected.

Document-sharing services allow users to share and collaborate on document files. These services originally targeted files such as PDFs, word processor documents, and spreadsheets. However many remote file storage services are now aimed at allowing users to share and sychronize all types of files across all the devices they use.

### File Sync and Sharing Services

File syncing and sharing services are file hosting services which allow users to create special folders on each of their computers or mobile devices, which the service then synchronizes so that it appears to be the same folder regardless of which computer is used to view it. Files placed in this folder also are typically accessible through a website and mobile apps, and can be easily shared with other users for viewing or collaboration.

Such services have become popular via consumer products such as Dropbox and Google Drive.

### Content Caching

Content providers who potentially encounter bandwidth congestion issues may use services specialized in distributing cached or static content. It is the case for companies with a major Internet presence.

### Storage Charges

Some online file storage services offer space on a per-gigabyte basis, and sometimes include a bandwidth cost component as well. Usually these will be charged monthly or yearly; for example, Carbonite. Some companies offer the service for free, relying on advertising revenue. Some hosting services do not place any limit on how much space the user's account can consume. Some services require a software download which makes files only available on computers which have that software installed, others allow users to retrieve files through any web browser. With the increased inbox space offered by webmail services, many users have started using their webmail service as an online drive. Some sites offer free unlimited file storage but have a limit on the file size. Some sites offer additional online storage capacity in exchange for new customer referrals.

### One-click Hosting

One-click hosting, sometimes referred to as cyberlocker, generally describes web services that allow internet users to easily upload one or more files from their hard drives (or from a remote location) onto the one-click host's server free of charge.

Most such services simply return a URL which can be given to other people, who can then fetch the file later. In many cases these URLs are predictable allowing potential misuse of the service. As of 2005 these sites have drastically increased in popularity, and subsequently, many of the smaller, less efficient sites have failed. Although one-click hosting can be used for many purposes, this type of file sharing has, to a degree, come to compete with P2P filesharing services.

The sites make money through advertising or charging for premium services such as increased downloading capacity, removing any wait restrictions the site may have or prolonging how long uploaded files remain on the site. Premium services include facilities like unlimited downloading, no waiting, maximum download speed etc. Many such sites implement a CAPTCHA to prevent automated downloading. Several programs aid in downloading files from these one-click hosts; examples are JDownloader, FreeRapid, Mipony, Tucan Manager and CryptLoad.

### Use for Copyright Infringement

File hosting services may be used as a means to distribute or share files without consent of the copyright owner. In such cases one individual uploads a file to a file hosting service, which others can then download. Legal assessments can be very diverse.

For example, in the case of Swiss-German file hosting service RapidShare, in 2010 the US government's congressional international anti-piracy caucus declared the site a "notorious illegal site", claiming that the site was "overwhelmingly used for the global exchange of illegal movies, music and other copyrighted works". But in the legal case *Atari Europe S.A.S.U. v. Rapidshare AG* in Germany, the Düsseldorf higher regional court examined claims related to alleged infringing activity and reached the conclusion on appeal that "most people utilize RapidShare for legal use cases" and that to assume otherwise was equivalent to inviting "a general suspicion against shared hosting services and their users which is not justified". The court also observed that the site removes copyrighted material when asked, does not provide search facilities for illegal material, noted previous cases siding with RapidShare, and after analysis the court concluded that the plaintiff's proposals for more strictly preventing sharing of copyrighted material – submitted as examples of anti-piracy measures RapidShare might have adopted – were found to be "unreasonable or pointless".

By contrast in January 2012 the United States Department of Justice seized and shut down the file hosting site Megaupload.com and commenced criminal cases against its owners and others. Their indictment concluded that Megaupload differed from other online file storage businesses, suggesting a number of design features of its operating model as being evidence showing a criminal intent and venture. Examples cited included reliance upon advertising revenue and other activities showing the business was funded by (and heavily promoted) downloads and not storage, defendants' communications helping users who sought infringing material, and defendants' communications discussing their own evasion and infringement issues. As of 2014 the case has not yet been heard.

The file hosting site Putlocker has been noted by the Motion Picture Association of America for being a major piracy threat, and Alfred Perry of Paramount Pictures listed Putlocker as one of the "top 5 rogue cyberlocker services", alongside Wupload, FileServe, Depositfiles, and MediaFire.

## Security

The emergence of cloud storage services have prompted much discussion on security. Security, as it relates to cloud storage can be broken down into:

### Access and Integrity Security

Deals with the questions: Will the user be able to continue accessing their data? Who else can access it? Who can change it?

Whether the user is able to continue accessing their data depends on a large number of factors, ranging from the location and quality of their internet connection and the physical integrity of the provider's data center to the financial stability of the storage provider.

The question of who can access and, potentially, change their data ranges from what physical access controls are in place in the provider's data center to what technical steps have been taken, such as access control, encryption, etc.

Many cloud storage services state that they either encrypt data before it is uploaded or while it is stored. While encryption is generally regarded as best practice in cloud storage how the encryption is implemented is very important.

Consumer-grade, public file hosting and synchronization services are popular, but for business use, they create the concern that corporate information is exported to devices and cloud services that are not controlled by the organization.

## Data Encryption

Secret key encryption is sometimes referred to as zero knowledge, meaning that only the user has the encryption key needed to decrypt the data. Since data is encrypted using the secret key, identical files encrypted with different keys will be different. To be truly zero knowledge, the file hosting service must not be able to store the user's passwords or see their data even with physical access to the servers. For this reason, secret key encryption is considered the highest level of access security in cloud storage. This form of encryption is rapidly gaining popularity, with companies such as SpiderOak being entirely zero knowledge file storage and sharing.

Since secret key encryption results in unique files, it makes data deduplication impossible and therefore may use more storage space.

Convergent encryption derives the key from the file content itself and means an identical file encrypted on different computers result in identical encrypted files. This enables the cloud storage provider to de-duplicate data blocks, meaning only one instance of a unique file (such as a document, photo, music or movie file) is actually stored on the cloud servers but made accessible to all uploaders. A third party who gained access to the encrypted files could thus easily determine if a user has uploaded a particular file simply by encrypting it themselves and comparing the outputs.

Some point out that there is a theoretical possibility that organizations such as the RIAA, MPAA, or a government could obtain a warrant for US law enforcement to access the cloud storage provider's servers and gain access to the encrypted files belonging to a user. By demonstrating to a court how applying the convergent encryption methodology to an unencrypted copyrighted file produces the same encrypted file as that possessed by the user would appear to make a strong case that the user is guilty of possessing the file in question and thus providing evidence of copyright infringement by the user.

There is, however, no easily accessible public record of this having been tried in court as of May 2013 and an argument could be made that, similar to the opinion expressed by Attorney Rick G. Sanders of Aaron | Sanders PLLC in regards to the iTunes Match "Honeypot" discussion, that a warrant to search the cloud storage provider's servers would be hard to obtain without other, independent, evidence establishing probable cause for copyright infringement. Such legal restraint would obviously not apply to the Secret Police of an oppressive government who could potentially gain access to the encrypted files through various forms of hacking or other cybercrime.

### Ownership Security

Deals with the questions: Who owns the data the user uploads? Will the act of uploading change the ownership?

## Cloud Storage Gateway

A cloud storage gateway is a network appliance or server which resides at the customer premises and translates cloud storage APIs such as SOAP or REST to block-based storage protocols such as iSCSI or Fibre Channel or file-based interfaces such as NFS or SMB.

According to a 2011 report by Gartner Group, cloud gateways were expected to increase the use of cloud storage by lowering monthly charges and eliminating the concern of data security.

### Market

The cloud storage gateway market was estimated at $74 million in 2012, up from $11 million at the end of 2010.

One analyst predicted in 2013 that the cloud storage gateway market might reach US$860 million by 2016. In January 2013, some vendors were CTERA Networks, Emulex, Panzura, Riverbed Technology, Seven10, Sonian Inc., StorSimple, Avere Systems and TwinStrata.

### Characteristics

Unlike the cloud storage services which they complement, cloud storage gateways use standard network protocols which integrate with existing applications. Cloud storage gateways can also serve as intermediaries to multiple cloud storage providers. Some cloud storage gateways also include additional storage features such as backup and recovery, caching, compression, encryption, storage de-duplication and provisioning.

### SOAP

SOAP (originally Simple Object Access Protocol) is a protocol specification for exchanging structured information in the implementation of web services in computer networks. Its purpose is to induce extensibility, neutrality and independence. It uses XML Information Set for its message format, and relies on application layer protocols, most often Hypertext Transfer Protocol (HTTP) or Simple Mail Transfer Protocol (SMTP), for message negotiation and transmission.

SOAP allows processes running on disparate operating systems (such as Windows and Linux) to communicate using Extensible Markup Language (XML). Since Web protocols like HTTP are installed and running on all operating systems, SOAP allows clients to invoke web services and receive responses independent of language and platforms.

## Characteristics

SOAP provides the Messaging Protocol layer of a web services protocol stack for web services. It is an XML-based protocol consisting of three parts:

- an envelope, which defines the message structure and how to process it
- a set of encoding rules for expressing instances of application-defined datatypes
- a convention for representing procedure calls and responses

SOAP has three major characteristics:

1. *extensibility* (security and WS-Addressing are among the extensions under development)
2. *neutrality* (SOAP can operate over any protocol such as HTTP, SMTP, TCP, UDP, or JMS)
3. *independence* (SOAP allows for any programming model)

As an example of what SOAP procedures can do, an application can send a SOAP request to a server that has web services enabled—such as a real-estate price database—with the parameters for a search. The server then returns a SOAP response (an XML-formatted document with the resulting data), e.g., prices, location, features. Since the generated data comes in a standardized machine-parsable format, the requesting application can then integrate it directly.

The SOAP architecture consists of several layers of specifications for:

- message format
- Message Exchange Patterns (MEP)
- underlying transport protocol bindings
- message processing models
- protocol extensibility

SOAP evolved as a successor of XML-RPC, though it borrows its transport and interaction neutrality from Web Service Addressing and the envelope/header/body from elsewhere (probably from WDDX).

## History

SOAP was designed as an object-access protocol in 1998 by Dave Winer, Don Box, Bob Atkinson, and Mohsen Al-Ghosein for Microsoft, where Atkinson and Al-Ghosein were working. Due to politics within Microsoft, the specification was not made available until it was submitted to IETF 13 September 1999. Because of Microsoft's hesitation, Dave Winer shipped XML-RPC in 1998.

The submitted Internet Draft did not reach RFC status and is therefore not considered a "standard" as such. Version 1.1 of the specification was published as a W3C Note on 8 May 2000. Since version 1.1 did not reach W3C Recommendation status, it can not be considered a "standard" either. Version 1.2 of the specification, however, became a W3C recommendation on June 24, 2003.

The SOAP specification was maintained by the XML Protocol Working Group of the World Wide Web Consortium until the group was closed 10 July 2009. *SOAP* originally stood for "Simple Object Access Protocol" but version 1.2 of the standard dropped this acronym.

After SOAP was first introduced, it became the underlying layer of a more complex set of Web services, based on Web Services Description Language (WSDL), XML schema and Universal Description Discovery and Integration (UDDI). These different services, especially UDDI, have proved to be of far less interest, but an appreciation of them gives a complete understanding of the expected role of SOAP compared to how web services have actually evolved.

## SOAP Terminology

SOAP specification can be broadly defined to be consisting of the following 3 conceptual components: Protocol concepts, encapsulation concepts and Network concepts.

## Protocol Concepts

- SOAP: The set of rules formalizing and governing the format and processing rules for information exchanged between a SOAP sender and a SOAP receiver.
- SOAP Nodes: These are physical/logical machines with processing units which are used to transmit/forward, receive and process SOAP messages. These are analogous to Node (networking).
- SOAP Roles: Over the path of a SOAP message, all nodes assume a specific role. The role of the node defines the action that the node performs on the message it receives. For example, a role "*none*" means that no node will process the SOAP header in any way and simply transmit the message along its path.
- SOAP protocol binding : A SOAP message needs to work in conjunction with other protocols to be transferred over a network. For example, a SOAP message

could use TCP as a lower layer protocol to transfer messages. These bindings are defined in the SOAP protocol binding framework.

- SOAP features: SOAP provides a messaging framework only. However, it can be extended to add features such as reliability, security etc. There are rules to be followed when adding features to the SOAP framework.
- SOAP module : A collection of specifications regarding the semantics of SOAP header to describe any new features being extended upon SOAP. A module needs to realize 0 or more features. SOAP requires modules to adhere to prescribed rules.

## Data Encapsulation Concepts

- SOAP message: Represents the information being exchanged between 2 soap nodes.
- SOAP envelope : As per its name, it is the enclosing element of an XML message identifying it as a SOAP message.
- SOAP header block: A SOAP header can contain more than one of these blocks, each being a discrete computational block within the header. In general, the SOAP *role* information is used to target nodes on the path. A header block is said to be targeted at a SOAP node if the SOAP role for the header block is the name of a role in which the SOAP node operates. (ex: A SOAP header block with role attribute as *ultimateReceiver* is targeted only at the destination node which has this role. A header with a role attribute as *next* is targeted at each intermediary as well as the destination node.)
- SOAP header : A collection of one or more header blocks targeted at each SOAP receiver.
- SOAP body : Contains the body of the message intended for the SOAP receiver. The interpretation and processing of SOAP body is defined by header blocks.
- SOAP fault: In case a SOAP node fails to process a SOAP message, it adds the fault information to the SOAP fault element. This element is contained within the SOAP body as a child element.

## Message Sender and Receiver Concepts

- SOAP sender: The node that transmits a SOAP message.
- SOAP receiver : The node receiving a SOAP message. (Could be an intermediary or the destination node.)
- SOAP message path : The path consisting of all the nodes that the SOAP message traversed to reach the destination node.

- Initial SOAP sender: This is the node which originated the SOAP message to be transmitted. This is the root of the SOAP message path.
- SOAP intermediary: All the nodes in between the SOAP originator and the intended SOAP destination. It processes the SOAP header blocks targeted at it and acts to forward a SOAP message towards an ultimate SOAP receiver.
- Ultimate SOAP receiver: The destination receiver of the SOAP message. This node is responsible for processing the message body and any header blocks targeted at it .

## Specification

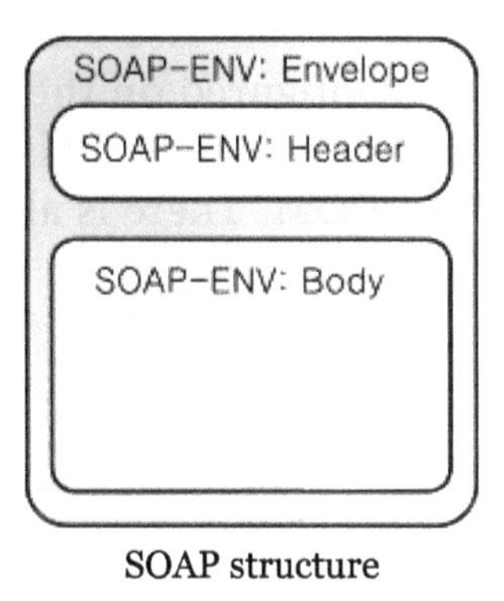


SOAP structure

The SOAP specification defines the messaging framework, which consists of:

- The *SOAP processing model* defining the rules for processing a SOAP message
- The *SOAP extensibility model* defining the concepts of SOAP features and SOAP modules
- The *SOAP underlying protocol binding* framework describing the rules for defining a binding to an underlying protocol that can be used for exchanging SOAP messages between SOAP nodes
- The *SOAP message construct* defining the structure of a SOAP message

## SOAP Building Blocks

A SOAP message is an ordinary XML document containing the following elements:

| Element | Description | Required |
|---|---|---|
| Envelope | Identifies the XML document as a SOAP message. | Yes |
| Header | Contains header information. | No |
| Body | Contains call, and response information. | Yes |
| Fault | Provides information about errors that occurred while processing the message. | No |

## Transport Methods

Both SMTP and HTTP are valid application layer protocols used as transport for SOAP, but HTTP has gained wider acceptance as it works well with today's internet infrastructure; specifically, HTTP works well with network firewalls. SOAP may also be used over HTTPS (which is the same protocol as HTTP at the application level, but uses an encrypted transport protocol underneath) with either simple or mutual authentication; this is the advocated WS-I method to provide web service security as stated in the WS-I Basic Profile 1.1.

This is a major advantage over other distributed protocols like GIOP/IIOP or DCOM, which are normally filtered by firewalls. SOAP over AMQP is yet another possibility that some implementations support. SOAP also has an advantage over DCOM that it is unaffected by security rights configured on the machines that require knowledge of both transmitting and receiving nodes. This lets SOAP be loosely coupled in a way that is not possible with DCOM. There is also the SOAP-over-UDP OASIS standard.

## Message Format

XML Information Set was chosen as the standard message format because of its widespread use by major corporations and open source development efforts. Typically, XML Information Set is serialized as XML. A wide variety of freely available tools significantly eases the transition to a SOAP-based implementation. The somewhat lengthy syntax of XML can be both a benefit and a drawback. While it promotes readability for humans, facilitates error detection, and avoids interoperability problems such as byte-order (endianness), it can slow processing speed and can be cumbersome. For example, CORBA, GIOP, ICE, and DCOM use much shorter, binary message formats. On the other hand, hardware appliances are available to accelerate processing of XML messages. Binary XML is also being explored as a means for streamlining the throughput requirements of XML. XML messages by their self-documenting nature usually have more 'overhead' (headers, footers, nested tags, delimiters) than actual data in contrast to earlier protocols where the overhead was usually a relatively small percentage of the overall message.

In financial messaging SOAP was found to result in a 2–4 times larger message than previous protocols FIX (Financial Information Exchange) and CDR (Common Data Representation).

XML Information Set does not have to be serialized in XML. For instance, CSV and JSON XML-infoset representations exist. There is also no need to specify a generic transformation framework. The concept of SOAP bindings allows for specific bindings for a specific application. The drawback is that both the senders and receivers have to support this newly defined binding.

### Example Message (Encapsulated in HTTP)

```
POST /InStock HTTP/1.1

Host: www.example.org

Content-Type: application/soap+xml; charset=utf-8

Content-Length: 299

SOAPAction: "http://www.w3.org/2003/05/soap-envelope"

<?xml version="1.0"?>

<soap:Envelope   xmlns:soap="http://www.w3.org/2003/05/soap-envelope"
xmlns:m="http://www.example.org/stock/Surya">

  <soap:Header>

  </soap:Header>

  <soap:Body>

     <m:GetStockPrice>

       <m:StockName>GOOGLE</m:StockName>

     </m:GetStockPrice>

   </soap:Body>

</soap:Envelope>
```

### Technical Critique

### Advantages

- SOAP's neutrality characteristic explicitly makes it suitable for use with any transport protocol. Implementations often use HTTP as a transport protocol, but other popular transport protocols can be used. For example, SOAP can also be used over SMTP, JMS and message queues.
- SOAP, when combined with HTTP post/response exchanges, tunnels easily through existing firewalls and proxies, and consequently doesn't require modifying the widespread computing and communication infrastructures that exist for processing HTTP post/response exchanges.
- SOAP has available to it all the facilities of XML, including easy internationalization and extensibility with XML Namespaces.

### Disadvantages

- When using standard implementations and the default SOAP/HTTP binding, the XML infoset is serialized as XML. To improve performance for the special case of XML with embedded binary objects, the Message Transmission Optimization Mechanism was introduced.

- When relying on HTTP as a transport protocol and not using WS-Addressing or an ESB, the roles of the interacting parties are fixed. Only one party (the client) can use the services of the other.
- The verbosity of the protocol, slow parsing speed of XML, and lack of a standardized interaction model led to the domination in the field by services using the HTTP protocol more directly. For example, REST.

## Representational State Transfer

Representational state transfer (REST) or RESTful web services is one way of providing interoperability between computer systems on the Internet. REST-compliant Web services allow requesting systems to access and manipulate textual representations of Web resources using a uniform and predefined set of stateless operations. Other forms of Web service exist, which expose their own arbitrary sets of operations such as WSDL and SOAP.

"Web resources" were first defined on the World Wide Web as documents or files identified by their URLs, but today they have a much more generic and abstract definition encompassing every thing or entity that can be identified, named, addressed or handled, in any way whatsoever, on the Web. In a RESTful Web service, requests made to a resource's URI will elicit a response that may be in XML, HTML, JSON or some other defined format. The response may confirm that some alteration has been made to the stored resource, and it may provide hypertext links to other related resources or collections of resources. Using HTTP, as is most common, the kind of operations available include those predefined by the HTTP verbs GET, POST, PUT, DELETE and so on.

By making use of a stateless protocol and standard operations, REST systems aim for fast performance, reliability, and the ability to grow, by re-using components that can be managed and updated without affecting the system as a whole, even while it is running.

The term *representational state transfer* was introduced and defined in 2000 by Roy Fielding in his doctoral dissertation. Fielding used REST to design HTTP 1.1 and Uniform Resource Identifiers (URI). The term is intended to evoke an image of how a well-designed Web application behaves: it is a network of Web resources (a virtual state-machine) where the user progresses through the application by selecting links, such as /user/tom, and operations such as GET or DELETE (state transitions), resulting in the next resource (representing the next state of the application) being transferred to the user for their use.

## History

Roy Fielding speaking at OSCON 2008

REST was defined by Roy Fielding in his 2000 PhD dissertation "Architectural Styles and the Design of Network-based Software Architectures" at UC Irvine. Fielding developed the REST architectural style in parallel with HTTP 1.1 of 1996–1999, based on the existing design of HTTP 1.0 of 1996.

In a retrospective look at the development of REST, Roy Fielding said:

Throughout the HTTP standardization process, I was called on to defend the design choices of the Web. That is an extremely difficult thing to do within a process that accepts proposals from anyone on a topic that was rapidly becoming the center of an entire industry. I had comments from well over 500 developers, many of whom were distinguished engineers with decades of experience, and I had to explain everything from the most abstract notions of Web interaction to the finest details of HTTP syntax. That process honed my model down to a core set of principles, properties, and constraints that are now called REST.

## Architectural Properties

The architectural properties affected by the constraints of the REST architectural style are:

- Performance - component interactions can be the dominant factor in user-perceived performance and network efficiency
- Scalability to support large numbers of components and interactions among components. Roy Fielding, one of the principal authors of the HTTP specification, describes REST's effect on scalability as follows:

  REST's client–server separation of concerns simplifies component implementation, reduces the complexity of connector semantics, improves the effectiveness of performance tuning, and increases the scalability of pure server components. Layered system constraints allow intermediaries—proxies, gateways, and firewalls—to be introduced at various points in the communication without changing the interfaces between components, thus allowing them to assist in communication translation or improve performance via large-scale, shared caching. REST enables intermediate processing by constraining messages to be self-descriptive: interaction is stateless between requests, standard methods and media types are used to indicate semantics and exchange information, and responses explicitly indicate cacheability.

- Simplicity of a uniform Interface
- Modifiability of components to meet changing needs (even while the application is running)
- Visibility of communication between components by service agents
- Portability of components by moving program code with the data
- Reliability is the resistance to failure at the system level in the presence of failures within components, connectors, or data

## Architectural Constraints

There are six guiding constraints that define a RESTful system. These constraints restrict the ways that the server may process and respond to client requests so that, by operating within these constraints, the service gains desirable non-functional properties, such as performance, scalability, simplicity, modifiability, visibility, portability, and reliability. If a service violates any of the required constraints, it cannot be considered RESTful.

The formal REST constraints are as follows:

### Client-server

The first constraints added to our hybrid style are those of the client-server architectural style. Separation of concerns is the principle behind the client-server constraints. By separating the user interface concerns from the data storage concerns, we improve the portability of the user interface across multiple platforms and improve scalability by simplifying the server components. Perhaps most significant to the Web, however, is that the separation allows the components to evolve independently, thus supporting the Internet-scale requirement of multiple organizational domains.

### Stateless

The client–server communication is constrained by no client context being stored on the server between requests. Each request from any client contains all the information necessary to service the request, and session state is held in the client. The session state can be transferred by the server to another service such as a database to maintain a persistent state for a period and allow authentication. The client begins sending requests when it is ready to make the transition to a new state. While one or more requests are outstanding, the client is considered to be *in transition*. The representation of each application state contains links that may be used the next time the client chooses to initiate a new state-transition.

### Cacheable

As on the World Wide Web, clients and intermediaries can cache responses. Responses must therefore, implicitly or explicitly, define themselves as cacheable or not to prevent clients from reusing stale or inappropriate data in response to further requests. Well-managed caching partially or completely eliminates some client–server interactions, further improving scalability and performance.

### Layered System

A client cannot ordinarily tell whether it is connected directly to the end server, or to an intermediary along the way. Intermediary servers may improve system scalability by enabling load balancing and by providing shared caches. They may also enforce security policies.

### Code on Demand (Optional)

Servers can temporarily extend or customize the functionality of a client by transferring executable code. Examples of this may include compiled components such as Java applets and client-side scripts such as JavaScript.

### Uniform Interface

The uniform interface constraint is fundamental to the design of any REST service. It simplifies and decouples the architecture, which enables each part to evolve independently. The four constraints for this uniform interface are

### Identification of Resources

Individual resources are identified in requests, for example using URIs in Web-based REST systems. The resources themselves are conceptually separate from the representations that are returned to the client. For example, the server may send data from its database as HTML, XML or JSON, none of which are the server's internal representation.

### Manipulation of Resources through Representations

When a client holds a representation of a resource, including any metadata attached, it has enough information to modify or delete the resource.

### Self-descriptive Messages

Each message includes enough information to describe how to process the message. For example, which parser to invoke may be specified by an Internet media type (previously known as a MIME type).

### Hypermedia as the Engine of Application State (HATEOAS)

Having accessed an initial URI for the REST application—analogous to a human Web user accessing the home page of a website—a REST client should then be able to use server-provided links dynamically to discover all the available actions and resources it needs. As access proceeds, the server responds with text that includes hyperlinks to other actions that are currently available. There is no need for the client to be hard-coded with information regarding the structure or dynamics of the REST service.

## Applied to Web Services

Web service APIs that adhere to the REST architectural constraints are called RESTful APIs. HTTP-based RESTful APIs are defined with the following aspects:

- base URL, such as `http://api.example.com/resources/`
- an internet media type that defines state transition data elements (e.g., Atom, microformats, application/vnd.collection+json, etc.) The current representation tells the client how to compose requests for transitions to all the next available application states. This could be as simple as a URL or as complex as a Java applet.
- standard HTTP methods (e.g., OPTIONS, GET, PUT, POST, and DELETE)

## Relationship between URL and HTTP Methods

The following table shows how HTTP methods are typically used in a RESTful API:

| HTTP methods | | | | |
|---|---|---|---|---|
| **Uniform Resource Locator (URL)** | **GET** | **PUT** | **POST** | **DELETE** |
| Collection, such as http://api.example.com/resources/ | List the URIs and perhaps other details of the collection's members. | Replace the entire collection with another collection. | Create a new entry in the collection. The new entry's URI is assigned automatically and is usually returned by the operation. | Delete the entire collection. |

| Element, such as http://api.example.com/resources/item17 | Retrieve a representation of the addressed member of the collection, expressed in an appropriate Internet media type. | Replace the addressed member of the collection, or if it does not exist, create it. | Not generally used. Treat the addressed member as a collection in its own right and create a new entry within it. | Delete the addressed member of the collection. |
|---|---|---|---|---|

The GET method is a safe method (or *nullipotent*), meaning that calling it produces no side-effects: retrieving or accessing a record does not change it. The PUT and DELETE methods are idempotent, meaning that the state of the system exposed by the API is unchanged no matter how many times more than once the same request is repeated.

Unlike SOAP-based Web services, there is no "official" standard for RESTful Web APIs. This is because REST is an architectural style, while SOAP is a protocol. REST is not a standard in itself, but RESTful implementations make use of standards, such as HTTP, URI, JSON, and XML. Many developers also describe their APIs as being RESTful, even though these APIs actually don't fulfill all of the architectural constraints described above (especially the uniform interface constraint).

## iSCSI

In computing, iSCSI is an acronym for Internet Small Computer Systems Interface, an Internet Protocol (IP)-based storage networking standard for linking data storage facilities. It provides block-level access to storage devices by carrying SCSI commands over a TCP/IP network. iSCSI is used to facilitate data transfers over intranets and to manage storage over long distances. It can be used to transmit data over local area networks (LANs), wide area networks (WANs), or the Internet and can enable location-independent data storage and retrieval.

The protocol allows clients (called *initiators*) to send SCSI commands (*CDBs*) to storage devices (*targets*) on remote servers. It is a storage area network (SAN) protocol, allowing organizations to consolidate storage into storage arrays while providing clients (such as database and web servers) with the illusion of locally attached SCSI disks. It mainly competes with Fibre Channel, but unlike traditional Fibre Channel which usually requires dedicated cabling, iSCSI can be run over long distances using existing network infrastructure. iSCSI was pioneered by IBM and Cisco in 1998 and submitted as a draft standard in March 2000.

### Concepts

In essence, iSCSI allows two hosts to negotiate and then exchange SCSI commands using Internet Protocol (IP) networks. By doing this, iSCSI takes a popular high-performance local storage bus and emulates it over a wide range of networks, creating a storage area network (SAN). Unlike some SAN protocols, iSCSI requires no dedicated cabling; it can be run over existing IP infrastructure. As a result, iSCSI is often seen as a low-cost alternative to Fibre Channel, which requires dedicated infrastructure except in its FCoE (Fibre Channel over Ethernet) form. However, the performance of an iSCSI SAN deployment can be severely degraded if not operated on a dedicated network or subnet (LAN or VLAN), due to competition for a fixed amount of bandwidth.

Although iSCSI can communicate with arbitrary types of SCSI devices, system administrators almost always use it to allow server computers (such as database servers) to access disk volumes on storage arrays. iSCSI SANs often have one of two objectives:

#### Storage Consolidation

Organizations move disparate storage resources from servers around their network to central locations, often in data centers; this allows for more efficiency in the allocation of storage, as the storage itself is no longer tied to a particular server. In a SAN environment, a server can be allocated a new disk volume without any changes to hardware or cabling.

#### Disaster Recovery

Organizations mirror storage resources from one data center to a remote data center, which can serve as a hot standby in the event of a prolonged outage. In particular, iSCSI SANs allow entire disk arrays to be migrated across a WAN with minimal configuration changes, in effect making storage "routable" in the same manner as network traffic.

### Initiator

An *initiator* functions as an iSCSI client. An initiator typically serves the same purpose to a computer as a SCSI bus adapter would, except that, instead of physically cabling SCSI devices (like hard drives and tape changers), an iSCSI initiator sends SCSI commands over an IP network. An initiator falls into two broad types:

A software initiator uses code to implement iSCSI. Typically, this happens in a kernel-resident device driver that uses the existing network card (NIC) and network stack to emulate SCSI devices for a computer by speaking the iSCSI protocol. Software initiators are available for most popular operating systems and are the most common method of deploying iSCSI.

A hardware initiator uses dedicated hardware, typically in combination with firmware running on that hardware, to implement iSCSI. A hardware initiator mitigates the overhead of iSCSI and TCP processing and Ethernet interrupts, and therefore may improve the performance of servers that use iSCSI. An iSCSI host bus adapter (more commonly,

HBA) implements a hardware initiator. A typical HBA is packaged as a combination of a Gigabit (or 10 Gigabit) Ethernet network interface controller, some kind of TCP/IP offload engine (TOE) technology and a SCSI bus adapter, which is how it appears to the operating system. An iSCSI HBA can include PCI option ROM to allow booting from an iSCSI SAN.

An *iSCSI offload engine*, or *iSOE card*, offers an alternative to a full iSCSI HBA. An iSOE "offloads" the iSCSI initiator operations for this particular network interface from the host processor, freeing up CPU cycles for the main host applications. iSCSI HBAs or iSOEs are used when the additional performance enhancement justifies the additional expense of using an HBA for iSCSI, rather than using a software-based iSCSI client (initiator). iSOE may be implemented with additional services such as TCP offload engine (TOE) to further reduce host server CPU usage.

### Target

The iSCSI specification refers to a storage resource located on an iSCSI server (more generally, one of potentially many *instances* of iSCSI storage nodes running on that server) as a *target*.

An iSCSI target is often a dedicated network-connected hard disk storage device, but may also be a general-purpose computer, since as with initiators, software to provide an iSCSI target is available for most mainstream operating systems.

Common deployment scenarios for an iSCSI target include:

### Storage Array

In a data center or enterprise environment, an iSCSI target often resides in a large storage array. These arrays can be in the form of commodity hardware with free-software-based iSCSI implementations, or as commercial products such as in CloudByte, StorTrends, Pure Storage, HP StorageWorks, EqualLogic, Tegile Systems, Nimble storage, Reduxio, IBM Storwize family, Isilon, NetApp filer, EMC Corporation NS-series, CX4, VNX, VNXe, VMAX, Hitachi Data Systems HNAS, or Pivot3 vSTAC.

A storage array usually provides distinct iSCSI targets for numerous clients.

### Software Target

Nearly all modern mainstream server operating systems (such as BSD, Linux, Solaris or Windows Server) can provide iSCSI target functionality, either as a built-in feature or with supplemental software. Some specific-purpose operating systems implement iSCSI target support.

## Logical Unit Number

In SCSI terminology, LUN stands for *logical unit*, which are specified by unique *logical unit numbers*. A LUN represents an individually addressable (logical) SCSI device that is part of a physical SCSI device (target). In an iSCSI environment, LUNs are essentially numbered disk drives. An initiator negotiates with a target to establish connectivity to a LUN; the result is an iSCSI connection that emulates a connection to a SCSI hard disk. Initiators treat iSCSI LUNs the same way as they would a raw SCSI or IDE hard drive; for instance, rather than mounting remote directories as would be done in NFS or CIFS environments, iSCSI systems format and directly manage filesystems on iSCSI LUNs.

In enterprise deployments, LUNs usually represent subsets of large RAID disk arrays, often allocated one per client. iSCSI imposes no rules or restrictions on multiple computers sharing individual LUNs; it leaves shared access to a single underlying filesystem as a task for the operating system.

## Network Booting

For general data storage on an already-booted computer, any type of generic network interface may be used to access iSCSI devices. However, a generic consumer-grade network interface is not able to boot a diskless computer from a remote iSCSI data source. Instead, it is commonplace for a server to load its initial operating system from a TFTP server or local boot device, and then use iSCSI for data storage once booting from the local device has finished.

A separate DHCP server may be configured to assist interfaces equipped with network boot capability to be able to boot over iSCSI. In this case, the network interface looks for a DHCP server offering a PXE or bootp boot image. This is used to kick off the iSCSI remote boot process, using the booting network interface's MAC address to direct the computer to the correct iSCSI boot target. One can then use a software-only approach to load a small boot program which can in turn mount a remote iSCSI target as if it was a local SCSI drive and then fire the boot process from said iSCSI target. This can be achieved using an existing Preboot Execution Environment (PXE) boot ROM, which is available on many wired Ethernet adapters. The boot code can also be loaded from CD/DVD, floppy disk (or floppy disk image) and USB storage, or it can replace existing PXE boot code on adapters that can be re-flashed. The most popular free software to offer iSCSI boot support is iPXE.

Most Intel Ethernet controllers for servers support iSCSI boot.

## Addressing

iSCSI uses TCP (typically TCP ports 860 and 3260) for the protocols itself, with higher-level names used to address the objects within the protocol. Special names refer to both iSCSI initiators and targets. iSCSI provides three name-formats:

iSCSI Qualified Name (IQN)

Format: The iSCSI Qualified Name is documented in RFC 3720, with further examples of names in RFC 3721. Briefly, the fields are:

- literal iqn (iSCSI Qualified Name)
- date (yyyy-mm) that the naming authority took ownership of the domain
- reversed domain name of the authority (e.g. org.alpinelinux, com.example, to.yp.cr)
- Optional ":" prefixing a storage target name specified by the naming authority.

From the RFC:

| Type | Date | Naming Auth | String defined by *example.com* Naming Authority |
|---|---|---|---|
| iqn | 1992-01 | com.example | storage:diskarrays-sn-a8675309 |
| iqn | 1992-01 | com.example | |
| iqn | 1992-01 | com.example | storage.tape1.sys1.xyz |
| iqn | 1992-01 | com.example | storage.disk2.sys1.xyz |

Extended Unique Identifier (EUI)

Format: eui.{EUI-64 bit address} (e.g. eui.02004567A425678D)

T11 Network Address Authority (NAA)

Format: naa.{NAA 64 or 128 bit identifier} (e.g. naa.52004567BA64678D)

IQN format addresses occur most commonly. They are qualified by a date (yyyy-mm) because domain names can expire or be acquired by another entity.

The IEEE Registration authority provides EUI in accordance with the EUI-64 standard. NAA is part OUI which is provided by the IEEE Registration Authority. NAA name formats were added to iSCSI in RFC 3980, to provide compatibility with naming conventions used in Fibre Channel and Serial Attached SCSI (SAS) storage technologies.

Usually, an iSCSI participant can be defined by three or four fields:

1. Hostname or IP Address (e.g., "iscsi.example.com")
2. Port Number (e.g., 3260)
3. iSCSI Name (e.g., the IQN "iqn.2003-01.com.ibm:00.fcd0ab21.shark128")
4. An optional CHAP Secret (e.g., "secretsarefun")

## iSNS

iSCSI initiators can locate appropriate storage resources using the Internet Storage Name Service (iSNS) protocol. In theory, iSNS provides iSCSI SANs with the same management model as dedicated Fibre Channel SANs. In practice, administrators can satisfy many deployment goals for iSCSI without using iSNS.

## Security

### Authentication

iSCSI initiators and targets prove their identity to each other using CHAP, which includes a mechanism to prevent cleartext passwords from appearing on the wire. By itself, CHAP is vulnerable to dictionary attacks, spoofing, and reflection attacks. If followed carefully, the best practices for using CHAP within iSCSI reduce the surface for these attacks and mitigate the risks.

Additionally, as with all IP-based protocols, IPsec can operate at the network layer. The iSCSI negotiation protocol is designed to accommodate other authentication schemes, though interoperability issues limit their deployment.

### Logical Network Isolation

To ensure that only valid initiators connect to storage arrays, administrators most commonly run iSCSI only over logically isolated backchannel networks. In this deployment architecture, only the management ports of storage arrays are exposed to the general-purpose internal network, and the iSCSI protocol itself is run over dedicated network segments or virtual LANs (VLAN). This mitigates authentication concerns; unauthorized users are not physically provisioned for iSCSI, and thus cannot talk to storage arrays. However, it also creates a transitive trust problem, in that a single compromised host with an iSCSI disk can be used to attack storage resources for other hosts.

### Physical Network Isolation

While iSCSI can be logically isolated from the general network using VLANs only, it is still no different from any other network equipment and may use any cable or port as long as there is a completed signal path between source and target. Just a single cabling mistake by a network technician can compromise the barrier of logical separation, and an accidental bridging may not be immediately detected because it does not cause network errors.

In order to further differentiate iSCSI from the regular network and prevent cabling mistakes when changing connections, administrators may implement self-defined color-coding and labeling standards, such as only using yellow-colored cables for the iSCSI connections and only blue cables for the regular network, and clearly labeling ports and switches used only for iSCSI.

While iSCSI could be implemented as just a VLAN cluster of ports on a large multi-port switch that is also used for general network usage, the administrator may instead choose to use physically separate switches dedicated to iSCSI VLANs only, to further prevent the possibility of an incorrectly connected cable plugged into the wrong port bridging the logical barrier.

## Authorization

Because iSCSI aims to consolidate storage for many servers into a single storage array, iSCSI deployments require strategies to prevent unrelated initiators from accessing storage resources. As a pathological example, a single enterprise storage array could hold data for servers variously regulated by the Sarbanes–Oxley Act for corporate accounting, HIPAA for health benefits information, and PCI DSS for credit card processing. During an audit, storage systems must demonstrate controls to ensure that a server under one regime cannot access the storage assets of a server under another.

Typically, iSCSI storage arrays explicitly map initiators to specific target LUNs; an initiator authenticates not to the storage array, but to the specific storage asset it intends to use. However, because the target LUNs for SCSI commands are expressed both in the iSCSI negotiation protocol and in the underlying SCSI protocol, care must be taken to ensure that access control is provided consistently.

## Confidentiality and Integrity

For the most part, iSCSI operates as a cleartext protocol that provides no cryptographic protection for data in motion during SCSI transactions. As a result, an attacker who can listen in on iSCSI Ethernet traffic can:

- Reconstruct and copy the files and filesystems being transferred on the wire
- Alter the contents of files by injecting fake iSCSI frames
- Corrupt filesystems being accessed by initiators, exposing servers to software flaws in poorly tested filesystem code.

These problems do not occur only with iSCSI, but rather apply to any SAN protocol without cryptographic security. IP-based security protocols, such as IPsec, can provide standards-based cryptographic protection to this traffic, generally at a severe performance penalty.

## Implementations

## Operating Systems

The dates in the following table denote the first appearance of a native driver in each operating system. Third-party drivers for Windows and Linux were available as early as 2001, specifically for attaching IBM's IP Storage 200i appliance.

| OS | First release date | Version | Features |
|---|---|---|---|
| **i5/OS** | 2006-10 | i5/OS V5R4M0 | Target, Multipath |
| **VMware ESX** | 2006-06 | ESX 3.0, ESX 4.0, ESXi 5.x, ESXi 6.x | Initiator, Multipath |
| **AIX** | 2002-10 | AIX 5.3 TL10, AIX 6.1 TL3 | Initiator, Target |
| **Windows** | 2003-06 | 2000, XP Pro, 2003, Vista, 2008, 2008 R2, Windows 7, Windows 8, Windows Server 2012, Windows 8.1, Windows Server 2012 R2, Windows 10, Windows Server 2016 | Initiator, Target, Multipath |
| **NetWare** | 2003-08 | NetWare 5.1, 6.5, & OES | Initiator, Target |
| **HP-UX** | 2003-10 | HP 11i v1, HP 11i v2, HP 11i v3 | Initiator |
| **Solaris** | 2002-05 | Solaris 10, OpenSolaris | Initiator, Target, Multipath, iSER |
| **Linux** | 2005-06 | 2.6.12, 3.1 | Initiator (2.6.12), Target (3.1), Multipath, iSER, VAAI |
| **OpenBSD** | 2009-10 | 4.9 | Initiator |
| **NetBSD** | 2002-06 | 4.0, 5.0 | Initiator (5.0), Target (4.0) |
| **FreeBSD** | 2008-02 | 7.0 | Initiator (7.0), Target (10.0), Multipath, iSER, VAAI |
| **OpenVMS** | 2002-08 | 8.3-1H1 | Initiator, Multipath |
| **macOS** | 2008-07 | 10.4– | N/A |

## Targets

Most iSCSI targets involve disk, though iSCSI tape and medium-changer targets are popular as well. So far, physical devices have not featured native iSCSI interfaces on a component level. Instead, devices with Parallel SCSI or Fibre Channel interfaces are bridged by using iSCSI target software, external bridges, or controllers internal to the device enclosure.

Alternatively, it is possible to virtualize disk and tape targets. Rather than representing an actual physical device, an emulated virtual device is presented. The underlying implementation can deviate drastically from the presented target as is done with virtual tape library (VTL) products. VTLs use disk storage for storing data written to virtual tapes. As with actual physical devices, virtual targets are presented by using iSCSI target software, external bridges, or controllers internal to the device enclosure.

In the security products industry, some manufacturers use an iSCSI RAID as a target, with the initiator being either an IP-enabled encoder or camera.

## Converters and Bridges

Multiple systems exist that allow Fibre Channel, SCSI and SAS devices to be attached to an IP network for use via iSCSI. They can be used to allow migration from older storage technologies, access to SANs from remote servers and the linking of SANs over IP networks. An iSCSI gateway bridges IP servers to Fibre Channel SANs. The TCP connection is terminated at the gateway, which is implemented on a Fibre Channel switch or as a standalone appliance.

## Fibre Channel

Fibre Channel, or FC, is a high-speed network technology (commonly running at 1, 2, 4, 8, 16, 32, and 128 gigabit per second rates) primarily used to connect computer data storage to servers. Fibre Channel is mainly used in storage area networks (SAN) in commercial data centers. Fibre Channel networks form a switched fabric because they operate in unison as one big switch. Fibre Channel typically runs on optical fiber cables within and between data centers.

Most block storage runs over Fibre Channel Fabrics and supports many upper level protocols. Fibre Channel Protocol (FCP) is a transport protocol that predominantly transports SCSI commands over Fibre Channel networks. Mainframe computers run the FICON command set over Fibre Channel because of its high reliability and throughput. Fibre Channel can be used for flash memory being transported over the NVMe interface protocol.

### Etymology

To promote the fiber optic aspects of the technology and to make a unique name, the industry decided to use the British English spelling *fibre* for the standard.

### History

Fibre Channel is standardized in the T11 Technical Committee of the International Committee for Information Technology Standards (INCITS), an American National Standards Institute (ANSI)-accredited standards committee. Fibre Channel started in 1988, with ANSI standard approval in 1994, to merge the benefits of multiple physical layer implementations including SCSI, HIPPI and ESCON.

Fibre Channel was designed as a serial interface to overcome limitations of the SCSI and HIPPI interfaces. FC was developed with leading edge multi-mode fiber technologies that overcame the speed limitations of the ESCON protocol. By appealing to the large base of SCSI disk drives and leveraging mainframe technologies, Fibre Channel developed economies of scale for advanced technologies and deployments became economical and widespread.

Initially, the standard also ratified lower speed Fibre Channel versions with 132.8125 Mbit/s ("12,5 MB/s»), 265.625 Mbit/s («25 MB/s»), and 531.25 Mbit/s («50 MB/s») that were already growing out of use at the time. Fibre Channel saw adoption at 1 Gigabit/s Fibre Channel (1GFC) and its success grew with each successive speed. Fibre Channel has doubled in speed every few years since 1996.

Fibre channel has seen active development since its inception, with numerous speed improvements on a variety of underlying transport media. For example, the following table shows native Fibre Channel speeds:

| Fibre Channel Variants | | | | | |
|---|---|---|---|---|---|
| NAME | Line-rate (gigabaud) | Line coding | Nominal throughput per direction; MB/s | Net throughput per direction; MB/s | Availability |
| 1GFC | 1.0625 | 8b10b | 100 | 103.2 | 1997 |
| 2GFC | 2.125 | 8b10b | 200 | 206.5 | 2001 |
| 4GFC | 4.25 | 8b10b | 400 | 412.9 | 2004 |
| 8GFC | 8.5 | 8b10b | 800 | 825.8 | 2005 |
| 10GFC | 10.51875 | 64b66b | 1,200 | 1,239 | 2008 |
| 16GFC | 14.025 | 64b66b | 1,600 | 1,652 | 2011 |
| 32GFC "Gen 6" | 28.05 | 64b66b | 3,200 | 3,303 | 2016 |
| 128GFC "Gen 6" | 28.05 ×4 | 64b66b | 12,800 | 13,210 | 2016 |

In addition to a cutting edge physical layer, Fibre Channel also added support for any number of "upper layer" protocols, including ATM, IP and FICON, with SCSI being the predominant usage.

## Topologies

There are three major Fibre Channel topologies, describing how a number of ports are connected together. A *port* in Fibre Channel terminology is any entity that actively communicates over the network, not necessarily a hardware port. This port is usually implemented in a device such as disk storage, an HBA on a server or a Fibre Channel switch.

- Point-to-point (FC-FS-3). Two devices are connected directly to each other. This is the simplest topology, with limited connectivity.

- Arbitrated Loop (*FC-AL-2*). In this design, all devices are in a loop or ring, similar to token ring networking. Adding or removing a device from the loop causes all activity on the loop to be interrupted. The failure of one device causes a break in the ring. Fibre Channel hubs exist to connect multiple devices together and may bypass failed ports. A loop may also be made by cabling each port to the next in a ring.

- o A minimal loop containing only two ports, while appearing to be similar to point-to-point, differs considerably in terms of the protocol.
- o Only one pair of ports can communicate concurrently on a loop.
- o Maximum speed of 8GFC.
- o Arbitrated Loop has been rarely used after 2010.

- Switched Fabric (*FC-SW-6*). In this design, all devices are connected to Fibre Channel switches, similar conceptually to modern Ethernet implementations. Advantages of this topology over point-to-point or Arbitrated Loop include:
  - o The Fabric can scale to tens of thousands of ports.
  - o The switches manage the state of the Fabric, providing optimized paths via Fabric Shortest Path First (FSPF).
  - o The traffic between two ports flows through the switches and not through any other ports like in Arbitrated Loop.
  - o Failure of a port is isolated to a link and should not affect operation of other ports.
  - o Multiple pairs of ports may communicate simultaneously in a Fabric.

| **Attribute** | **Point-to-Point** | **Arbitrated Loop** | **Switched Fabric** |
|---|---|---|---|
| Max ports | 2 | 127 | ~16777216 ($2^{24}$) |
| Address size | N/A | 8-bit ALPA | 24-bit port ID |
| Side effect of port failure | Link fails | Loop fails (until port bypassed) | N/A |
| Access to medium | Dedicated | Arbitrated | Dedicated |

## Layers

Fibre Channel does not follow the OSI model layering, and is split into five layers:

- FC-4 – Protocol-mapping layer, in which upper level protocols such as SCSI, IP or FICON, are encapsulated into Information Units (IUs) for delivery to FC-2. Current FC-4s include FCP-4, FC-SB-5, and FC-NVMe.
- FC-3 – Common services layer, a thin layer that could eventually implement functions like encryption or RAID redundancy algorithms; multiport connections;

- FC-2 – Signaling Protocol, defined by the Fibre Channel Framing and Signaling 4 (FC-FS-4) standard, consists of the low level Fibre Channel protocols; port to port connections;
- FC-1 – Transmission Protocol, which implements line coding of signals;
- FC-0 – PHY, includes cabling, connectors etc.;

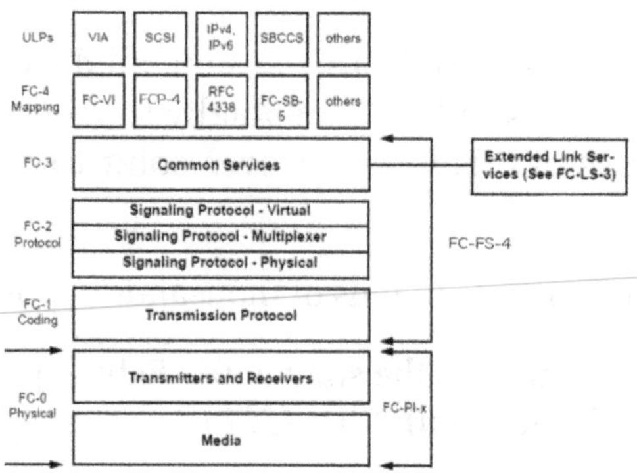


Fibre Channel is a layered technology that starts at the physical layer and progresses through the protocols to the upper level protocols like SCSI and SBCCS.

This diagram from FC-FS-4 defines the layers.

Layers FC-0 are defined in Fibre Channel Physical Interfaces (FC-PI-6), the physical layers of Fibre Channel.

Fibre Channel products are available at 1, 2, 4, 8, 10, 16 and 32 and 128 Gbit/s; these protocol flavors are called accordingly 1GFC, 2GFC, 4GFC, 8GFC, 10GFC, 16GFC, 32GFC or 128GFC. The 32GFC standard was approved by the INCITS T11 committee in 2013, and those products became available in 2016. The 1GFC, 2GFC, 4GFC, 8GFC designs all use 8b/10b encoding, while the 10GFC and 16GFC standard uses 64b/66b encoding. Unlike the 10GFC standards, 16GFC provides backward compatibility with 4GFC and 8GFC since it provides exactly twice the throughput of 8GFC or four times that of 4GFC.

## Ports

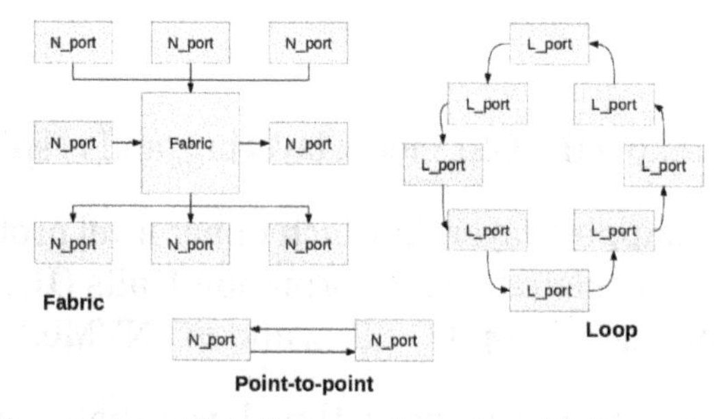


FC topologies and port types: This diagram shows how N_Ports can be connected to a fabric or to another N_Port. A Loop Port (L_Port) communicates through a shared loop and is rarely used anymore.

Fibre Channel ports come in a variety of logical configurations. The most common types of ports are:

- N_Port (Node port) An N_Port is typically an HBA port that connects to a switch's F_Port or another N_Port. Nx_Port communicating through a PN_ Port that is not operating a Loop Port State Machine.
- F_Port (Fabric port) An F_Port is a switch port that is connected to an N_Port.
- E_Port (Expansion port) Switch port that attaches to another E_Port to create an Inter-Switch Link.

Fibre Channel Loop protocols create multiple types of Loop Ports:

- L_Port (Loop port) FC_Port that contains Arbitrated Loop functions associated with the Arbitrated Loop topology.
- FL_Port (Fabric Loop port) L_Port that is able to perform the function of an F_Port, attached via a link to one or more NL_Ports in an Arbitrated Loop topology.
- NL_Port (Node Loop port) PN_Port that is operating a Loop port state machine.

If a port can support loop and non-loop functionality, the port is known as:

- Fx_Port switch port capable of operating as an F_Port or FL_Port.
- Nx_Port end point for Fibre Channel frame communication, having a distinct address identifier and Name_Identifier,providing an independent set of FC-2V functions to higher levels, and having the ability to act as an Originator, a Responder, or both.

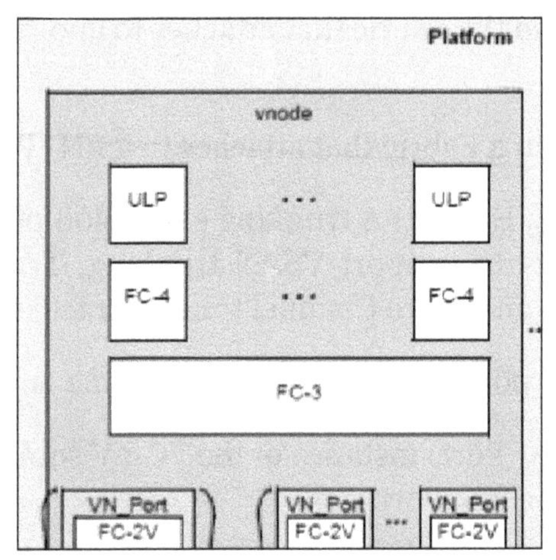


A Port has a physical structure as well as logical or virtual structure. This diagram shows how a virtual port may have multiple physical ports and vice versa.

Ports have virtual components and physical components and are described as:

- PN_Port entity that includes a Link_Control_Facility and one or more Nx_Ports.
- VF_Port (Virtual F_Port) instance of the FC-2V sublevel that connects to one or more VN_Ports.
- VN_Port (Virtual N_Port) instance of the FC-2V sublevel. VN_Port is used when it is desired to emphasize support for multiple Nx_Ports on a single Multiplexer (e.g., via a single PN_Port).
- VE_Port (Virtual E_Port) instance of the FC-2V sublevel that connects to another VE_Port or to a B_Port to create an Inter-Switch Link.

The following types of ports are also used in Fibre Channel:

- A_Port (Adjacent port) combination of one PA_Port and one VA_Port operating together.
- B_Port (Bridge Port) Fabric inter-element port used to connect bridge devices with E_Ports on a Switch.
- D_Port (Diagnostic Port) A configured port used to perform diagnostic tests on a link with another D_Port.
- EX_Port A type of E_Port used to connect to an FC router fabric.
- G_Port (Generic Fabric port) Switch port that may function either as an E_Port, A_Port, or as an F_Port.
- GL_Port (Generic Fabric Loop port) Switch port that may function either as an E_Port, A_Port, or as an Fx_Port.
- PE_Port LCF within the Fabric that attaches to another PE_Port or to a B_Port through a link.
- PF_Port LCF within a Fabric that attaches to a PN_Port through a link.
- TE_Port (Trunking E_Port) A trunking expansion port that expands the functionality of E ports to support VSAN trunking, Transport quality of service (QoS) parameters, and Fibre Channel trace (fctrace) feature.
- U_Port (Universal port) A port waiting to become another port type
- VA_Port (Virtual A_Port) instance of the FC-2V sublevel of Fibre Channel that connects to another VA_Port.
- VEX_Port VEX_Ports are no different from EX_Ports, except underlying transport is IP rather than FC.

## Media and Modules

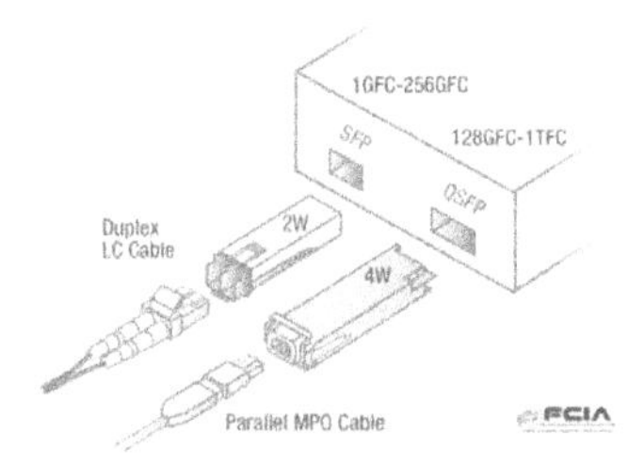


Fibre Channel predominantly uses the SFP module with the LC connector and duplex cabling, but 128GFC uses the QSFP28 module and the MPO connectors and ribbon cabling.

The Fibre Channel physical layer is based on serial connections that use corresponding modules. The small form-factor pluggable transceiver (SFP) module and its enhanced version SFP+ are common form factors for ports, supporting a variety of distances via multi-mode and single-mode fiber as shown in the table below. The SFP module uses duplex fiber cabling that has LC connectors.

The quad small form-factor pluggable (QSFP) module began being used for 4-lane implementations of 128GFC. The QSFP uses either the LC connector for 128GFC-CWDM4 or an MPO connector for 128GFC-SW4 or 128GFC-PSM4. The MPO cabling uses 8- or 12-fiber cabling infrastructure that connects to another 128GFC port or may be broken out into four duplex LC connections to 32GFC SFP+ ports. Fibre Channel switches use either SFP or QSFP modules.

| Fiber Type | Speed (MB/s) | Transmitter | Medium variant | Distance |
|---|---|---|---|---|
| Single-mode Fiber (SMF) | 12,800 | 1,310 nm longwave light | 128GFC-PSM4 | 0.5m - 0.5 km |
| | | 1,270, 1,290, 1,310 and 1,330 nm longwave light | 128GFC-CWDM4 | 0.5 m – 2 km |
| | 3,200 | 1,310 nm longwave light | 3200-SM-LC-L | 0.5 m - 10 km |
| | 1,600 | 1,310 nm longwave light | 1600-SM-LC-L | 0.5 m – 10 km |
| | | 1,490 nm longwave light | 1600-SM-LZ-I | 0.5 m – 2 km |
| | 800 | 1,310 nm longwave light | 800-SM-LC-L | 2 m – 10 km |
| | | | 800-SM-LC-I | 2 m – 1.4 km |
| | 400 | 1,310 nm longwave light | 400-SM-LC-L | 2 m – 10 km |
| | | | 400-SM-LC-M | 2 m – 4 km |
| | | | 400-SM-LL-I | 2 m – 2 km |
| | 200 | 1,550 nm longwave light | 200-SM-LL-V | 2 m – 50 km |
| | | 1,310 nm longwave light | 200-SM-LC-L | 2 m – 10 km |
| | | | 200-SM-LL-I | 2 m – 2 km |
| | 100 | 1,550 nm longwave light | 100-SM-LL-V | 2 m – 50 km |
| | | 1,310 nm longwave light | 100-SM-LL-L 100-SM-LC-L | 2 m – 10 km |
| | | | 100-SM-LL-I | 2 m – 2 km |

| Fiber Type | Speed (MB/s) | Transmitter | Medium variant | Distance |
|---|---|---|---|---|
| Multimode Fiber (MMF) | 12,800 | 850 nm shortwave light | 128GFC-SW4 | 0 – 100 m |
| | 3,200 | | 3200-SN | 0 – 100 m |
| | 1,600 | | 1600-M5F-SN-I | 0.5 m – 125 m |
| | | | 1600-M5E-SN-I | 0.5–100 m |
| | | | 1600-M5-SN-S | 0.5–35 m |
| | | | 1600-M6-SN-S | 0.5–15 m |
| | 800 | | 800-M5F-SN-I | 0.5–190 m |
| | | | 800-M5E-SN-I | 0.5–150 m |
| | | | 800-M5-SN-S | 0.5–50 m |
| | | | 800-M6-SN-S | 0.5–21 m |
| | 400 | | 400-M5F-SN-I | 0.5–400 m |
| | | | 400-M5E-SN-I | 0.5–380 m |
| | | | 400-M5-SN-I | 0.5–150 m |
| | | | 400-M6-SN-I | 0.5–70 m |
| | 200 | | 200-M5E-SN-I | 0.5–500 m |
| | | | 200-M5-SN-I | 0.5–300 m |
| | | | 200-M6-SN-I | 0.5–150 m |
| | 100 | | 100-M5E-SN-I | 0.5–860 m |
| | | | 100-M5-SN-I | 0.5–500 m |
| | | | 100-M6-SN-I | 0.5–300 m |
| | | | 100-M5-SL-I | 2–500 m |
| | | | 100-M6-SL-I | 2–175 m |

| Multimode fiber | Fiber diameter | FC media designation |
|---|---|---|
| OM1 | 62.5 µm | M6 |
| OM2 | 50 µm | M5 |
| OM3 | 50 µm | M5E |
| OM4 | 50 µm | M5F |

Modern Fibre Channel devices support SFP transceiver, mainly with LC (Lucent Connector) fiber connector. Older 1GFC devices used GBIC transceiver, mainly with SC (Subscriber Connector) fiber connector.

## Fibre Channel Storage Area Networks

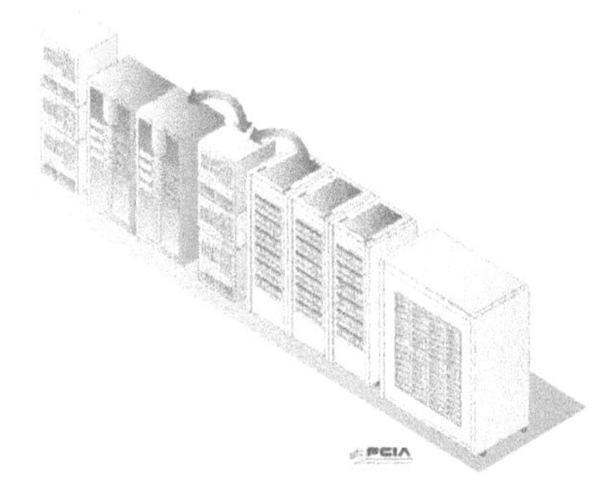

The Fibre Channel SAN connects servers to storage via Fibre Channel switches.

The goal of Fibre Channel is to create a storage area network (SAN) to connect servers to storage.

The SAN is a dedicated network that enables multiple servers to access the same storage. Enterprise storage uses the SAN to backup to tape libraries while the storage is still accessible to the server. Servers may access storage from multiple storage devices over the network as well.

SANs are often designed with dual fabrics to increase fault tolerance. Two completely separate fabrics are operational and if the primary fabric fails, then the second fabric becomes the primary.

## Fibre Channel Switches

Fibre Channel switch with SFP+ modules and LC optical fiber connectors with Optical Multimode 3 (OM3) fiber (aqua).

Fibre Channel switches can be divided into two classes. These classes are not part of the standard, and the classification of every switch is a marketing decision of the manufacturer:

- Directors offer a high port-count in a modular (slot-based) chassis with no single point of failure (high availability).
- Switches are typically smaller, fixed-configuration (sometimes semi-modular), less redundant devices.

A fabric consisting entirely of one vendors products is considered to be *homogeneous*. This is often referred to as operating in its "native mode" and allows the vendor to add proprietary features which may not be compliant with the Fibre Channel standard.

If multiple switch vendors are used within the same fabric it is *heterogeneous*, the switches may only achieve adjacency if all switches are placed into their interoperability modes. This is called the "open fabric" mode as each vendor's switch may have to disable its proprietary features to comply with the Fibre Channel standard.

Some switch manufacturers offer a variety of interoperability modes above and beyond the "native" and "open fabric" states. These "native interoperability" modes allow switches to operate in the native mode of another vendor and still maintain some of the proprietary behaviors of both. However, running in native interoperability mode may still disable some proprietary features and can produce fabrics of questionable stability.

## Fibre Channel Host Bus Adapters

Dual port 8Gb FC host bus adapter card.

Fibre Channel HBAs, as well as CNAs, are available for all major open systems, computer architectures, and buses, including PCI and SBus. Some are OS dependent. Each HBA has a unique World Wide Name (WWN), which is similar to an Ethernet MAC address in that it uses an Organizationally Unique Identifier (OUI) assigned by the IEEE. However, WWNs are longer (8 bytes). There are two types of WWNs on a HBA; a node WWN (WWNN), which can be shared by some or all ports of a device, and a port WWN (WWPN), which is necessarily unique to each port.

## Network File System

Network File System (NFS) is a distributed file system protocol originally developed by Sun Microsystems in 1984, allowing a user on a client computer to access files over a computer network much like local storage is accessed. NFS, like many other protocols, builds on the Open Network Computing Remote Procedure Call (ONC RPC) system. The NFS is an open standard defined in Request for Comments (RFC), allowing anyone to implement the protocol.

## Versions and Variations

Sun used version 1 only for in-house experimental purposes. When the development team added substantial changes to NFS version 1 and released it outside of Sun, they decided to release the new version as v2, so that version interoperation and RPC version fallback could be tested.

### NFSv2

Version 2 of the protocol (defined in RFC 1094, March 1989) originally operated only over User Datagram Protocol (UDP). Its designers meant to keep the server side stateless, with locking (for example) implemented outside of the core protocol. People involved in the creation of NFS version 2 include Russel Sandberg, Bob Lyon, Bill Joy, Steve Kleiman, and others.

The Virtual File System interface allows a modular implementation, reflected in a simple protocol. By February 1986, implementations were demonstrated for operating systems such as System V release 2, DOS, and VAX/VMS using Eunice. NFSv2 only allows the first 2 GB of a file to be read due to 32-bit limitations.

### NFSv3

Version 3 (RFC 1813, June 1995) added:

- support for 64-bit file sizes and offsets, to handle files larger than 2 gigabytes (GB);
- support for asynchronous writes on the server, to improve write performance;
- additional file attributes in many replies, to avoid the need to re-fetch them;
- a READDIRPLUS operation, to get file handles and attributes along with file names when scanning a directory;
- assorted other improvements.

The first NFS Version 3 proposal within Sun Microsystems was created not long after the release of NFS Version 2. The principal motivation was an attempt to mitigate the performance issue of the synchronous write operation in NFS Version 2. By July 1992, implementation practice had solved many shortcomings of NFS Version 2, leaving only lack of large file support (64-bit file sizes and offsets) a pressing issue. This became an acute pain point for Digital Equipment Corporation wih the intodution of a 64-bit version of Ultrix to support their newly released 64-bit RISC processor, the Alpha 21064. At the time of introduction of Version 3, vendor support for TCP as a transport-layer protocol began increasing. While several vendors had already added support for NFS Version 2 with TCP as a transport, Sun Microsystems added support for TCP as a transport for NFS at the same time it added support for Version 3. Using TCP as a transport made using NFS over a WAN more feasible, and allowed the use of larger read and write transfer sizes beyond the 8 KB limit imposed by User Datagram Protocol (UDP).

### NFSv4

Version 4 (RFC 3010, December 2000; revised in RFC 3530, April 2003 and again in RFC 7530, March 2015), influenced by Andrew File System (AFS) and Server Message Block (SMB, also termed CIFS), includes performance improvements, mandates strong security, and introduces a stateful protocol. Version 4 became the first version developed with the Internet Engineering Task Force (IETF) after Sun Microsystems handed over the development of the NFS protocols.

NFS version 4.1 (RFC 5661, January 2010) aims to provide protocol support to take advantage of clustered server deployments including the ability to provide scalable parallel access to files distributed among multiple servers (pNFS extension). NFS version 4.2 (RFC 7862) was published in November 2016.

### Other Extensions

WebNFS, an extension to Version 2 and Version 3, allows NFS to integrate more easily into Web-browsers and to enable operation through firewalls. In 2007 Sun Microsystems open-sourced their client-side WebNFS implementation.

Various side-band protocols have become associated with NFS. Note:

- the byte-range advisory Network Lock Manager (NLM) protocol (added to support UNIX System V file locking APIs)
- the remote quota-reporting (RQUOTAD) protocol, which allows NFS users to view their data-storage quotas on NFS servers
- NFS over RDMA, an adaptation of NFS that uses remote direct memory access (RDMA) as a transport
- NFS-Ganesha, an NFS server, running in user-space and supporting the CephFS FSAL (File System Abstraction Layer) using libcephfs

### Platforms

NFS is often used with Unix operating systems (such as Solaris, AIX, HP-UX), Apple's macOS, and Unix-like operating systems (such as Linux and FreeBSD). It is also available to operating systems such as Acorn RISC OS, the classic Mac OS, OpenVMS, MS-DOS, Microsoft Windows, Novell NetWare, and IBM AS/400. Alternative remote file access protocols include the Server Message Block (SMB, also termed CIFS), Apple Filing Protocol (AFP), NetWare Core Protocol (NCP), and OS/400 File Server file system (QFileSvr.400).

SMB and NetWare Core Protocol (NCP) occur more often than NFS on systems running Microsoft Windows; AFP occurs more often than NFS in Apple Macintosh systems; and QFileSvr.400 occurs more often in AS/400 systems. Haiku recently added NFSv4 support as part of a Google Summer of Code project.

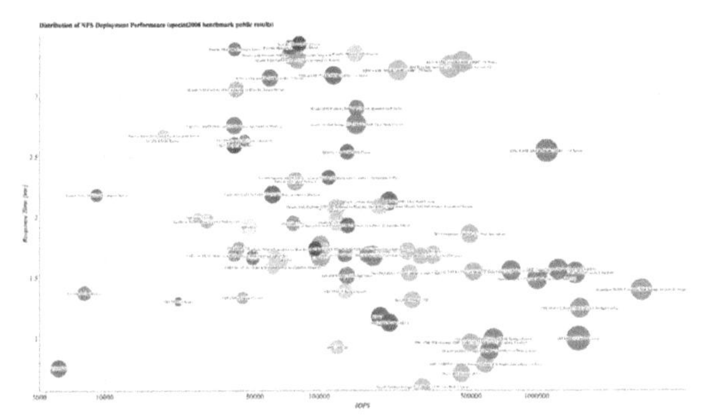

NFS specint2008 performance comparison, as of 22 November 2013

## Typical Implementation

Assuming a Unix-style scenario in which one machine (the client) needs access to data stored on another machine (the NFS server):

1. The server implements NFS daemon processes, running by default as nfsd, to make its data generically available to clients.
2. The server administrator determines what to make available, exporting the names and parameters of directories, typically using the /etc/exports configuration file and the exportfs command.
3. The server security-administration ensures that it can recognize and approve validated clients.
4. The server network configuration ensures that appropriate clients can negotiate with it through any firewall system.
5. The client machine requests access to exported data, typically by issuing a mount command. (The client asks the server (rpcbind) which port the NFS server is using, the client connects to the NFS server (nfsd), nfsd passes the request to mountd)
6. If all goes well, users on the client machine can then view and interact with mounted filesystems on the server within the parameters permitted.

Note that automation of the NFS mounting process may take place — perhaps using /etc/fstab and/or automounting facilities.

## Protocol Development

During the development of the ONC protocol (called SunRPC at the time), only Apollo's Network Computing System (NCS) offered comparable functionality. Two competing groups developed over fundamental differences in the two remote procedure call systems. Arguments focused on the method for data-encoding — ONC's External Data Representation (XDR) always rendered integers in big-endian order, even if both peers of the connection had little-endian machine-architectures, whereas NCS's method attempted to avoid byte-swap whenever two peers shared a common endianness in their machine-architectures. An industry-group called the Network Computing Forum formed (March 1987) in an (ultimately unsuccessful) attempt to reconcile the two network-computing environments.

Later, Sun and AT&T announced they would jointly develop AT&T's UNIX System V Release 4. This caused many of AT&T's other licensees of UNIX System to become concerned that this would put Sun in an advantaged position, and ultimately led to Digital Equipment, HP, IBM, and others forming the Open Software Foundation (OSF) in 1988. Ironically, Sun and AT&T had formerly competed over Sun's NFS versus AT&T's Remote File System (RFS), and the quick adoption of NFS over RFS by Digital Equipment, HP, IBM, and many other computer vendors tipped the majority of users in favor of NFS. NFS interoperability was aided by events called "Connectathons" starting in 1986 that allowed vendor-neutral testing of implementations with each other. OSF adopted the Distributed Computing Environment (DCE) and the DCE Distributed File System (DFS) over Sun/ONC RPC and NFS. DFS used DCE as the RPC, and DFS derived from the Andrew File System (AFS); DCE itself derived from a suite of technologies, including Apollo's NCS and Kerberos.

### 1990s

Sun Microsystems and the Internet Society (ISOC) reached an agreement to cede "change control" of ONC RPC so that the ISOC's engineering-standards body, the Internet Engineering Task Force (IETF), could publish standards documents (RFCs) related to ONC RPC protocols and could extend ONC RPC. OSF attempted to make DCE RPC an IETF standard, but ultimately proved unwilling to give up change control. Later, the IETF chose to extend ONC RPC by adding a new authentication flavor based on Generic Security Services Application Program Interface (GSSAPI), RPCSEC GSS, to meet IETF requirements that protocol standards have adequate security.

Later, Sun and ISOC reached a similar agreement to give ISOC change control over NFS, although writing the contract carefully to exclude NFS version 2 and version 3. Instead, ISOC gained the right to add new versions to the NFS protocol, which resulted in IETF specifying NFS version 4 in 2003.

### 2000s

By the 21st century, neither DFS nor AFS had achieved any major commercial success as compared to SMB-CIFS or NFS. IBM, which had formerly acquired the primary commercial vendor of DFS and AFS, Transarc, donated most of the AFS source code to the free software community in 2000. The OpenAFS project lives on. In early 2005, IBM announced end of sales for AFS and DFS.

In January, 2010, Panasas proposed an NFSv4.1 based on their *Parallel NFS* (pNFS) technology claiming to improve data-access parallelism capability. The NFSv4.1 protocol defines a method of separating the filesystem meta-data from file data location; it goes beyond the simple name/data separation by striping the data amongst a set of data servers. This differs from the traditional NFS server which holds the names of files and their data under the single umbrella of the server. Some products are multi-node NFS servers, but the participation of the client in separation of meta-data and data is limited.

The NFSv4.1 pNFS server is a set of server resources or components; these are assumed to be controlled by the meta-data server.

The pNFS client still accesses one meta-data server for traversal or interaction with the namespace; when the client moves data to and from the server it may directly interact with the set of data servers belonging to the pNFS server collection. The NFSv4.1 client can be enabled to be a direct participant in the exact location of file data and to avoid solitary interaction with one NFS server when moving data.

In addition to pNFS, NFSv4.1 provides:

- Sessions
- Directory Delegation and Notifications
- Multi-server Namespace
- access control lists and discretionary access control
- Retention Attributions
- SECINFO_NO_NAME

## Cloud E-commerce

Cloud e-commerce refers to the process of outsourcing of a remote network of servers hosted on the Internet to use application services, store, and process data. Essentially, it is a cloud-based e-commerce solution versus software installed on a local server.

Cloud e-commerce provides a wide range of benefits over traditional on-premise storage used for commerce. Within the last years, the cloud has gained popularity due to reduced complexity and lower cost of maintenance. Nowadays, cloud e-commerce has become one of the most optimal solutions on the market.

### Scalability on Demand

The extreme traffic variability in e-commerce with its seasonal spikes creates a unique workload for e-commerce hosting. Required hardware capacity must conform to the traffic peaks (ex. Black Friday, Cyber Monday, etc.). But for most of the year, the servers are not in use.

The cloud offers an elastic solution, that allows for substantial variations in workload and meets the needs for seasonal or even hourly promotional spikes in traffic, including unpredictable outbreaks. This way cloud e-commerce store resources can be scaled up and down to support your actual needs.

The other side of scalability is business growth. An increase in store's popularity, integration of new services and further store evolution force the infrastructure to grow accordingly. A flexible platform at the heart of your e-commerce solution, as well as scalable environment responds quickly to business challenges and opportunities.

Cloud allows to avoid physical superstructure. The e-commerce business doesn't have to purchase additional equipment and hire new maintenance staff.

### Reliable Pro Protection

When hosting your business in the cloud, the e-commerce website doesn't need to worry about maintaining and monitoring servers. Security and protection of network, physical facilities, applications, including data encryption and customers' personal data safety can be excluded from the list of concerns. E-commerce cloud vendors take all the risks. The cloud hosting providers complete a third-party certification, and proper security is a priority for them. Besides, constant accessibility of ecommerce storefront and regular data backup ensure that the e-commerce store will be available without any data loss in case of an emergency.

### Cost-effective Performance

Cloud fits e-commerce solutions perfectly because the business pays for resources only when it needs them. A cloud-based solution may save a company over 70% of the costs associated with building static environments scaled for traffic peaks - the hardware that may only be in use a few days a year.

### Easy Accessibility from any Place

If the e-commerce project operates in multiple countries, a cloud-based e-commerce solution offers clear advantages considering the speed required to roll out and manage an e-commerce application. With cloud-based e-commerce, there's a remote network of servers that responds dynamically to business demands to deliver content fast no matter where your customer is.

## How to Pick a Service for your Commerce?

The cloud computing service categories fall under several distinct categories. Each of these models or their combinations allows users to create the perfect foundation for the e-commerce suite.

IaaS (Infrastructure as a Service)

This type of cloud service focuses on providing on-demand data storage on disks and virtual servers. Customers purchase a remote data center infrastructure service instead of having to purchase their own hardware.

Examples include cloud services offered by established well-known brands, such as Amazon, Microsoft, and others.

PaaS (Platform as a Service)

A cloud development platform that allows its users to develop, manage, and launch applications within a self-service portal with a ready-to-use cloud computing infrastructure. Most platforms provide the basics so that you don't have to start from scratch. The operating system is supported and frequently upgraded, and the services for your e-commerce solution can be built, using certain modules.

Examples of Platform-as-a-Service are Google App Engine, Cloudfy, and Cloudsuite.

SaaS (Software as a Service)

Software-as-a-Service means that a third-party hosting service provider gives clients access to various software solutions on a pay-as-you-go basis.

This service type is very popular among e-commerce vendors. Modern applications allow your business to improve its customer experience and expand the online store with advanced features, such as smart shopping cart or mobile-friendly applications.

Among the most popular SaaS solutions are Salesforce, NetSuite, Slack and others.

An optimal choice for an e-commerce business willing to use cloud, however, would be a solution that combines a platform with a ready-to-use set of software tools. In other words, PaaS and SaaS built specifically for e-commerce. Examples of cloud e-commerce solutions include:

- Magento

- Demandware
- Commerce Cloud from Oracle
- Commerce Cloud from SalesForce

Enterprise e-commerce cloud solutions can be based on different public clouds, including Azure from Microsoft, Google Cloud or AWS from Amazon.

## Cooperative Storage Cloud

A cooperative storage cloud is a decentralized model of networked online storage where data is stored on multiple computers (nodes), hosted by the participants cooperating in the cloud. For the cooperative scheme to be viable, the total storage contributed in aggregate must be at least equal to the amount of storage needed by end users. However, some nodes may contribute less storage and some may contribute more. There may be reward models to compensate the nodes contributing more.

Unlike a traditional storage cloud, a cooperative does not directly employ dedicated servers for the actual storage of the data, thereby eliminating the need for a significant dedicated hardware investment. Each node in the cooperative runs specialized software which communicates with a centralized control and orchestration server, thereby allowing the node to both consume and contribute storage space to the cloud. The centralized control and orchestration server requires several orders of magnitude less resources (storage, computing power, and bandwidth) to operate, relative to the overall capacity of the cooperative.

### Data Security

Files hosted in the cloud are fragmented and encrypted before leaving the local machine. They are then distributed randomly using a load balancing and geo-distribution algorithm to other nodes in the cooperative. Users can add an additional layer of security and reduce storage space by compressing and encrypting files before they are copied to the cloud.

### Data Redundancy

In order to maintain data integrity and high availability across a relatively unreliable set of computers over a wide area network like the Internet, the source node will add some level of redundancy to each data block. This allows the system to recreate the entire block even if some nodes are temporarily unavailable (due to loss of network connectivity, the machine being powered off or a hardware failure). The most storage and bandwidth efficient forms of redundancy use erasure coding techniques like

Reed-Solomon. A simple, less CPU intensive but more expensive form of redundancy is duplicate copies.

## Flexible Contribution

Due to bandwidth or hardware constraints some nodes may not be able to contribute as much space as they consume in the cloud. On the other hand, nodes with large storage space and limited or no bandwidth constraints may contribute more than they consume, thereby the cooperative can always stay in balance.

## Examples

The University of California's OceanStore project, MIT's Chord, is a non-commercial example.

Sia is a fully distributed system using a blockchain where a cryptocurrency is exchanged for storage, and a daemon that can act both as a file host and as a "renter" of storage, using Merkle trees to provide strong guarantees that hosts will only get paid if they successfully hold data for the duration of a "storage contract". Data is encrypted and spread among hosts in a redundant manner, using erasure coding, to maximize availability. According to one of its creators, Sia was the first platform of its kind to launch an end-user product.

On June 1, 2016 Minebox GMBH announced that their forthcoming Minebox Networked Attached Storage device (NAS) will utilize the Sia network to persist its backups. Users of the Minebox will also be able to rent their free disk space via Sia.

Storj is another example: based on the Bitcoin blockchain technology and a peer-to-peer architecture, it intends to provide cloud storage to people. It is currently developing two applications to achieve this goal: *MetaDisk*, which lets the user upload files to the network, and *DriveShare*, allowing users to rent out their storage space to MetaDisk users.

A partly centralized system was operated by Symform, Inc., a startup company based in Seattle. Symform generated and kept the keys used to encrypt and decrypt, and since it also decided which server will host which parts of a file, users have to trust Symform not to share those with any other party or misuse the information. Symform discontinued its service on Jul 31, 2016.

## References


- Mellor, Chris (6 January 2015). "IDC: Who's HOT and who's NOT (in object storage) in 2014". The Register. Retrieved 26 January 2015
- Hirsch, Frederick; Kemp, John; Ilkka, Jani (2007). Mobile Web Services: Architecture and Implementation. John Wiley & Sons. p. 27. ISBN 9780470032596. Retrieved 2014-09-15

- Butler, Brandon (2 June 2014). "Cloud's worst-case scenario: What to do if your provider goes belly up". Network World. Retrieved 20 June 2015
- Chu, Cheng-Kang; Chow, S.S.M.; Tzeng, Wen-Guey; Zhou, Jianying; Deng, R.H. (2014-02-01). "Key-Aggregate Cryptosystem for Scalable Data Sharing in Cloud Storage". IEEE Transactions on Parallel and Distributed Systems. 25 (2): 468–477. ISSN 1045-9219. doi:10.1109/TPDS.2013.112
- "Box.net lets you store, share, work in the computing cloud". Silicon Valley Business Journal. December 6, 2009. Retrieved October 2, 2016
- Thomas Erl, Benjamin Carlyle, Cesare Pautasso, Raj Balasubramanian (2013). "5.1". In Thomas Erl. SOA with REST. Prentice Hall. ISBN 978-0-13-701251-0
- Mesnier, Mike; Gregory R. Ganger; Erik Riedel (August 2003). "Object-Based Storage" (PDF). IEEE Communications Magazine: 84–90. doi:10.1109/mcom.2003.1222722. Retrieved 27 October 2013
- Gupta, P (20 October 2013). "The usage and adoption of cloud computing by small and medium businesses". International Journal of Information Management (33): 861–874. doi:10.1016/j.ijinfomgt.2013.07.001
- Richardson, Leonard; Amundsen, Mike (2013), RESTful Web APIs, O'Reilly Media, ISBN 978-1-449-35806-8, retrieved 15 September 2015
- Sanjay Ghemawat; Howard Gobioff; Shun-Tak Leung (October 2003). "The Google File System" (PDF). Google. Retrieved 7 November 2013
- Subashini, S.; Kavitha, V. (2011-01-01). "A survey on security issues in service delivery models of cloud computing". Journal of Network and Computer Applications. 34 (1): 1–11. doi:10.1016/j.jnca.2010.07.006
- Preston, W. Curtis (2002). "Fibre Channel Architecture". Using SANs and NAS. Sebastopol, CA: O'Reilly Media. pp. 19–39. ISBN 978-0-596-00153-7. OCLC 472853124
- Sandoval, Greg (31 March 2012). "MPAA wants more criminal cases brought against 'rogue' sites". CNET. Retrieved 10 November 2016

# 3

# Cloud Computing as Service

Commercially, cloud computing is used in providing various services such as Platform as a service (PaaS), cloud engineering, Security as a service (SECaaS), etc. Such services aid businesses and entrepreneurships. The aspects elucidated in this chapter are of vital importance, and provide a better understanding of cloud computing.

## Cloud Engineering

Cloud engineering is the application of engineering disciplines to cloud computing. It brings a systematic approach to concerns of commercialization, standardization, and governance of cloud computing applications. In practice, it leverages the methods and tools of engineering in conceiving, developing, operating and maintaining cloud computing systems and solutions. It is about the process of designing the systems necessary to leverage the power and economics of cloud resources to solve business problems.

### Core Features

Cloud engineering is a field of engineering that focuses on cloud services, such as "software as a service", "platform as a service", and "infrastructure as a service". It is a multidisciplinary method encompassing contributions from diverse areas such as *systems engineering*, *software engineering*, *web engineering*, *performance engineering*, *information engineering*, *security engineering*, platform engineering, service engineering, risk engineering, and quality engineering. The nature of commodity-like capabilities delivered by cloud services and the inherent challenges in this business model drive the need for cloud engineering as the core discipline.

Elements of Cloud Engineering include:

- Foundation: the fundamental basics, concepts, guiding principles, and taxonomy
- Implementation: the building blocks and practice guides for Cloud realization
- Lifecycle: the end-to-end iteration of Cloud development and delivery
- Management: the design-time and run-time Cloud management from multiple perspectives

## Profession

The professionals who work in the field of cloud engineering are primarily cloud architects and engineers. The key skills possessed by cloud engineering professionals are:

- Know the language of business and domain knowledge
- Understand the conceptual, logical and physical architecture
- Master various cloud technologies, frameworks, and platforms
- Implement the solutions for quality of cloud services, e.g. HA, DR, scaling, performance
- Work on the security at multiple levels
- Develop applications for flexible deployment, provisioning, and management
- Leverage open source packages and products
- Apply agile and lean principles in design and construction

The demand for skills in advanced ICT (Information and Communication Technology) has rapidly expanded in recent years as business and society are being transformed by the emergence of Internet and Web as ubiquitous media for enabling knowledge-based global economy. This in turn has created a huge demand for networked-enabled parallel and distributed computing technologies that are changing the way we conduct science, operate business, and tackle challenging problems such as epidemic diseases and climate change.

## Software

There are many platforms available for cloud engineering. There are the CAD-Tools Onshape and Autodesk Revit, for CAE-purposes, users can use the software ExaCloud or SimScale.

## History

The notion of cloud engineering in the context of cloud computing had been sparsely used in discussions, presentations and talks in various occasions in the middle of the 2000s. The term of cloud engineering was formally coined around 2007 and the concept of cloud engineering was officially introduced in April 2009. Various aspects and topics of this subject have been extensively covered in a number of industry events. Extensive research has been conducted on specific areas in cloud engineering, such as development support for cloud patterns, and cloud business continuity services. The first IEEE International Conference on Cloud Engineering (IC2E) took place on March 25–28, 2013 and the second conference was held on March 10–14, 2014.

# Platform as a Service

Platform as a service (PaaS) or application platform as a service (aPaaS) is a category of cloud computing services that provides a platform allowing customers to develop, run, and manage applications without the complexity of building and maintaining the infrastructure typically associated with developing and launching an app. PaaS can be delivered in two ways: as a public cloud service from a provider, where the consumer controls software deployment with minimal configuration options, and the provider provides the networks, servers, storage, operating system (OS), 'middleware' (e.g. Java runtime, .NET runtime, integration, etc.), database and other services to host the consumer's application; or as a private service (software or appliance) inside the firewall, or as software deployed on a public infrastructure as a service.

## Development and uses

Fotango, a London-based (Old Street) company owned by Canon Europe launched the world's first public platform as a service known as 'Zimki'. It was developed in 2005 with a beta launch in March 2006 and a public launch at EuroOSCON in 2006. Zimki was an end-to-end JavaScript web application development and utility computing platform that removed all the repetitive tasks encountered when creating web applications and web services. All aspects of infrastructure and operations from provisioning and setting up virtual servers, scaling, configuration, security and backups were done automatically by Zimki. Zimki introduced the tagline 'Pre-Shaved Yaks' to describe the removal of all these repetitive tasks.

Zimki was a pure 'pay as you go' code execution platform which enabled developers to build and deploy applications or web services without incurring any start-up costs on a true utility based computing platform. Charging was done on storage used, network traffic and JSOPs (Javascript Operations). It provided a multi-tenant platform where developers could create entire applications (front and back end through SSJS) by using a single language - Javascript, with all development, billing, monitoring and application control exposed through APIs and a range of component services from a NoSQL object store to Message Queue services. Furthermore, all functions within Zimki could be exposed as web services and Zimki provided billing analysis down to individual functions.

Whilst the Zimki platform was rapidly growing and Fotango was profitable, the parent company decided this area was not core and the service was closed in Dec 2007. At the time of its closure, Zimki had several thousand developer accounts and had demonstrated the technical viability of Platform as a Service but also provided the first example of the perils of being dependent upon a single provider. This risk had been highlighted in July 2007, when the CEO gave a presentation on Zimki at OSCON 2007 which announced that Zimki would no longer be open sourced and discussed the future of what was then called Framework as a Service (later renamed to Platform as a Service) covering the importance of a market of providers based upon an open source reference model.

In April 2008, Google launched App Engine, with a free trial version limited to 10,000 developers. This was said to have "turned the Internet cloud computing space into a fully-fledged industry virtually overnight."

The original intent of PaaS was to simplify the code-writing process for developers, with the infrastructure and operations handled by the PaaS provider. Originally, all PaaSes were in the public cloud. Because many companies did not want to have everything in the public cloud, private and hybrid PaaS options (managed by internal IT departments) were created.

PaaS provides an environment for developers and companies to create, host and deploy applications, saving developers from the complexities of the infrastructure side (setting up, configuring and managing elements such as servers and databases). PaaS can improve the speed of developing an app, and allow the consumer to focus on the application itself. With PaaS, the consumer manages applications and data, while the provider (in public PaaS) or IT department (in private PaaS) manages runtime, middleware, operating system, virtualization, servers, storage and networking. Development tools provided by the vendor are customized according to the needs of the user. The user can choose to maintain the software, or have the vendor maintain it.

PaaS offerings may also include facilities for application design, application development, testing and deployment, as well as services such as team collaboration, web service integration, and marshalling, database integration, security, scalability, storage, persistence, state management, application versioning, application instrumentation, and developer community facilitation. Besides the service engineering aspects, PaaS offerings include mechanisms for service management, such as monitoring, workflow management, discovery and reservation.

## Advantages and Disadvantages

The advantages of PaaS are primarily that it allows for higher-level programming with dramatically reduced complexity; the overall development of the application can be more effective, as it has built-in infrastructure; and maintenance and enhancement of the application is easier. It can also be useful in situations where multiple developers are working on a single project involving parties who are not located nearby.

One disadvantage of PaaS offerings is that developers may not be able to use a full range of conventional tools (e.g. relational databases, with unrestricted joins). Another possible disadvantage is being locked in to a certain platform. However, most PaaSes are relatively lock-in free.

## Types

### Public, Private and Hybrid

There are several types of PaaS, including public, private and hybrid. PaaS was originally intended for applications on public cloud services, before expanding to include private and hybrid options.

Public PaaS is derived from software as a service (SaaS), and is situated in cloud computing between SaaS and infrastructure as a service (IaaS). SaaS is software that is hosted in the cloud, so that it doesn't take up hard drive from the computer of the user or the servers of a company. IaaS provides virtual hardware from a provider with adjustable scalability. With IaaS, the user still has to manage the server, whereas with PaaS the server management is done by the provider. IBM Bluemix (also private and hybrid), Amazon AWS and Heroku are some of the commercial public cloud PaaS providers.

A private PaaS can typically be downloaded and installed either in a company's on-premises data center, or in a public cloud. Once the software is installed on one or more machines, the private PaaS arranges the application and database components into a single hosting platform. Private PaaS vendors include Apprenda, which started out on the Microsoft .NET platform before rolling out a Java PaaS; Red Hat's OpenShift and Pivotal Cloud Foundry. Apprenda and Microsoft once considered to be two of the only PaaSes that provide superior .NET support. Now joined by the publicly announced Microsoft and IBM Partnership programme.

Hybrid PaaS is typically a deployment consisting of a mix of public and private deployments. An example here is IBM Bluemix which is delivered as a single, integrated cloud platform across public, dedicated, and on-premise deployment models.

### Mobile PaaS

Initiated in 2012, mobile PaaS (mPaaS) provides development capabilities for mobile app designers and developers. The Yankee Group identified mPaaS as one of its themes for 2014, naming a number of providers including Kinvey, CloudMine, AnyPresence, FeedHenry, FatFractal and Point.io.

### Open PaaS

Open PaaS does not include hosting, but rather it provides open source software allowing a PaaS provider to run applications in an open source environment. For example, AppScale allows a user to deploy some applications written for Google App Engine to their own servers, providing datastore access from a standard SQL or NoSQL database. Some open platforms let the developer use any programming language, database, operating system or server to deploy their applications.

## PaaS for Rapid Development

In 2014, Forrester Research defined enterprise public cloud platforms for rapid developers as an emerging trend, naming a number of providers including Mendix, Salesforce.com, OutSystems and Acquia.

## System Types

PaaS is found on the following types of systems:

### Add-on Development Facilities

These facilities allow customization of existing SaaS applications, often requiring PaaS developers and their users to purchase subscriptions to the add-on SaaS application.

### Stand Alone Environments

Stand-alone PaaS environments do not include technical, licensing or financial dependencies on specific SaaS applications or web services, and are intended to provide a generalized development environment.

### Application Delivery-only Environments

Delivery-only PaaS offerings generally focus on hosting services, such as security and on-demand scalability. The service does not include development, debugging and test capabilities, though they may be supplied offline (via an Eclipse plugin, for example).

## Providers

There are various types of PaaS providers. All offer application hosting and a deployment environment, along with various integrated services. Services offer varying levels of scalability and maintenance. Developers can write an application and upload it to a PaaS that supports their software language of choice, and the application runs on that PaaS.

# Serverless Computing

Serverless computing, also known as function as a service (FaaS), is a cloud computing code execution model in which the cloud provider fully manages starting and stopping of a function's container platform as a service (PaaS) as necessary to serve requests, and requests are billed by an abstract measure of the resources required to satisfy the request, rather than per virtual machine, per hour.

Despite the name, it does not actually involve running code without servers. The name "serverless computing" is used because the business or person that owns the system does not have to purchase, rent or provision servers or virtual machines for the back-end code to run on.

Serverless code can be used in conjunction with code written in traditional server style, such as microservices. For example, part of a web application could be written as microservices and another part could be written as serverless code. Alternatively, an application could be written that uses no provisioned servers at all, being completely serverless.

Serverless code can either be triggered by specific events (such as user registration with Amazon Cognito), or be configured to run behind an API management platform in order to expose it as a REST API endpoint.

### History

The first 'pay as you go' code execution platform where developers simply wrote code online including billing at a functional level, creation of virtual resources by the system as needed, exposure of functions as APIs was Zimki in 2006. AWS Lambda, introduced by Amazon in November 2014, was the first major provider considered to have a serverless offering. AWS Lambda initially launched with Node.js as the only runtime, but as of 2016 it now officially supports Python, Java, C# and other languages such as Haskell can also be used by using Node.js as an invoker.

Google has released an alpha version of its serverless platform, which is called Google Cloud Functions, and supports Node.js.

IBM announced OpenWhisk as an open source serverless platform of its own at InterConnect 2016. IBM donated the source code to the Apache Software Foundation as part of an Incubation project bearing the same name in December 2016.

In addition to supporting functions as a service, OpenWhisk has a programming model that offers features that include user-defined triggers, function execution rules, function composition via sequences, and a model for sharing assets via packages. OpenWhisk may be hosted on premise or hosted as a service as is the case with IBM Bluemix Serverless offering that is built on the Apache OpenWhisk project; the source code is available on GitHub. At launch, OpenWhisk included support for Node.js and Swift, as well as black box functions (in any language or runtime) via Docker containers. It now officially also includes support for Python and Java as well.

Microsoft followed up in 2016 by announcing Azure Functions, a technology usable in both the Azure public cloud and on any other cloud environment, public or private. Azure functions have been generally available for production use since November 2016.

## Advantages

### Cost

Serverless computing can be more cost-efficient just in terms of computing resources, than renting or purchasing a fixed quantity of servers, which generally involves periods of underutilisation or non-use. It can even be more cost-efficient than provisioning an autoscaling group, because even autoscaling groups are typically designed to have underutilisation to allow time for new instances to start up.

In addition, a serverless architecture means that developers and operations specialists do not need to spend time setting up and tuning autoscaling policies or systems; the cloud provider is responsible for ensuring that the capacity meets the demand.

### Programming Model

In serverless computing, the units of code exposed to the outside world are simple functions. For example, in AWS Lambda, they are essentially functions that both consume and produce JSON, although they can make calls to other APIs, and the JSON may be automatically serialized from and deserialized to data structures at the option of the programmer. This means that typically, the programmer does not have to worry about multithreading or directly handling HTTP requests in their code, simplifying the task of back-end software development.

## Disadvantages

### Performance

Infrequently-used serverless code may suffer from greater response latency than code that is continuously running on a dedicated server, virtual machine, or container. This is because, unlike with autoscaling, the cloud provider typically "spins down" the serverless code completely when not in use. This means that if the runtime (for example, the Java runtime) in use requires a significant amount of time to start up, that will introduce latency into request handling. However, not all code is latency-sensitive; for example, batch processing operations run by cron jobs might not be significantly affected by small, infrequent latencies such as this.

### Resource Limits

Serverless computing is not suited to some computing workloads, such as high-performance computing, because of the resource limits imposed by cloud providers, and also because it would likely be cheaper to bulk-provision the number of servers believed to be required at any given point in time.

## Monitoring and Debugging

Diagnosing performance or excessive resource usage problems with serverless code may be more difficult than with traditional server code, because although entire functions can be timed, there is typically no ability to dig into more detail by attaching profilers, debuggers or APM tools. Furthermore, the environment in which the code runs is typically not open source, so its performance characteristics cannot be precisely replicated in a local environment. However, Amazon plans to provide AWS Lambda support in its APM and tracing technology called AWS X-Ray.

## Serverless Frameworks

Multiple serverless frameworks have been published:

- Serverless Framework, a software framework for creating serverless systems on AWS Lambda with Node.js or Python
- Kubeless, a proof of concept to develop a serverless framework for Kubernetes. It uses a ThirdPartyResource to be able to create functions as custom resources
- Fission, a framework for serverless functions on Kubernetes. It is extensible to any programming language (Python, NodeJS, Go, C#, PHP are supported).
- Funktion, an open source event based lambda programming for kubernetes.
- Apache OpenWhisk, a serverless, open source cloud platform that executes functions in response to events at any scale.

## Execution (Computing)

Execution in computer and software engineering is the process by which a computer or a virtual machine performs the instructions of a computer program. The instructions in the program trigger sequences of simple actions on the executing machine. Those actions produce effects according to the semantics of the instructions in the program.

Programs for a computer may execute in a batch process without human interaction, or a user may type commands in an interactive session of an interpreter. In this case the "commands" are simply programs, whose execution is chained together.

The term run is used almost synonymously. A related meaning of both "to run" and "to execute" refers to the specific action of a user starting (or *launching* or *invoking*) a program, as in "Please run the application."

## Context of Execution

The context in which execution takes place is crucial. Very few programs execute on a bare machine. Programs usually contain implicit and explicit assumptions about resources available at the time of execution. Most programs execute with the support of an operating system and run-time libraries specific to the source language that provide crucial services not supplied directly by the computer itself. This supportive environment, for instance, usually decouples a program from direct manipulation of the computer peripherals, providing more general, abstract services instead.

### Process

Prior to execution, a program must first be written. This is generally done in source code, which is then compiled at compile time (and statically linked at link time) to an executable. This executable is then invoked, most often by an operating system, which loads the program into memory (load time), possibly performs dynamic linking, and then begins execution by moving control to the entry point of the program; all these steps depend on the Application Binary Interface of the operating system. At this point execution begins and the program enters run time. The program then runs until it ends, either normal termination or a crash.

### Interpreter

A system that executes a program is called an interpreter of the program. Loosely speaking, an interpreter actually does what the program says to do. This contrasts with a language translator that converts a program from one language to another. The most common language translators are compilers. Translators typically convert their source from a high-level, human readable language into a lower-level language (sometimes as low as native machine code) that is simpler and faster for the processor to directly execute. The idea is that the ratio of executions to translations of a program will be large; that is, a program need only be compiled once and can be run any number of times. This can provide a large benefit for translation versus direct interpretation of the source language. One trade-off is that development time is increased, because of the compilation. In some cases, only the changed files must be recompiled. Then the executable needs to be relinked. For some changes, the executable must be rebuilt from scratch. As computers and compilers become faster, this fact becomes less of an obstacle. Also, the speed of the end product is typically more important to the user than the development time.

Translators usually produce an abstract result that is not completely ready to execute. Frequently, the operating system will convert the translator's object code into the final executable form just before execution of the program begins.

## Security as a Service

Security as a service (SECaaS) is a business model in which a large service provider integrates their security services into a corporate infrastructure on a subscription basis more cost effectively than most individuals or corporations can provide on their own, when total cost of ownership is considered. In this scenario, security is delivered as a service from the cloud, without requiring on-premises hardware avoiding substantial capital outlays. These security services often include authentication, anti-virus, anti-malware/spyware, intrusion detection, and security event management, among others.

Outsourced security licensing and delivery is boasting a multibillion-dollar market. SECaaS provides users with Internet security services providing protection from online threats and attacks such as DDoS that are constantly searching for access points to compromise websites. As the demand and use of cloud computing skyrockets, users are more vulnerable to attacks due to accessing the Internet from new access points. SECaaS serves as a buffer against the most persistent online threats.

## Categories of SECaaS

The Cloud Security Alliance (CSA) is and organization that is dedicated to defining and raising awareness of secure cloud computing. In doing so, the CSA has defined the following categories of SECaaS tools and created a series of technical and implementation guidance documents to help businesses implement and understand SECaaS. These categories include:

- Business Continuity and Disaster Recovery (BCDR)
- Continuous Monitoring
- Data Loss Prevention (DLP)
- Email Security
- Encryption
- Identity and Access Management (IAM)
- Intrusion Management
- Network Security
- Security Assessment
- Security Information and Event Management (SIEM)
- Vulnerability Scanning
- Web Security

## SECaaS Models

SECaaS are typically offered in several forms:

- Subscription

- Payment for utilized services
- Free of charge: Examples include AIONCLOUD, Cloudbric, CloudFlare, and Incapsula.

## Benefits

Security as a service offers a number of benefits, including:

- Cost-cutting: SECaaS eases the financial constraints and burdens for online businesses, integrating security services without on-premises hardware or a huge budget. Using a cloud-based security product also bypasses the need for costly security experts and analysts.
- Consistent and uniform protection:SECaaS services provide continued protection as databases are constantly being updated to provide up-to-date security coverage. It also alleviates the issue of having separate infrastructures, instead combining all elements in one manageable system.
- Constant virus definition updates that are not reliant on user compliance
- Greater security expertise than is typically available within an organization
- Faster user provisioning
- Outsourcing of administrative tasks, such as log management, to save time and money and allow an organization to devote more time to its core competencies
- A web interface that allows in-house administration of some tasks as well as a view of the security environment and ongoing activities

## Challenges

SECaas has a number of deficiencies that make it insecure for many applications. Each individual security service request adds at least one across-the-'Net round-trip (not counting installer packages), four opportunities for the hacker to intercept the conversation:

1. At the send connection point going up
2. At the receive connection point going up
3. At the sending point for the return; and
4. At the receiving point for the return.

SECaas makes all security handling uniform so that once there is a security breach for one request, security is broken for all requests, the very broadest attack surface there can be. It also multiplies the rewards incentive to a hacker because the value of what can be gained for the effort is dramatically increased. Both these factors are especially tailored to the resources of the nation/state-sponsored hacker.

The biggest challenge for the SECaaS market is maintaining a reputation of reliability and superiority to standard non-cloud services still used by some. SECaaS as a whole has seemingly become a mainstay in the cloud market.

Cloud-based website security doesn't cater to all businesses, and specific requirements must be properly assessed by individual needs. Business who cater to the end consumers cannot afford to keep their data loose and vulnerable to hacker attacks. The heaviest part in SECaaS is educating the businesses. Since data is the biggest asset for the businesses, it is up to CIOs and CTOs to take care of the overall security in the company.

## Mobile Backend as a Service

Mobile backend as a service (MBaaS), also known as "backend as a service" (BaaS), is a model for providing web app and mobile app developers with a way to link their applications to backend cloud storage and APIs exposed by back end applications while also providing features such as user management, push notifications, and integration with social networking services. These services are provided via the use of custom software development kits (SDKs) and application programming interfaces (APIs). BaaS is a relatively recent development in cloud computing, with most BaaS startups dating from 2011 or later. Although a fairly nascent industry, trends indicate that these services are gaining mainstream traction with enterprise consumers.

### Purpose

Web and mobile apps require a similar set of features on the backend, including push notifications, integration with social networks, and cloud storage. Each of these services has its own API that must be individually incorporated into an app, a process that can be time-consuming and complicated for app developers. BaaS providers form a bridge between the frontend of an application and various cloud-based backends via a unified API and SDK.

Providing a consistent way to manage backend data means that developers do not need to redevelop their own backend for each of the services that their apps need to access, potentially saving both time and money.

Although similar to other cloud-computing developer tools, such as software as a service (SaaS), infrastructure as a service (IaaS), and platform as a service (PaaS), BaaS is distinct from these other services in that it specifically addresses the cloud-computing needs of web and mobile app developers by providing a unified means of connecting their apps to cloud services.

## Service Providers

Each BaaS provider offers a slightly different set of backend tools and resources. Among the most common services provided are push notifications, file storage and sharing, integration with social networks such as Facebook and Twitter, location services, database persistence and queries, messaging and chat functions, user management, running business logic, and usage analysis tools.

BaaS providers have a broad focus, providing SDKs and APIs that work for app development on multiple platforms, such as iOS, Android, Blackberry, Windows Phone, HTML5, and others.

## Business Model

BaaS providers generate revenue from their services in various ways, often using a freemium model. Under this model, a client receives a certain number of free active users or API calls per month, and pays a fee for each user or call over this limit. Alternatively, clients can pay a set fee for a package which allows for a greater number of calls or active users per month. There are also flat fee plans that make the pricing more predictable. Kumulos is an example. Some of the providers offer the unlimited API calls inside their free plan offerings. While BaaS is most commonly offered as a commercial service, Open Source options are available.

## List of MBaaS Providers

- AnyPresence
- Apps Panel
- Back4App
- Backand
- Backendless
- Baqend
- Blazesoft
- Firebase
- Coriunder

- GoDB
- Halosys
- Kinvey
- Kony
- Kumulos
- Kuzzle
- Microsoft Visual Studio Mobile Center
- Odesso
- Protogrid
- Red Hat
- Soul
- Syncano
- Skygear
- ZetaPush

## Software Development Kit

A software development kit (SDK or devkit) is typically a set of software development tools that allows the creation of applications for a certain software package, software framework, hardware platform, computer system, video game console, operating system, or similar development platform. To enrich applications with advanced functionalities, advertisements, push notifications and more, most app developers implement specific software development kits. Some SDKs are critical for developing an iOS/Android app. For example, the development of an Android application requires an SDK with Java, for iOS apps an iOS SDK with Swift, and for MS Windows the .NET Framework SDK with .NET. There are also SDKs that are installed in apps to provide analytics and data about activity. Prominent examples include Google, InMobi and Facebook.

It may be something as simple as the implementation of one or more application programming interfaces (APIs) in the form of some libraries to interface to a particular programming language or to include sophisticated hardware that can communicate with a particular embedded system. Common tools include debugging facilities and other utilities, often presented in an integrated development environment (IDE). SDKs also frequently include sample code and supporting technical notes or other supporting documentation to help clarify points made by the primary reference material.

## Details

SDKs may have attached licenses that make them unsuitable for building software intended to be developed under an incompatible license. For example, a proprietary SDK will probably be incompatible with free software development, while a GPL-licensed SDK could be incompatible with proprietary software development. LGPL SDKs are typically safe for proprietary development.

The average Android mobile app implements 15.6 SDKs, with gaming apps implementing an average of 17.5 SDKs. The most popular SDK categories for Android mobile apps are analytics and advertising.

SDKs may be unsafe (as SDKs are implemented within apps, but are running an independent code). Malicious SDKs (with honest intentions or not) may violate users' data privacy, damage the apps' performance or even get apps banned from Google Play or iTunes. New technologies allow app developers to control and monitor SDKs in real time.

A software engineer typically receives the SDK from the target system developer. Often the SDK can be downloaded directly via the Internet or via SDKs marketplaces. Many SDKs are provided for free to encourage developers to use the system or language. Sometimes this is used as a marketing tool. Freely offered SDKs may still be able to monetize, based on user data taken from the apps, which may serve the interests of big players in the ecosystem, for example the operating system.

A SDK for an operating system add-on (for instance, QuickTime for classic Mac OS) may include the add-on software itself to be used for development purposes, albeit not necessarily for redistribution together with the developed product. Between platforms where it is possible to develop applications that can at least start up on a system configuration without the add-on installed, and use a Gestalt-style run-time *environment query* to determine whether the add-on is present, and ones where the application will simply fail to start, it is possible to build a single binary that will run on configurations with and without the add-on present, albeit operating with reduced functionality in the latter situation.

Providers of SDKs for specific systems or subsystems may sometimes substitute a more specific term instead of *software*. For instance, both Microsoft and Apple provide driver development kits (DDK) for developing device drivers.

## Application Programming Interface

In computer programming, an application programming interface (API) is a set of subroutine definitions, protocols, and tools for building application software. In general terms, it is a set of clearly defined methods of communication between various software components. A good API makes it easier to develop a computer program by providing all the building blocks, which are then put together by the programmer. An API may be for a web-based system, operating system, database system, computer hardware or software library. An API specification can take many forms, but often includes specifications for routines, data structures, object classes, variables or remote calls. POSIX, Microsoft Windows API, the C++ Standard Template Library and Java APIs are examples of different forms of APIs. Documentation for the API is usually provided to facilitate usage.

## Purpose

Just as a graphical user interface makes it easier for people to use programs, application programming interfaces make it easier for developers to use certain technologies in building applications. By abstracting the underlying implementation and only exposing objects or actions the developer needs, an API simplifies programming. While a graphical interface for an email client might provide a user with a button that performs all the steps for fetching and highlighting new emails, an API for file input/output might give the developer a function that copies a file from one location to another without requiring that the developer understand the file system operations occurring behind the scenes.

## Uses

### Libraries and Frameworks

An API is usually related to a software library. The API describes and prescribes the *expected behavior* (a specification) while the library is an *actual implementation* of this set of rules. A single API can have multiple implementations (or none, being abstract) in the form of different libraries that share the same programming interface. The separation of the API from its implementation can allow programs written in one language to use a library written in another. For example, because Scala and Java compile to compatible bytecode, Scala developers can take advantage of any Java API.

API use can vary depending on the type of programming language involved. An API for a procedural language such as Lua could primarily consist of basic routines to execute code, manipulate data or handle errors, while an API for an object-oriented language such as Java would provide a specification of classes and their class methods.

Language bindings are also APIs. By mapping the features and capabilities of one language to an interface implemented in another language, a language binding allows a library or service written in one language to be used when developing in another language. Tools such as SWIG and F2PY, a Fortran-to-Python interface generator, facilitate the creation of such interfaces.

An API can also be related to a software framework: a framework can be based on several libraries implementing several APIs, but unlike the normal use of an API, the access to the behavior built into the framework is mediated by extending its content with new classes plugged into the framework itself. Moreover, the overall program flow of control can be out of the control of the caller and in the hands of the framework via inversion of control or a similar mechanism.

### Operating Systems

An API can specify the interface between an application and the operating system. POSIX, for example, specifies a set of common APIs that aim to enable an application written for a POSIX conformant operating system to be compiled for another POSIX conformant operating system. Linux and Berkeley Software Distribution are examples of operating systems that implement the POSIX APIs.

Microsoft has shown a strong commitment to a backward-compatible API, particularly within their Windows API (Win32) library, so older applications may run on newer versions of Windows using an executable-specific setting called "Compatibility Mode".

An API differs from an application binary interface (ABI) in that an API is source code based while an ABI is binary based. For instance, POSIX provides APIs, while the Linux Standard Base provides an ABI.

### Remote APIs

Remote APIs allow developers to manipulate remote resources through protocols, specific standards for communication that allow different technologies to work together, regardless of language or platform. For example, the Java Database Connectivity API allows developers to query many different types of databases with the same set of functions, while the Java remote method invocation API uses the Java Remote Method Protocol to allow invocation of functions that operate remotely, but appear local to the developer. Therefore, remote APIs are useful in maintaining the object abstraction in object-oriented programming; a method call, executed locally on a proxy object, invokes the corresponding method on the remote object, using the remoting protocol, and acquires the result to be used locally as return value. A modification on the proxy object will also result in a corresponding modification on the remote object.

### Web APIs

Web APIs are the defined interfaces through which interactions happen between an enterprise and applications that use its assets. An API approach is an architectural approach that revolves around providing programmable interfaces to a set of services to different applications serving different types of consumers. When used in the context of web development, an API is typically defined as a set of Hypertext Transfer Protocol (HTTP) request messages, along with a definition of the structure of response messages, which is usually in an Extensible Markup Language (XML) or JavaScript Object Notation (JSON) format. An example might be a shipping company API that can be added to an eCommerce-focused web site, to facilitate ordering shipping services and automatically include current shipping rates, without the site developer having to enter the shipper's rate table into a web database. While "web API" historically has been virtually synonymous for web service, the recent trend (so-called Web 2.0) has been moving away from Simple Object Access Protocol (SOAP) based web services and service-oriented architecture (SOA) towards more direct representational state transfer (REST) style web resources and resource-oriented architecture (ROA). Part of this trend is related to the Semantic Web movement toward Resource Description Framework (RDF), a concept to promote web-based ontology engineering technologies. Web APIs allow the combination of multiple APIs into new applications known as mashups. In the social media space, web APIs have allowed web communities to facilitate sharing content and data between communities and applications. In this way, content that is created in one place can be dynamically posted and updated in multiple locations on the web.

## Design

The design of an API has significant impacts on its usability. The principle of information hiding describes the role of programming interfaces as enabling modular programming by hiding the implementation details of the modules so that users of modules need not understand the complexities inside the modules. Thus, the design of an API attempts to provide only the tools a user would expect. The design of programming interfaces represents an important part of software architecture, the organization of a complex piece of software.

Several authors have created recommendations for how to design APIs, such as Joshua Bloch, Kin Lane, and Michi Henning.

## Release Policies

APIs are one of the most common ways technology companies integrate with each other. Those that provide and use APIs are considered as being members of a business ecosystem.

The main policies for releasing an API are:

- Private: The API is for internal company use only.
- Partner: Only specific business partners can use the API. For example, car service companies such as Uber and Lyft allow approved third party developers to directly order rides from within their apps. This allows the companies to exercise quality control by curating which apps have access to the API, and provides them with an additional revenue stream.
- Public: The API is available for use by the public. For example, Microsoft makes the Microsoft Windows API public, and Apple releases its APIs Carbon and Cocoa, so that software can be written for their platforms.

## Public API Implications

An important factor when an API becomes public is its *interface stability*. Changes by a developer to a part of it—for example adding new parameters to a function call—could break compatibility with clients that depend on that API.

When parts of a publicly presented API are subject to change and thus not stable, such parts of a particular API should be explicitly documented as *unstable*. For example, in the Google Guava library the parts that are considered unstable, and that might change in the near future, are marked with the Java annotation @Beta.

A public API can sometimes declare parts of itself as *deprecated*. This usually means that such part of an API should be considered candidates for being removed, or modified in a backward incompatible way. Therefore, deprecation allows developers to transition away from parts of the API that will be removed or unsupported in the future.

## Documentation

API documentation describes what services an API offers and how to use those services, aiming to cover everything a client would need to know to use the API. Documentation is crucial for the development and maintenance of applications that use the API. API documentation is traditionally found in documentation files, but can also be found in social media such as blogs, forums, and Q&A websites. Traditional documentation files are often presented via a documentation system, such as Javadoc or Pydoc, that has a consistent appearance and structure. However, the types of content included in the documentation differs from API to API. To facilitate understanding, API documentation can include description of classes and methods in the API as well as "typical usage scenarios, code snippets, design rationales, performance discussions, and contracts", but implementation details of the API services themselves are usually omitted. Restrictions and limitations on how the API can be used are also covered by the documentation. For example, documentation for an API function could note that its parameters cannot be null, or that the function itself is not thread safe. Because API documentation is so comprehensive, it can be difficult for the writers to keep the documentation updated and for the users to read it carefully, potentially resulting in bugs.

API documentation can be enriched with metadata information like Java annotations. This metadata can be used by the compiler, tools, and by the *run-time* environment to implement custom behaviors or custom handling.

## Copyright Controversy

In 2010, Oracle Corporation sued Google for having distributed a new implementation of Java embedded in the Android operating system. Google had not acquired any permission to reproduce the Java API, although permission had been given to the similar OpenJDK project. Judge William Alsup ruled in the *Oracle v. Google* case that

APIs cannot be copyrighted in the U.S, and that a victory for Oracle would have widely expanded copyright protection and allowed the copyrighting of simple software commands:

To accept Oracle's claim would be to allow anyone to copyright one version of code to carry out a system of commands and thereby bar all others from writing their own different versions to carry out all or part of the same commands.

In 2014, however, Alsup's ruling was overturned on appeal, though the question of whether such use of APIs constitutes fair use was left unresolved.

In 2016, following a two-week trial, a jury determined that Google's reimplementation of the Java API constituted fair use, but Oracle vowed to appeal the decision.

### Examples

- ASPI for SCSI device interfacing
- Cocoa and Carbon for the Macintosh
- DirectX for Microsoft Windows
- EHLLAPI
- Java APIs
- ODBC for Microsoft Windows
- OpenAL cross-platform sound API
- OpenCL cross-platform API for general-purpose computing for CPUs & GPUs
- OpenGL cross-platform graphics API
- OpenMP API that supports multi-platform shared memory multiprocessing programming in C, C++ and Fortran on many architectures, including Unix and Microsoft Windows platforms.
- Server Application Programming Interface (SAPI)
- Simple DirectMedia Layer (SDL)

## Fabasoft Folio Cloud

Fabasoft Folio Cloud is a cloud computing service developed by Fabasoft in Linz, Austria announced in April 2010. It focuses on enabling secure collaboration and is web-based with iOS and Android apps for use on mobile devices. The software is object-oriented and offers a wide range of sophisticated functionality for document management and global collaboration, which can be extended by specialist cloud applications. Fabasoft places a large amount of focus on usability and accessibility.

Folio Cloud operates a freemium financial model, offering both free and fee-requiring services. The free service includes 5 GB of online storage and the core functionality of Folio Cloud. The fee-requiring services include storage packages and further editions with added functionality.

## Collaboration

The core element for collaboration in Folio Cloud is the team room – a team room is a protected area in the cloud for storing data. Users may have read only access, change access or full control within a team room.

Workflows can be set up for structured collaboration. For example, it allows the definition of the business process for approving a document via different users or groups. Such structured collaboration is supported with the integration of Skype and other direct communication tools such as news feeds and instant messaging.

## Security

Folio Cloud is certified and tested according to the following security standards : ISO 27001:2005, ISO 20000, ISO 9001, SAS 70 Type II. Fabasoft was also the first software manufacturer to receive MoReq2 certification – the European standard for records management.

All Folio Cloud data is saved in data centers in Europe, where European standards for security, reliability and data protection apply. Cloud data is kept permanently synchronized in two mirrored data centers in Austria so that a fail over is possible at any time. A backup of data is constantly maintained in a third data center. Further data center locations are being integrated in Germany and Switzerland and in future users will be able to decide at which data center location their data is stored.

Folio Cloud is based on open source and does not contain any US-owned software. This prevents access to European cloud data by US authorities under the "US Patriot Act".

All communication and transfer of data within Folio Cloud is encrypted via SSL/TLS. Cloud access is protected by secure forms of authentication including two factor authentication with Motoky or SMS and login via digital ID. Folio Cloud has integrated the new German digital ID card, the Austrian Citizen Card with mobile signature and the SuisseID as forms of digital authentication. Fabasoft is active in the support of the advancement of European cloud infrastructure.

### Mobile Cloud

Folio Cloud supports all common web browsers, different operating systems and end user devices. Folio Cloud apps are also available on Google Play and the Apple App Store for use on Android and iOS devices. Folio Cloud supports open standards such as WebDAV, CalDAV and CMIS.

Folio Cloud uses Fabasoft Mindbreeze as its integrated search.

### Apps

Apps are online applications that extend the functionality of Folio Cloud to fulfill concrete use cases and needs. All Folio Cloud Apps are available in the Fabasoft Cloud App Store.

Fabasoft held its first Cloud Developer Conference (CDC) from December 15–17, 2010 as a free event for Cloud developers. Since then the event has taken place twice a year, once in the summer and once in the winter.

## Rackspace Cloud

The Rackspace Cloud is a set of cloud computing products and services billed on a utility computing basis from the US-based company Rackspace. Offerings include web application hosting or platform as a service ("*Cloud Sites*"), Cloud Storage ("*Cloud Files*"), virtual private server ("*Cloud Servers*"), load balancers, databases, backup, and monitoring.

### History

Rackspace Cloud announced Mosso LLC in March, 2006, as a wholly owned subsidiary billed as a utility computing offering. As it pre-dated mainstream adoption of the term cloud computing, it was "retooled" and relaunched on February 19, 2008, adopting the tagline "Mosso: The Hosting Cloud". The "Mosso" branding (including the mosso.com domain) was then dropped on June 17, 2009 in favour of "The Rackspace Cloud" branding (including the rackspacecloud.com domain name). Since then, customer contracts were executed with Rackspace US, Inc. d/b/a The Rackspace Cloud rather than with the Mosso LLC subsidiary.

Other companies (such as EMC Corporation with its "Decho" subsidiary) also use alternative branding for their cloud computing offerings.

In 2011, the "Rackspace Cloud" brand merged with Rackspace.com. In 2012, Rackspace rebranded as "Rackspace, the open cloud company". In 2014, Rackspace rebranded as "Rackspace, the #1 managed cloud company".

## Services

## Cloud Files

Cloud files is a cloud hosting service that provides "unlimited online storage and CDN" for media (examples given include backups, video files, user content) on a utility computing basis. It was originally launched as *Mosso CloudFS* as a private beta release on May 5, 2008 and is similar to Amazon Simple Storage Service. Unlimited files of up to 5 GB can be uploaded, managed via the online control panel or RESTful API and optionally served out via Akamai Technologies' Content Delivery Network.

### API

In addition to the online control panel, the service can be accessed over a RESTful API with open source client code available in C#/.NET, Python, PHP, Java, and Ruby. Rackspace-owned Jungle Disk allows Cloud Files to be mounted as a local drive within supported operating systems (Linux, Mac OS X, and Windows).

### Security

Redundancy is achieved by replicating three full copies of data across multiple computers in multiple "zones" within the same data center, where "zones" are physically (though not geographically) separate and supplied separate power and Internet services. Uploaded files can be distributed via Akamai Technologies to "hundreds of endpoints across the world" which provides an additional layer of data redundancy.

The control panel and API are protected by SSL and the requests themselves are signed and can be safely delivered to untrusted clients. Deleted data is zeroed out immediately.

### Use Cases

Use cases considered as "well suited" include backing up or archiving data, serving images and videos (which are streamed directly to the users' browsers), serving content over content delivery networks, storing secondary static web-accessible data, developing data storage applications, storing fluctuating and/or unpredictable amounts of data and reducing costs.

### Caveats

There is no native operating system support for the Cloud Files API so it is not yet possible to "map" or "mount" it as a virtual drive without third-party software like JungleDisk that translates to a supported standard such as WebDAV. There are no concepts of "appending" or "locking" data within Cloud Files (which may affect some disk mirroring or backup solutions), nor support for permissions or transcoding. Data is organised into "containers" but it is not possible to create nested folders without a translation layer.

## Cloud Servers

Cloud Servers is a cloud infrastructure service that allows users to deploy "one to hundreds of cloud servers instantly" and create "advanced, high availability architectures" similar to the Amazon Elastic Compute Cloud. The "cloud servers" are virtual machines running on the Xen hypervisor for Linux-based instances, and Citrix XenServer for Windows and Linux instances. Each quad core hardware node has between 16 and 32 GB of RAM, allowing for allocations between 256 MB and 30 GB. Disk and CPU allocations scale up with memory, with disk sizes ranging from 10 GB to 620 GB. Various distributions of Linux are supported, including Arch, CentOS, Debian, Fedora, Gentoo, Red Hat Enterprise Linux and Ubuntu.

The technology behind the service was purchased in Rackspace's October 22, 2008 acquisition of *Slicehost* and the servers were formerly known as "slices". These are "much cheaper and generally easier to use than a traditional dedicated server", though it is still necessary to maintain the operating system and solution stack which is not required for the *Cloud Sites* product. This is one of the main differentiators between the two services; where Cloud Servers includes full root access and thus allows for more customisation, the Cloud Sites product is less flexible but requires less maintenance.

On December 14, 2010, Rackspace began offering a managed service level on the Cloud Servers product, which added additional support for the operating system and common applications as well as patching and other routine services. This additional support level does come at an increased cost, however.

During 2014, Rackspace ceased to advertise the First Generation Cloud Servers and the Standard Next Generation Cloud Servers on its main Cloud Servers product page, opting to only disclose the Next Generation Performance 1 and Performance 2 products that require a minimum $50/month service charge per account for support service. The First Generation and Standard Next Generation platforms are now referred to as "Legacy Infrastructure" buried in the pricing page for the old products. The minimum charge for the lowest product on the First Generation platform is $10.95/month for the 256MB instance while the minimum charge on the Standard Next Generation platform is $16.06/month for the 512MB instance. On the Performance platform, the minimum charge for one server is $23.36 for the 1GB instance + $50 minimum service charge, for a total of $73.36/month. Rackspace is quietly phasing out its older, less expensive products in transition to a managed platform where mandatory support charges are incorporated into the cost of the services.

Cloud Tools are applications and infrastructure software built to run on the RackSpace cloud. Applications listed include Zend, a PHP stack, Cloudkick, a cloud performance testing services, CopperEgg, a real-time cloud server and application monitoring service, Xeround, a MySQL cloud database, and MongoLab, the cloud version of the popular NoSQL database MongoDB.

## API

The Cloud Servers API launched on July 14, 2009 under the Creative Commons Attribution 3.0 license allows clients to create, configure and control virtual servers. In addition to issuing basic management commands this "enables elastic scenarios" whereby servers are instantiated and destroyed in response to fluctuating load (one of the key characteristics of cloud computing). RightScale is among third-party providers to have announced support for this API.

## Cloud Sites

Cloud Sites is a platform as a service offering, similar to traditional web hosting only built on horizontally scalable hardware infrastructure. A fixed monthly credit card payment gives users access to the service with an allocation of compute, storage and bandwidth resources. Should this allocation be exhausted then subsequent usage is billed on a utility computing basis. It allows an "unlimited" number of sites, databases and email accounts and includes reseller options such as client billing and support. Touted as "the fastest way to put sites on the cloud", it runs Windows or Linux applications across "hundreds of servers".

Cloud Sites supports the PHP 5, Perl, Python, MySQL, .NET 2.0+, ASP and Microsoft SQL Server 2008 application frameworks.

## Compute Cycles

The service includes up to 10,000 "compute cycles" per month which "is roughly equivalent to running a server with a 2.8 GHz modern processor for the same period of time" (with additional cycles priced at USD 0.01). This non-standard unit of measurement primarily reflects CPU processing time but also includes I/O operations so pages with many database queries will consume more "compute cycles". It can however be difficult to compare services between providers without standard units of measurement.

## Caveats

Cloud Sites does not support Java, Tomcat, ColdFusion, SSH, RDP, API access, Microsoft Exchange or custom server-side components at this time. It is also not possible to set up multiple top level domains to point to the same web root directory. The .NET environment dropped support for "full trust" in favour of "modified medium trust" despite having previously announced on their blog that they had been able to work directly with Microsoft to engineer a system that could accommodate Full Trust without compromising the security, scalability, and performance of other users.

## Locations

Cloud servers and most other cloud products are physically located in any of six data centers: Chicago, Northern Virginia, Dallas, London, Sydney, or Hong Kong. A separate "UK" account is required to access the London-based cloud products, however a single "US" Rackspace cloud account can access all US data centers along with the Sydney and Hong Kong regions. Cloud Sites are available in the Dallas and Chicago data centers only.

## Control Panel

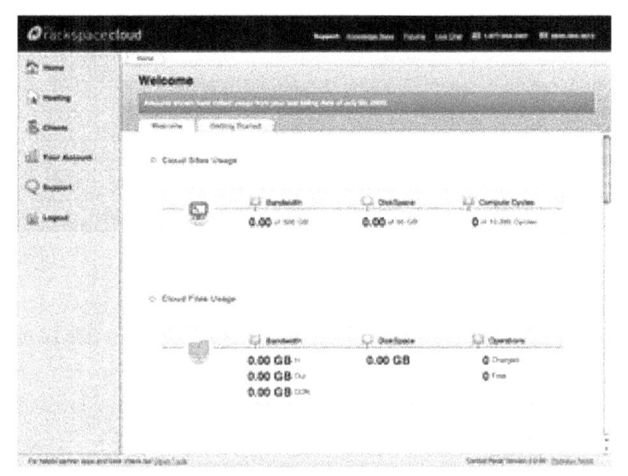

Rackspace Cloud online control panel

The online control panel was custom built by and for the Rackspace Cloud service (as opposed to using control panel software like cPanel).

The control panel includes management interfaces for the Cloud Sites, Cloud Servers and Cloud Files services. There was once a web based file manager, but this was removed for undisclosed reasons. It also allows users to manage multiple clients and the plans and products (e.g. databases, 24x7 support) that apply to them, with white label branding options for messaging. The clients themselves have access to a restricted version of the control panel that allows them to conduct administrative tasks such as managing mail accounts.

The control panel is also home to the billing and reporting functions and provides access to support materials including developer resources, a knowledge base, forums and live chat.

## OpenStack

In 2010, RackSpace contributed the source code of its Cloud Files product to the OpenStack project under the Apache License to become the OpenStack Object Storage component.

In April 2012, Rackspace announced it would implement OpenStack Compute as the underlying technology for their Cloud Servers product. The change will come a new control panel as well as add-on cloud services offering databases, server monitoring, block storage, and virtual networking.

## Citrix Cloud

Citrix Cloud is a cloud management platform that allows organizations to deploy cloud-hosted desktops and apps to end users. It was developed by Citrix Systems and released in 2015.

### Overview

Citrix Cloud is a cloud-based platform for managing and deploying Citrix products and desktops and applications to end users using any type of cloud, whether public, private or hybrid, or on-premises hardware. The product supports cloud-based versions of every major Citrix product. These can be accessed together as an integrated "workspace" or independently.

### Features

Citrix Cloud enables cloud services for Citrix products XenApp, XenDesktop, XenMobile, ShareFile, and NetScaler. In addition, Citrix has developed several cloud-native services, including its Secure Browser Service.

Citrix Cloud is compatible with any device and cloud or data center and can be synced via Citrix Cloud Connector. As of May 2016, Citrix states that Microsoft Azure is its preferred cloud partner. Citrix platforms reside in Citrix Cloud, however other applications and resources may make use of other clouds and infrastructures. A company's IT department retains the ability to choose a custom combination of data centers and cloud providers. Citrix continuously updates Citrix Cloud so that users are automatically running the most current version.

As of 2015, Citrix Cloud offers four different service packages.

### History

Citrix Workspace Cloud was announced in May 2015 at the company's industry conference, Citrix Synergy. The offering launched in August 2015 with four core services: App and Desktop Service, Lifecycle Management, Secure Documents, and Mobility. The company positioned Workspace Cloud as an alternative to XenDesktop and XenApp, the company's traditional desktop and application virtualization platforms.

The company renamed Citrix Workspace Cloud to Citrix Cloud in May 2016.r In addition, cloud services were renamed with cloud-based versions of other Citrix products.

XenDesktop and XenApp Service, ShareFile, and XenMobile Service replaced Desktop and App Service, Secure Documents Service, and Mobility Service, respectively. The company also announced in 2016 that Citrix Cloud users that are Windows 10 Enterprise customers would be able to access Windows 10 images on Azure via XenDesktop without having to pay an additional license fee.

### Reception

Prior to its release, Citrix Workspace Cloud was praised by desktop virtualization blogger Brian Madden for its concept and *CMSWire* noted that it stood out among competitors as the only product of its kind.

Following its release, *TechTarget* stated that the platform was "intriguing" that it "provide[s] something IT professionals have wanted for a very long time: centralized management of on-premises and cloud desktop and application workloads", but "also surprisingly expensive". A review in *Computerworld* suggested the hybrid nature of the product was compatible with the rising use of hybrid cloud implementations by businesses, but that Citrix would need to ensure "adequate support for critical applications and [make] sure that company policies, such as access rules, are followed properly".

## Sun Cloud

Sun Cloud was an on-demand Cloud computing service operated by Sun Microsystems prior to its acquisition by Oracle Corporation. The Sun Cloud Compute Utility provided access to a substantial computing resource over the Internet for US$1 per CPU-hour. It was launched as Sun Grid in March 2006. It was based on and supported open source technologies such as Solaris 10, Sun Grid Engine, and the Java platform.

Sun Cloud delivered enterprise computing power and resources over the Internet, enabling developers, researchers, scientists and businesses to optimize performance, speed time to results, and accelerate innovation without investment in IT infrastructure.

In early 2010 Oracle announced it was discontinuing the Sun Cloud project. Since Sunday, March 7, 2010, the network.com web site has been inaccessible.

### Suitable Applications

A typical application that could run on the Compute Utility fit the following parameters:

- must be self-contained
- runs on the Solaris 10 Operating System (OS)

- is implemented with standard object libraries included with the Solaris 10 OS or user libraries packaged with the executable
  - o all executable code must be available on the Compute Utility at time of execution
- runs to completion under control of shell scripts (no requirement for interactive access)
- has a total maximum size of applications and data that does not exceed 10 gigabytes
- can be packaged for upload to Sun Cloud as one or more ZIP files of 300 megabytes or smaller

### Resources, Jobs, and Runs

Resources are collections of files that contain the user's data and executable.

Jobs are a Compute Utility concept that define the elements of the unit of work that is submitted to the Sun Cloud Compute Utility. The major elements of a job include the name of the shell script controlling program execution, required arguments to the shell script, and a list of resources that must be in place for the job to run.

A run is a specific instantiation of a Job description submitted to the Sun Cloud Compute Utility. Runs occur when the job is submitted to the Compute Utility for execution.

### CPU-hour

For each job one submits and runs on the Cloud, the Sun Cloud CPU usage is aggregated and then rounded up to the nearest whole hour. For example, if a job used 1000 CPUs for one minute, it would be aggregated as 1000 CPU minutes or 16.67 CPU hours. The software rounds this up to 17 hours and the job would be billed as US $17.

### Application Catalog

On March 13, 2007, Sun announced the launch of Application Catalog, an online service that allows developers and ISVs to develop and publish their applications, enabling communities of scientists and academics in life sciences, education, engineering, and other fields to accelerate innovation and complete research projects quickly and less expensively.

The Network.com Application Catalog gives users immediate online access to popular ISV and open source applications through an easy-to-use Web portal with no contractual obligation. Users can upload and run their own applications and create a personal library of favorites or take advantage of the pre-installed and configured applications giving them instant productivity. The portal gives them everything they need to conduct analysis and complete complex computational tasks to help speed scientific discovery and shorten the time to market for new products. They simply select the application, upload their data, and get results fast.

Network.com enables anyone to publish applications to the Application Catalog and take advantage of the powerful Solaris 10-based Cloud platform. Users can publish their own applications to a private library and access them whenever they want; they can also share their applications with others while retaining their data securely in their private space.

## Available Applications

Applications available on the Catalog include(by category):

- General - Blender, FDS
- Computer Aided Engineering - Calculix, deal.II, Elmer Solver, Impact, FreeFEM, OFELI
- Life Sciences - BLAST, FASTA, GROMACS, Clustalw, eHITS, T-Coffee, fastD-NAml, READSEQ

Examples of types of suitable applications include:

- Bio informatics
- Financial domain applications, like Monte Carlo method, Black–Scholes option pricing models
- Computer Arts, like Fractal landscape generation
- Speech synthesis applications, like Festival
- Scientific applications, like Computer simulation

## References


- Wardley, Simon (20 Feb 2015). "On open source, gameplay and cloud". Bits or pieces?. Simon Wardley. Archived from the original (HTML) on 8 Mar 2016. Retrieved 29 December 2016
- Tony Shan, "Smart Cloud Engineering, Nomenclature, and Enablement", in Proceedings of the 1st International, May 7-9, 2011. SciTePress. ISBN 978-989-8425-52-2
- Dan Rowinski (17 April 2012). "The Rise of Mobile Cloud Services: BaaS Startups Grow Up". ReadWrite. Retrieved 23 October 2012
- Furfaro, A.; Garro, A.; Tundis, A. (2014-10-01). "Towards Security as a Service (SecaaS): On the modeling of Security Services for Cloud Computing". 2014 International Carnahan Conference on Security Technology (ICCST): 1–6. doi:10.1109/CCST.2014.6986995

- Baqend. "High-Performance Backend-as-a-Service | Baqend". High-Performance Backend-as-a-Service | Baqend. Retrieved 6 February 2017
- Henning, Michi; Vinoski, Steve (1999). "Advanced CORBA Programming with C++". Addison-Wesley. ISBN 978-0201379273. Retrieved 16 June 2015
- Rosenblatt, Seth (May 9, 2014). "Court sides with Oracle over Android in Java patent appeal". CNET. Retrieved 2014-05-10
- Monperrus, Martin; Eichberg, Michael; Tekes, Elif; Mezini, Mira (3 December 2011). "What should developers be aware of? An empirical study on the directives of API documentation" (PDF). Empirical Software Engineering. 17 (6): 703–737. doi:10.1007/s10664-011-9186-4. Retrieved 22 July 2016

4

# Various Software Applications of Cloud Computing

Popular software are now hosted in clouds for easy access to users. They are often referred to as "on-demand software". Google Cloud Connect, Adobe Marketing Cloud, Cloudike and CloudMe are some of the software listed in this section. The chapter on cloud computing offers an insightful focus, keeping in mind the complex subject matter.

## Software as a Service

Software as a service is a software licensing and delivery model in which software is licensed on a subscription basis and is centrally hosted. It is sometimes referred to as "on-demand software", and was formerly referred to as "software plus services" by Microsoft. SaaS is typically accessed by users using a thin client via a web browser. SaaS has become a common delivery model for many business applications, including office and messaging software, payroll processing software, DBMS software, management software, CAD software, development software, gamification, virtualization, accounting, collaboration, customer relationship management (CRM), Management Information Systems (MIS), enterprise resource planning (ERP), invoicing, human resource management (HRM), talent acquisition, content management (CM), and service desk management. SaaS has been incorporated into the strategy of nearly all leading enterprise software companies.

According to a Gartner Group estimate, SaaS sales in 2010 reached $10 billion and were projected to increase to $12.1 billion in 2011, up 20.7% from 2010. Gartner Group estimates that SaaS revenue will be more than double its 2010 numbers by 2015 and reach a projected $21.3 billion. Customer relationship management (CRM) continues to be the largest market for SaaS. SaaS revenue within the CRM market was forecast to reach $3.8 billion in 2011, up from $3.2 billion in 2010.

The term "software as a service" (SaaS) is considered to be part of the nomenclature of cloud computing, along with infrastructure as a service (IaaS), platform as a service (PaaS), desktop as a service (DaaS), managed software as a service (MSaaS), mobile backend as a service (MBaaS), and information technology management as a service (ITMaaS).

## History

Centralized hosting of business applications dates back to the 1960s. Starting in that decade, IBM and other mainframe providers conducted a service bureau business, often referred to as time-sharing or utility computing. Such services included offering computing power and database storage to banks and other large organizations from their worldwide data centers.

The expansion of the Internet during the 1990s brought about a new class of centralized computing, called Application Service Providers (ASP). ASPs provided businesses with the service of hosting and managing specialized business applications, with the goal of reducing costs through central administration and through the solution provider's specialization in a particular business application. Two of the world's pioneers and largest ASPs were USI, which was headquartered in the Washington, DC area, and Futurelink Corporation, headquartered in Irvine, California.

Software as a Service essentially extends the idea of the ASP model. The term *Software as a Service (SaaS)*, however, is commonly used in more specific settings:

- While most initial ASPs focused on managing and hosting third-party independent software vendors' software, as of 2012 SaaS vendors typically develop and manage their own software.
- Whereas many initial ASPs offered more traditional client-server applications, which require installation of software on users' personal computers, SaaS solutions of today rely predominantly on the Web and only require a web browser to use.
- Whereas the software architecture used by most initial ASPs mandated maintaining a separate instance of the application for each business, as of 2012 SaaS solutions normally utilize a multitenant architecture, in which the application serves multiple businesses and users, and partitions its data accordingly.

The acronym allegedly first appeared in an article called "Strategic Backgrounder: Software As A Service," internally published in February 2001 by the Software & Information Industry Association's (SIIA) eBusiness Division.

DbaaS (Database as a Service) has emerged as a sub-variety of SaaS.

## Distribution

The cloud (or SaaS) model has no physical need for indirect distribution because it is not distributed physically and is deployed almost instantaneously, therefore partners and middlemen of the traditional kind are not necessary. However, as the market has grown, SaaS and managed service players have been forced to try to redefine their role.

## Pricing

Unlike traditional software, which is conventionally sold as a perpetual license with an up-front cost (and an optional ongoing support fee), SaaS providers generally price applications using a subscription fee, most commonly a monthly fee or an annual fee. Consequently, the initial setup cost for SaaS is typically lower than the equivalent enterprise software. SaaS vendors typically price their applications based on some usage parameters, such as the number of users using the application. However, because in a SaaS environment customers' data reside with the SaaS vendor, opportunities also exist to charge per transaction, event, or other unit of value, such as the number of processors required.

The relatively low cost for user provisioning (i.e., setting up a new customer) in a multitenant environment enables some SaaS vendors to offer applications using the freemium model. In this model, a free service is made available with limited functionality or scope, and fees are charged for enhanced functionality or larger scope. Some other SaaS applications are completely free to users, with revenue being derived from alternative sources such as advertising.

A key driver of SaaS growth is SaaS vendors' ability to provide a price that is competitive with on-premises software. This is consistent with the traditional rationale for outsourcing IT systems, which involves applying economies of scale to application operation, i.e., an outside service provider may be able to offer better, cheaper, more reliable applications.

## Architecture

The vast majority of SaaS solutions are based on a multitenant architecture. With this model, a single version of the application, with a single configuration (hardware, network, operating system), is used for all customers ("tenants"). To support scalability, the application is installed on multiple machines (called horizontal scaling). In some cases, a second version of the application is set up to offer a select group of customers with access to pre-release versions of the applications (e.g., a beta version) for testing purposes. This is contrasted with traditional software, where multiple physical copies of the software — each potentially of a different version, with a potentially different configuration, and often customized — are installed across various customer sites. In this traditional model, each version of the application is based on a unique code.

Although an exception rather than the norm, some SaaS solutions do not use multitenancy, or use other mechanisms—such as virtualization—to cost-effectively manage a large number of customers in place of multitenancy. Whether multitenancy is a necessary component for software-as-a-service is a topic of controversy.

There are two main varieties of SaaS:

Vertical SaaS

A Software which answers the needs of a specific industry (e.g., software for the healthcare, agriculture, real estate, finance industries)

Horizontal SaaS

The products which focus on a software category (marketing, sales, developer tools, HR) but are industry agnostic.

## Characteristics

Although not all software-as-a-service applications share all traits, the characteristics below are common among many SaaS applications:

## Configuration and Customization

SaaS applications similarly support what is traditionally known as application *customization*. In other words, like traditional enterprise software, a single customer can alter the set of configuration options (a.k.a. parameters) that affect its functionality and look-and-feel. Each customer may have its own settings (or: parameter values) for the configuration options. The application can be customized to the degree it was designed for based on a set of predefined configuration options.

For example: to support customers' common need to change an application's look-and-feel so that the application appears to be having the customer's brand (or—if so desired—co-branded), many SaaS applications let customers provide (through a self service interface or by working with application provider staff) a custom logo and sometimes a set of custom colors. The customer cannot, however, change the page layout unless such an option was designed for.

## Accelerated Feature Delivery

SaaS applications are often updated more frequently than traditional software, in many cases on a weekly or monthly basis. This is enabled by several factors:

- The application is hosted centrally, so an update is decided and executed by the provider, not by customers.
- The application only has a single configuration, making development testing faster.
- The application vendor does not have to expend resources updating and maintaining backdated versions of the software, because there is only a single version.

- The application vendor has access to all customer data, expediting design and regression testing.
- The solution provider has access to user behavior within the application (usually via web analytics), making it easier to identify areas worthy of improvement.

Accelerated feature delivery is further enabled by agile software development methodologies. Such methodologies, which have evolved in the mid-1990s, provide a set of software development tools and practices to support frequent software releases.

## Open Integration Protocols

Because SaaS applications cannot access a company's internal systems (databases or internal services), they predominantly offer integration protocols and application programming interfaces (APIs) that operate over a wide area network. Typically, these are protocols based on HTTP, REST and SOAP.

The ubiquity of SaaS applications and other Internet services and the standardization of their API technology has spawned development of mashups, which are lightweight applications that combine data, presentation and functionality from multiple services, creating a compound service. Mashups further differentiate SaaS applications from on-premises software as the latter cannot be easily integrated outside a company's firewall.

## Collaborative (and "Social") Functionality

Inspired by the success of online social networks and other so-called *web 2.0* functionality, many SaaS applications offer features that let its users collaborate and share information.

For example, many project management applications delivered in the SaaS model offer—in addition to traditional project planning functionality—collaboration features letting users comment on tasks and plans and share documents within and outside an organization. Several other SaaS applications let users vote on and offer new feature ideas.

Although some collaboration-related functionality is also integrated into on-premises software, (implicit or explicit) collaboration between users or different customers is only possible with centrally hosted software.

## Adoption Drivers

Several important changes to the software market and technology landscape have facilitated acceptance and growth of SaaS solutions:

- The growing use of web-based user interfaces by applications, along with the proliferation of associated practices (e.g., web design), continuously decreased the need for traditional client-server applications. Consequently, traditional software vendor's investment in software based on fat clients has become a disadvantage (mandating ongoing support), opening the door for new software vendors offering a user experience perceived as more "modern".

- The standardization of web page technologies (HTML, JavaScript, CSS), the increasing popularity of web development as a practice, and the introduction and ubiquity of web application frameworks like Ruby on Rails or Laravel (PHP) gradually reduced the cost of developing new SaaS solutions, and enabled new solution providers to come up with competitive solutions, challenging traditional vendors.
- The increasing penetration of broadband Internet access enabled remote centrally hosted applications to offer speed comparable to on-premises software.
- The standardization of the HTTPS protocol as part of the web stack provided universally available lightweight security that is sufficient for most everyday applications.
- The introduction and wide acceptance of lightweight integration protocols such as REST and SOAP enabled affordable integration between SaaS applications (residing in the cloud) with internal applications over wide area networks and with other SaaS applications.

## Adoption Challenges

Some limitations slow down the acceptance of SaaS and prohibit it from being used in some cases:

- Because data are being stored on the vendor's servers, data security becomes an issue.
- SaaS applications are hosted in the cloud, far away from the application users. This introduces latency into the environment; so, for example, the SaaS model is not suitable for applications that demand response times in the milliseconds.
- Multitenant architectures, which drive cost efficiency for SaaS solution providers, limit customization of applications for large clients, inhibiting such applications from being used in scenarios (applicable mostly to large enterprises) for which such customization is necessary.
- Some business applications require access to or integration with customer's current data. When such data are large in volume or sensitive (e.g. end users' personal information), integrating them with remotely hosted software can be costly or risky, or can conflict with data governance regulations.

- Constitutional search/seizure warrant laws do not protect all forms of SaaS dynamically stored data. The end result is that a link is added to the chain of security where access to the data, and, by extension, misuse of these data, are limited only by the assumed honesty of 3rd parties or government agencies able to access the data on their own recognizance.
- Switching SaaS vendors may involve the slow and difficult task of transferring very large data files over the Internet.
- Organizations that adopt SaaS may find they are forced into adopting new versions, which might result in unforeseen training costs, an increase in probability that a user might make an error, or instability from bugs in the newer software.
- Should the vendor of the software go out of business or suddenly EOL the software, the user may lose access to their software unexpectedly, which could destabilize their organization's current and future projects, as well as leave the user with older data they can no longer access or modify.
- Relying on an Internet connection means that data are transferred to and from a SaaS firm at Internet speeds, rather than the potentially higher speeds of a firm's internal network.
- Can the SaaS hosting company guarantee the uptime level agreed in the SLA (Service Level Agreement)?

The standard model also has limitations:

- Compatibility with hardware, other software, and operating systems.
- Licensing and compliance problems (unauthorized copies of the software program putting the organization at risk of fines or litigation).
- Maintenance, support, and patch revision processes.

## Emerging Trends

As a result of widespread fragmentation in the SaaS provider space, there is an emerging trend towards the development of SaaS Integration Platforms (SIP). These SIPs allow subscribers to access multiple SaaS applications through a common platform. They also offer new application developers an opportunity to quickly develop and deploy new applications.

This trend is being referred to as the "third wave" in software adoption - where SaaS moves beyond standalone applications to become a comprehensive platform. The first of which was created by Bitium in 2012, which provides SSO services to businesses who operate on multiple applications. Zoho and SutiSoft are two companies that offer comprehensive SIPs today. Several other industry players, including Salesforce, Microsoft, Procurify and Oracle are aggressively developing similar integration platforms.

Another trend deals with the rise of software products that combine functions for human resource management, payroll accounting, and expense management as an all-in-one solution in promoting collaboration between an employer and an employee. This supplements the ongoing effort of many businesses to create employee self-service tools for their workforce.

### Engineering Applications

Engineering simulation software, traditionally delivered as an on-premises solution through the user's desktop, is an ideal candidate for SaaS delivery. The market for SaaS engineering simulation software is in its infancy, but interest in the concept is growing for similar reasons as interest in SaaS is growing in other industries. The main driver is that traditional engineering simulation software required a large up-front investment in order to access the simulation software. The large investment kept engineering simulation inaccessible for many startups and middle market companies who were reluctant or unable to risk a large software expenditure on unproven projects.

### Healthcare Applications

According to a survey by HIMSS Analytics, 83% of US IT healthcare organizations are now using cloud services with 9.3% planning to, whereas 67% of IT healthcare organizations are currently running SaaS-based applications.

### Data Escrow

*Software as a service data escrow* is the process of keeping a copy of critical software-as-a-service application data with an independent third party. Similar to source code escrow, where critical software source code is stored with an independent third party, SaaS data escrow is the same logic applied to the data within a SaaS application. It allows companies to protect and insure all the data that resides within SaaS applications, protecting against data loss.

There are many and varied reasons for considering SaaS data escrow including concerns about vendor bankruptcy unplanned service outages and potential data loss or corruption. Many businesses are also keen to ensure that they are complying with their own data governance standards or want improved reporting and business analytics against their SaaS data. A research conducted by Clearpace Software Ltd. into the growth of SaaS showed that 85 percent of the participants wanted to take a copy of their SaaS data. A third of these participants wanted a copy on a daily basis.

## Criticism

One notable criticism of SaaS comes from Richard Stallman of the Free Software Foundation referring to it as Service as a Software Substitute (SaaSS). He considers the use of SaaS to be a violation of the principles of free software. According to Stallman:

With SaaS, the users do not have a copy of the executable file: it is on the server, where the users can't see or touch it. Thus it is impossible for them to ascertain what it really does, and impossible to change it. SaaS inherently gives the server operator the power to change the software in use, or the users' data being operated on.

This criticism does not apply to all SaaS products. In 2010, *Forbes* contributor Dan Woods noted that Drupal Gardens, a free web hosting platform based on the open source Drupal content management system, is a "new open source model for SaaS". He added:

Open source provides the escape hatch. In Drupal Gardens, users will be able to press a button and get a source code version of the Drupal code that runs their site along with the data from the database. Then, you can take that code, put it up at one of the hosting companies, and you can do anything that you would like to do.

Similarly, MediaWiki, WordPress and their many extensions are increasingly used for a wide variety of internal applications as well as public web services. Duplicating the code is relatively simple, as it is an integration of existing extensions, plug-ins, templates, etc. Actual customizations are rare, and usually quickly replaced by more standard publicly available extensions. There is additionally no guarantee the software source code obtained through such means accurately reflects the software system it claims to reflect.

Andrew Hoppin, a former Chief Information Officer for the New York State Senate, refers to this combination of SaaS and open source software as OpenSaaS and points to WordPress as another successful example of an OpenSaaS software delivery model that gives customers "the best of both worlds, and more options. The fact that it is open source means that they can start building their websites by self-hosting WordPress and customizing their website to their heart's content. Concurrently, the fact that WordPress is SaaS means that they don't have to manage the website at all – they can simply pay WordPress.com to host it." The cloud (or SaaS) model has no physical need for indirect distribution because it is not distributed physically and is deployed almost instantaneously, therefore partners and middlemen of the traditional kind are not necessary.

## Open-source Software

Open-source software (OSS) is computer software with its source code made available with a license in which the copyright holder provides the rights to study, change, and distribute the software to anyone and for any purpose. Open-source software may be developed in a collaborative public manner. According to scientists who studied it, open-source software is a prominent example of open collaboration.

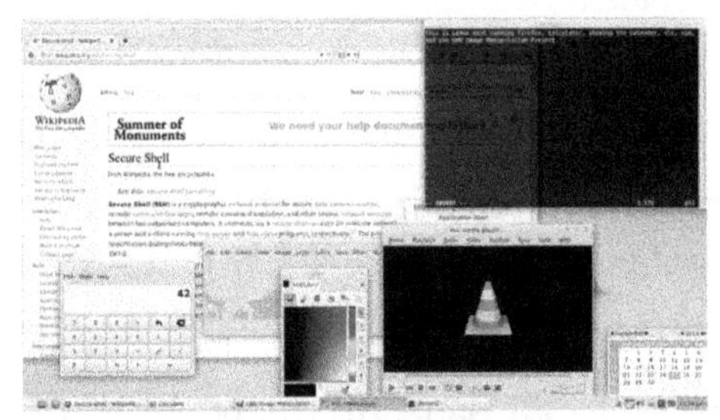

A screenshot of Linux Mint running the Xfce desktop environment, Mozilla Firefox browsing Wikipedia, a calculator program, the built in calendar, Vim, GIMP, and the VLC media player, all of which are open-source software.

The open-source software development, or collaborative development from multiple independent sources, generates an increasingly more diverse scope of design perspective than any one company is capable of developing and sustaining long term. A 2008 report by the Standish Group states that adoption of open-source software models has resulted in savings of about $60 billion (£48 billion) per year to consumers.

## History

### End of 1990s: Foundation of the Open Source Initiative

In the early days of computing, programmers and developers shared software in order to learn from each other and evolve the field of computing. Eventually the open source notion moved to the way side of commercialization of software in the years 1970-1980. In 1997, Eric Raymond published *The Cathedral and the Bazaar*, a reflective analysis of the hacker community and free software principles. The paper received significant attention in early 1998, and was one factor in motivating Netscape Communications Corporation to release their popular Netscape Communicator Internet suite as free software. This source code subsequently became the basis behind SeaMonkey, Mozilla Firefox, Thunderbird and KompoZer.

Netscape's act prompted Raymond and others to look into how to bring the Free Software Foundation's free software ideas and perceived benefits to the commercial software industry. They concluded that FSF's social activism was not appealing to companies like Netscape, and looked for a way to rebrand the free software movement to emphasize the business potential of sharing and collaborating on software source code. The new term they chose was "open source", which was soon adopted by Bruce Perens, publisher Tim O'Reilly, Linus Torvalds, and others. The Open Source Initiative was founded in February 1998 to encourage use of the new term and evangelize open-source principles.

While the Open Source Initiative sought to encourage the use of the new term and evangelize the principles it adhered to, commercial software vendors found themselves increasingly threatened by the concept of freely distributed software and universal access to an application's source code. A Microsoft executive publicly stated in 2001 that "open source is an intellectual property destroyer. I can't imagine something that could be worse than this for the software business and the intellectual-property business." However, while FOSS has historically played a role outside of the mainstream of private software development, companies as large as Microsoft have begun to develop official open-source presences on the Internet. IBM, Oracle, Google and State Farm are just a few of the companies with a serious public stake in today's competitive open-source market. There has been a significant shift in the corporate philosophy concerning the development of FOSS.

The free software movement was launched in 1983. In 1998, a group of individuals advocated that the term free software should be replaced by open-source software (OSS) as an expression which is less ambiguous and more comfortable for the corporate world. Software developers may want to publish their software with an open-source license, so that anybody may also develop the same software or understand its internal functioning. With open-source software, generally anyone is allowed to create modifications of it, port it to new operating systems and instruction set architectures, share it with others or, in some cases, market it. Scholars Casson and Ryan have pointed out several policy-based reasons for adoption of open source – in particular, the heightened value proposition from open source (when compared to most proprietary formats) in the following categories:

- Security
- Affordability
- Transparency
- Perpetuity
- Interoperability
- Flexibility
- Localization—particularly in the context of local governments (who make software decisions). Casson and Ryan argue that "governments have an inherent responsibility and fiduciary duty to taxpayers" which includes the careful analysis of these factors when deciding to purchase proprietary software or implement an open-source option.

The *Open Source Definition*, notably, presents an open-source philosophy, and further defines the terms of use, modification and redistribution of open-source software. Software licenses grant rights to users which would otherwise be reserved by copyright law to the copyright holder. Several open-source software licenses have qualified within the boundaries of the *Open Source Definition*. The most prominent and popular example is the GNU General Public License (GPL), which "allows free distribution under the condition that further developments and applications are put under the same licence", thus also free.

The *open source* label came out of a strategy session held on April 7, 1998 in Palo Alto in reaction to Netscape's January 1998 announcement of a source code release for Navigator (as Mozilla). A group of individuals at the session included Tim O'Reilly, Linus Torvalds, Tom Paquin, Jamie Zawinski, Larry Wall, Brian Behlendorf, Sameer Parekh, Eric Allman, Greg Olson, Paul Vixie, John Ousterhout, Guido van Rossum, Philip Zimmermann, John Gilmore and Eric S. Raymond. They used the opportunity before the release of Navigator's source code to clarify a potential confusion caused by the ambiguity of the word "free" in English.

Many people claimed that the birth of the Internet, since 1969, started the open source movement, while others do not distinguish between open-source and free software movements.

The Free Software Foundation (FSF), started in 1985, intended the word "free" to mean *freedom to distribute* (or "free as in free speech") and not *freedom from cost* (or "free as in free beer"). Since a great deal of free software already was (and still is) free of charge, such free software became associated with zero cost, which seemed anti-commercial.

The Open Source Initiative (OSI) was formed in February 1998 by Eric Raymond and Bruce Perens. With at least 20 years of evidence from case histories of closed software development versus open development already provided by the Internet developer community, the OSI presented the "open source" case to commercial businesses, like Netscape. The OSI hoped that the use of the label "open source", a term suggested by Peterson of the Foresight Institute at the strategy session, would eliminate ambiguity, particularly for individuals who perceive "free software" as anti-commercial. They sought to bring a higher profile to the practical benefits of freely available source code, and they wanted to bring major software businesses and other high-tech industries into open source. Perens attempted to register "open source" as a service mark for the OSI, but that attempt was impractical by trademark standards. Meanwhile, due to the presentation of Raymond's paper to the upper management at Netscape—Raymond only discovered when he read the Press Release, and was called by Netscape CEO Jim Barksdale's PA later in the day—Netscape released its Navigator source code as open source, with favorable results.

## Definitions

The Open Source Initiative's (OSI) definition is recognized by governments internationally as the standard or *de facto* definition. In addition, many of the world's largest open source software projects and contributors, including Debian, Drupal Association,

FreeBSD Foundation, Linux Foundation, Mozilla Foundation, Wikimedia Foundation, Wordpress Foundation have committed to upholding the OSI's mission and Open Source Definition through the OSI Affiliate Agreement.

The logo of the Open Source Initiative

OSI uses *The Open Source Definition* to determine whether it considers a software license open source. The definition was based on the Debian Free Software Guidelines, written and adapted primarily by Perens. Perens did not base his writing on the "four freedoms" from the Free Software Foundation (FSF), which were only widely available later.

Under Perens' definition, *open source* describes a broad general type of software license that makes source code available to the general public with relaxed or non-existent restrictions on the use and modification of the code. It is an explicit "feature" of open source that it puts very few restrictions on the use or distribution by any organization or user, in order to enable the rapid evolution of the software.

Despite initially accepting it, Richard Stallman of the FSF now flatly opposes the term "Open Source" being applied to what they refer to as "free software". Although he agrees that the two terms describe "almost the same category of software", Stallman considers equating the terms incorrect and misleading. Stallman also opposes the professed pragmatism of the Open Source Initiative, as he fears that the free software ideals of freedom and community are threatened by compromising on the FSF's idealistic standards for software freedom. The FSF considers free software to be a subset of open source software, and Richard Stallman explained that DRM software, for example, can be developed as open source, despite that it does not give its users freedom (it restricts them), and thus doesn't qualify as free software.

## Open-source Software Licensing

When an author contributes code to an open-source project (e.g., Apache.org) they do so under an explicit license (e.g., the Apache Contributor License Agreement) or an implicit license (e.g. the open-source license under which the project is already licensing code). Some open-source projects do not take contributed code under a license, but actually require joint assignment of the author's copyright in order to accept code contributions into the project.

Examples of free software license / open-source licenses include Apache License, BSD license, GNU General Public License, GNU Lesser General Public License, MIT License, Eclipse Public License and Mozilla Public License.

The proliferation of open-source licenses is a negative aspect of the open-source movement because it is often difficult to understand the legal implications of the differences between licenses. With more than 180,000 open-source projects available and more than 1400 unique licenses, the complexity of deciding how to manage open-source use within "closed-source" commercial enterprises has dramatically increased. Some are home-grown, while others are modeled after mainstream FOSS licenses such as Berkeley Software Distribution ("BSD"), Apache, MIT-style (Massachusetts Institute of Technology), or GNU General Public License ("GPL"). In view of this, open-source practitioners are starting to use classification schemes in which FOSS licenses are grouped (typically based on the existence and obligations imposed by the copyleft provision; the strength of the copyleft provision).

An important legal milestone for the open source / free software movement was passed in 2008, when the US federal appeals court ruled that free software licenses definitely do set legally binding conditions on the use of copyrighted work, and they are therefore enforceable under existing copyright law. As a result, if end-users violate the licensing conditions, their license disappears, meaning they are infringing copyright. Despite this licensing risk, most commercial software vendors are using open source software in commercial products while fulfilling the license terms, e.g. leveraging the Apache license.

## Certifications

Certification can help to build user confidence. Certification could be applied to the simplest component, to a whole software system. The United Nations University International Institute for Software Technology, initiated a project known as "The Global Desktop Project". This project aims to build a desktop interface that every end-user is able to understand and interact with, thus crossing the language and cultural barriers. The project would improve developing nations' access to information systems. UNU/IIST hopes to achieve this without any compromise in the quality of the software by introducing certifications.

## Open-source Software Development

## Development Model

In his 1997 essay *The Cathedral and the Bazaar*, open-source evangelist Eric S. Raymond suggests a model for developing OSS known as the *bazaar* model. Raymond likens the development of software by traditional methodologies to building a cathedral, "carefully crafted by individual wizards or small bands of mages working in splendid isolation". He suggests that all software should be developed using the bazaar style, which he described as "a great babbling bazaar of differing agendas and approaches."

In the traditional model of development, which he called the *cathedral* model, development takes place in a centralized way. Roles are clearly defined. Roles include people dedicated to designing (the architects), people responsible for managing the project, and people responsible for implementation. Traditional software engineering follows the cathedral model.

The bazaar model, however, is different. In this model, roles are not clearly defined. Gregorio Robles suggests that software developed using the bazaar model should exhibit the following patterns:

### Users should be Treated as Co-developers

The users are treated like co-developers and so they should have access to the source code of the software. Furthermore, users are encouraged to submit additions to the software, code fixes for the software, bug reports, documentation etc. Having more co-developers increases the rate at which the software evolves. Linus's law states, "Given enough eyeballs all bugs are shallow." This means that if many users view the source code, they will eventually find all bugs and suggest how to fix them. Note that some users have advanced programming skills, and furthermore, each user's machine provides an additional testing environment. This new testing environment offers that ability to find and fix a new bug.

### Early Releases

The first version of the software should be released as early as possible so as to increase one's chances of finding co-developers early.

### Frequent Integration

Code changes should be integrated (merged into a shared code base) as often as possible so as to avoid the overhead of fixing a large number of bugs at the end of the project life cycle. Some open source projects have nightly builds where integration is done automatically on a daily basis.

### Several Versions

There should be at least two versions of the software. There should be a buggier version with more features and a more stable version with fewer features. The buggy version (also called the development version) is for users who want the immediate use of the latest features, and are willing to accept the risk of using code that is not yet thoroughly tested. The users can then act as co-developers, reporting bugs and providing bug fixes.

### High Modularization

The general structure of the software should be modular allowing for parallel development on independent components.

### Dynamic Decision Making Structure

There is a need for a decision making structure, whether formal or informal, that makes strategic decisions depending on changing user requirements and other factors. Cf. Extreme programming.

Data suggests, however, that OSS is not quite as democratic as the bazaar model suggests. An analysis of five billion bytes of free/open source code by 31,999 developers shows that 74% of the code was written by the most active 10% of authors. The average number of authors involved in a project was 5.1, with the median at 2.

## Advantages and Disadvantages

Open source software is usually easier to obtain than proprietary software, often resulting in increased use. Additionally, the availability of an open source implementation of a standard can increase adoption of that standard. It has also helped to build developer loyalty as developers feel empowered and have a sense of ownership of the end product.

Moreover, lower costs of marketing and logistical services are needed for OSS. OSS also helps companies keep abreast of technology developments. It is a good tool to promote a company's image, including its commercial products. The OSS development approach has helped produce reliable, high quality software quickly and inexpensively.

Open source development offers the potential for a more flexible technology and quicker innovation. It is said to be more reliable since it typically has thousands of independent programmers testing and fixing bugs of the software. It is flexible because modular systems allow programmers to build custom interfaces, or add new abilities to it and it is innovative since open source programs are the product of collaboration among a large number of different programmers. The mix of divergent perspectives, corporate objectives, and personal goals speeds up innovation.

Moreover, free software can be developed in accord with purely technical requirements. It does not require thinking about commercial pressure that often degrades the quality of the software. Commercial pressures make traditional software developers pay more attention to customers' requirements than to security requirements, since such features are somewhat invisible to the customer.

It is sometimes said that the open source development process may not be well defined and the stages in the development process, such as system testing and documentation may be ignored. However this is only true for small (mostly single programmer) projects. Larger, successful projects do define and enforce at least some rules as they need them to make the teamwork possible. In the most complex projects these rules may be as strict as reviewing even minor change by two independent developers.

Not all OSS initiatives have been successful, for example SourceXchange and Eazel. Software experts and researchers who are not convinced by open source's ability to produce quality systems identify the unclear process, the late defect discovery and the lack of any empirical evidence as the most important problems (collected data concerning productivity and quality). It is also difficult to design a commercially sound business model around the open source paradigm. Consequently, only technical requirements may be satisfied and not the ones of the market. In terms of security, open source may allow hackers to know about the weaknesses or loopholes of the software more easily than closed-source software.It depends on control mechanisms in order to create effective performance of autonomous agents who participate in virtual organizations.

## Development Tools

In OSS development, tools are used to support the development of the product and the development process itself.

Revision control systems such as Concurrent Versions System (CVS) and later Subversion (SVN) and Git are examples of tools, often themselves open source, help manage the source code files and the changes to those files for a software project. The projects are frequently hosted and published on sites like Launchpad, Bitbucket, and GitHub.

Open source projects are often loosely organized with "little formalised process modelling or support", but utilities such as issue trackers are often used to organize open source software development. Commonly used bugtrackers include Bugzilla and Redmine.

Tools such as mailing lists and IRC provide means of coordination among developers. Centralized code hosting sites also have social features that allow developers to communicate.

## Organizations

Some of the "more prominent organizations" involved in OSS development include the Apache Software Foundation, creators of the Apache web server; the Linux Foundation, a nonprofit which as of 2012 employed Linus Torvalds, the creator of the Linux operating system kernel; the Eclipse Foundation, home of the Eclipse software development platform; the Debian Project, creators of the influential Debian GNU/Linux distribution; the Mozilla Foundation, home of the Firefox web browser; and OW2, European-born community developing open source middleware. New organizations tend to have a more sophisticated governance model and their membership is often formed by legal entity members.

Open Source Software Institute is a membership-based, non-profit (501 (c)(6)) organization established in 2001 that promotes the development and implementation of open source software solutions within US Federal, state and local government agencies. OSSI's efforts have focused on promoting adoption of open source software programs and policies within Federal Government and Defense and Homeland Security communities.

Open Source for America is a group created to raise awareness in the United States Federal Government about the benefits of open source software. Their stated goals are to encourage the government's use of open source software, participation in open source software projects, and incorporation of open source community dynamics to increase government transparency.

Mil-OSS is a group dedicated to the advancement of OSS use and creation in the military.

## Funding

Open-source software is widely used both as independent applications and as components in non-open-source applications. Many independent software vendors (ISVs), value-added resellers (VARs), and hardware vendors (OEMs or ODMs) use open-source frameworks, modules, and libraries inside their proprietary, for-profit products and services. From a customer's perspective, the ability to use open technology under standard commercial terms and support is valuable. They are willing to pay for the legal protection (e.g., indemnification from copyright or patent infringement), "commercial-grade QA", and professional support/training/consulting that are typical of commercial software, while also receiving the benefits of fine-grained control and lack of lock-in that comes with open-source.

## Comparisons with Other Software Licensing/Development Models

### Closed Source / Proprietary Software

The debate over *open source* vs. *closed source* (alternatively called proprietary software) is sometimes heated.

The top four reasons (as provided by Open Source Business Conference survey) individuals or organizations choose open source software are:

1. lower cost,
2. security,

3. no vendor 'lock in', and
4. better quality.

Since innovative companies no longer rely heavily on software sales, proprietary software has become less of a necessity. As such, things like open source content management system—or CMS—deployments are becoming more commonplace. In 2009, the US White House switched its CMS system from a proprietary system to Drupal open source CMS. Further, companies like Novell (who traditionally sold software the old-fashioned way) continually debate the benefits of switching to open source availability, having already switched part of the product offering to open source code. In this way, open source software provides solutions to unique or specific problems. As such, it is reported that 98% of enterprise-level companies use open source software offerings in some capacity.

With this market shift, more critical systems are beginning to rely on open source offerings, allowing greater funding (such as US Department of Homeland Security grants) to help "hunt for security bugs." According to a pilot study of organisations adopting (or not adopting) OSS; several factors of statistical significance were observed in the manager's beliefs in relation to (a) attitudes toward outcomes, (b) the influences and behaviours of others and (c) their ability to act.

Proprietary source distributors have started to develop and contribute to the open source community due to the market share shift, doing so by the need to reinvent their models in order to remain competitive.

Many advocates argue that open source software is inherently safer because any person can view, edit, and change code. A study of the Linux source code has 0.17 bugs per 1000 lines of code while proprietary software generally scores 20–30 bugs per 1000 lines.

## Free Software

According to the Free software movement's leader, Richard Stallman, the main difference is that by choosing one term over the other (i.e. either "open source" or "free software") one lets others know about what one's goals are: "Open source is a development methodology; free software is a social movement." Nevertheless, there is significant overlap between open source software and free software.

The FSF said that the term "open source" fosters an ambiguity of a different kind such that it confuses the mere availability of the source with the freedom to use, modify, and redistribute it. On the other hand, the "free software" term was criticized for the ambiguity of the word "free" as "available at no cost", which was seen as discouraging for business adoption, and for the historical ambiguous usage of the term.

Developers have used the alternative terms *Free and Open Source Software* (FOSS), or *Free/Libre and Open Source Software* (FLOSS), consequently, to describe open source software that is also free software. While the definition of open source software is very similar to the FSF's free software definition it was based on the Debian Free Software Guidelines, written and adapted primarily by Bruce Perens with input from Eric S. Raymond and others.

The term "open source" was originally intended to be trademarkable; however, the term was deemed too descriptive, so no trademark exists. The OSI would prefer that people treat open source as if it were a trademark, and use it only to describe software licensed under an OSI approved license.

OSI Certified is a trademark licensed only to people who are distributing software licensed under a license listed on the Open Source Initiative's list.

## Open-source Versus Source-available

Although the OSI definition of "open source software" is widely accepted, a small number of people and organizations use the term to refer to software where the source is available for viewing, but which may not legally be modified or redistributed. Such software is more often referred to as *source-available*, or as *shared source*, a term coined by Microsoft in 2001. While in 2007 two shared source licenses were certified by the OSI, most of the shared source licenses are still *source-available only*.

In 2007 Michael Tiemann, president of OSI, had criticized companies such as SugarCRM for promoting their software as "open source" when in fact it did not have an OSI-approved license. In SugarCRM's case, it was because the software is so-called "badgeware" since it specified a "badge" that must be displayed in the user interface (SugarCRM has since switched to GPLv3). Another example was Scilab prior to version 5, which called itself "the open source platform for numerical computation" but had a license that forbade commercial redistribution of modified versions.

## Open-sourcing

Open-sourcing is the act of propagating the open source movement, most often referring to releasing previously proprietary software under an open source/free software license, but it may also refer programing Open Source software or installing Open Source software.

Notable software packages, previously proprietary, which have been open sourced include:

- Netscape Navigator, the code of which became the basis of the Mozilla and Mozilla Firefox web browsers

- StarOffice, which became the base of the OpenOffice.org office suite and Libre-Office
- Global File System, was originally GPL'd, then made proprietary in 2001(?), but in 2004 was re-GPL'd.
- SAP DB, which has become MaxDB, and is now distributed (and owned) by MySQL AB
- InterBase database, which was open sourced by Borland in 2000 and presently exists as a commercial product and an open-source fork (Firebird)

Before changing the license of software, distributors usually audit the source code for third party licensed code which they would have to remove or obtain permission for its relicense. Backdoors and other malware should also be removed as they may easily be discovered after release of the code.

## Current Applications and Adoption

"We migrated key functions from Windows to Linux because we needed an operating system that was stable and reliable – one that would give us in-house control. So if we needed to patch, adjust, or adapt, we could."

*Official statement of the United Space Alliance, which manages the computer systems for the International Space Station (ISS), regarding why they chose to switch from Windows to Debian GNU/Linux on the ISS*

## Widely used Open-source Software

Open source software projects are built and maintained by a network of volunteer programmers and are widely used in free as well as commercial products. Prime examples of open-source products are the Apache HTTP Server, the e-commerce platform osCommerce, internet browsers Mozilla Firefox and Chromium (the project where the vast majority of development of the freeware Google Chrome is done) and the full office suite LibreOffice. One of the most successful open-source products is the GNU/ Linux operating system, an open-source Unix-like operating system, and its derivative Android, an operating system for mobile devices. In some industries, open source software is the norm.

## Extensions for Non-software use

While the term "open source" applied originally only to the source code of software, it is now being applied to many other areas such as Open source ecology, a movement to decentralize technologies so that any human can use them. However, it is often misapplied to other areas which have different and competing principles, which overlap only partially.

The same principles that underlie open source software can be found in many other ventures, such as open-source hardware, Wikipedia, and open-access publishing. Collectively, these principles are known as open source, open content, and open collaboration: "any system of innovation or production that relies on goal-oriented yet loosely coordinated participants, who interact to create a product (or service) of economic value, which they make available to contributors and non-contributors alike."

This "culture" or ideology takes the view that the principles apply more generally to facilitate concurrent input of different agendas, approaches and priorities, in contrast with more centralized models of development such as those typically used in commercial companies.

## H2O (Software)

H2O is open-source software for big-data analysis. It is produced by the company H2O.*ai* (formerly *oxdata*), which launched in 2011 in Silicon Valley. H2O allows users to fit thousands of potential models as part of discovering patterns in data.

H2O's mathematical core is developed with the leadership of Arno Candel, part of Fortune's 2014 "Big Data All Stars". The firm's scientific advisors are experts on statistical learning theory and mathematical optimization.

The H2O software runs can be called from the statistical package *R*, Python, and other environments. It is used for exploring and analyzing datasets held in cloud computing systems and in the Apache Hadoop Distributed File System as well as in the conventional operating-systems Linux, macOS, and Microsoft Windows. The H2O software is written in Java, Python, and *R*. Its graphical-user interface is compatible with four browsers: Chrome, Safari, Firefox, and Internet Explorer.

### H2O

The H2O project aims to develop an analytical interface for cloud computing, providing users with tools for data analysis.

### Leadership

H2O.ai was co-founded by Cliff Click and SriSatish Ambati.

H2O's chief executive, SriSatish Ambati, had helped to start Platfora, a big-data firm that develops software for the Apache Hadoop distributed file system. Ambati was frustrated with the performance of the *R* programming language on large data-sets and started the development of H2O software with encouragement from John Chambers, who created the *S* programming language at Bell Labs and who is a member of *R*'s core team (which leads the development of *R*).

Ambati co-founded oxdata with Cliff Click, who served as the chief technical officer of H2O and helped create much of H2O's product. Click helped to write the HotSpot Server Compiler and worked with Azul Systems to construct a big-data Java virtual machine (JVM). Click left H2O in February 2016. Leland Wilkinson, author of The Grammar of Graphics, serves as Chief Scientist and provides visualization leadership.

## Scientific advisory council

Stanford University professor Trevor J. Hastie serves as an advisor to H2O.ai.

H2O's Scientific Advisory Council lists three mathematical scientists, who are all professors at Stanford University: Professor Stephen P. Boyd is an expert in convex minimization and applications in statistics and electrical engineering. Robert Tibshirani, a collaborator with Bradley Efron on bootstrapping, is an expert on generalized additive models and statistical learning theory. Trevor Hastie, a collaborator of John Chambers on *S*, is an expert on generalized additive models and statistical learning theory.

## H2O.ai: A Silicon Valley Start-up

The software is open-source and freely distributed. The company receives fees for providing customer service and customized extensions. In November 2014, its twenty clients included Cisco, eBay, Nielsen, and PayPal, according to *VentureBeat*.

## Mining of Big Data

Big datasets are too large to be analyzed using traditional software like *R*. The H2O software provides data structures and methods suitable for big data. H2O allow users to analyze and visualize whole sets of data without using the Procrustean strategy of studying only a small subset with a conventional statistical package. H2O's statistical algorithms includes K-means clustering, generalized linear models, distributed random forests, gradient boosting machines, naive bayes, principal component analysis, and generalized low rank models.

H2O is also able to run on Spark.

## Iterative Methods for real-time Problems

H2O uses iterative methods that provide quick answers using all of the client's data. When a client cannot wait for an optimal solution, the client can interrupt the computations and use an approximate solution. In its approach to deep learning, H2O divides all the data into subsets and then analyzing each subset simultaneously using the same method. These processes are combined to estimate parameters by using the Hogwild scheme, a parallel stochastic gradient method. These methods allow H2O to provide answers that use all the client's data, rather than throwing away most of it and analyzing a subset with conventional software.

## Software

## Programming Languages

The H2O software has an interface to the following programming languages: Java (6 or later), Python (2.7.x, 3.5.x), *R* (3.0.0 or later) and Scala (1.4-1.6).

## Operating Systems

The H2O software can be run on conventional operating-systems: Microsoft Windows (7 or later), Mac OS X (10.9 or later), and Linux (Ubuntu 12.04 ; RHEL/CentOS 6 or later), It also runs on big-data systems, particularly Apache Hadoop Distributed File System (HDFS), several popular versions: Cloudera (5.1 or later), MapR (3.0 or later), and Hortonworks (HDP 2.1 or later). It also operates on cloud computing environments, for example using Amazon EC2, Google Compute Engine, and Microsoft Azure. The H2O Sparkling Water software is Databricks-certified on Apache Spark.

## Graphical user Interface and Browsers

Its graphical user interface is compatible with four browsers (unless specified, in their latest versions as of 1 June 2015): Chrome, Safari, Firefox, Internet Explorer (IE10).

## Cloudify

Cloudify is an open source software cloud orchestration product created by GigaSpaces Technologies.

### Overview

Cloudify uses the OASIS TOSCA technology and is written in the Python programming language. It is licensed under the Apache License Version 2.0, and its source files can be found and forked on GitHub. Built on a YAML DSL (Domain Specific Language) configuration files called "blueprints" define the application's configurations, services and their tier dependencies. With these Cloudify automates the deployment phases of applications to Cloud computing and Virtualization infrastructure. The blueprints describe how the application interacts with the data center through APIs to execute the defined blueprint configurations.

These blueprint files describe the execution plans for the lifecycle of the application for installing, starting, terminating, orchestrating and monitoring the application stack. Cloudify uses the blueprint as input that describes the deployment plan and is responsible for executing it on the cloud environments. The blueprint also employs cloud driver configuration files as well, to describe machines and their images for the chosen cloud, making it possible to manage the infrastructure as code. For each component it describe the location of your binaries, installation and monitoring configurations. By creating an abstraction layer that isolates the code from the underlying infrastructure, Cloudify is able to support any cloud.

Cloudify also supports configuration management tools like Chef Puppet, Ansible for the application deployment phase, as a method of deploying and configuring application services.

### Marketing

Cloudify was mentioned in marketing publications, including: the VentureBeat CloudBeat Showdown 2011, the CRN 20 Coolest Cloud Platforms & Development Vendors 2012 and 2014, the 2012 SD Times 100: A Software Development Superfecta as a cloud leader, was recognized by Frost & Sullivan with the 2015 Global Frost & Sullivan Award for New Product Innovation.

Cloudify, together with VMware and Athonet, won the 2016 "Best of Show" Award at the Tokyo Interop event, for the demonstration of the fastest and simplest cloud-based deployment of a virtualized LTE mobile packet core & VoLTE service.

The Agile Reference Implementation of Automation (ARIA), a open source MANO group spawned from Cloudify, won "MANO Software of the Year" at the Network Virtualization Industry 2016 Awards.

### Collaborative Projects and Community Memberships

Cloudify is a member of various collaborative projects and open source communities:

- Linux Foundation
- OPNFV
- MEF Forum
- OASIS TOSCA
- OpenStack
- OPEN-O
- ONAP - Open Network Automation Platform
- Project Clearwater

### Users

Cloudify is used in Open-O, AT&T, VMware, Deutsche Telekom, Orange S.A.#Orange Labs, within OPNFV, and Metaswitch among others.

## Adobe Marketing Cloud

Adobe Marketing Cloud (AMC) is a collection of integrated online marketing and Web analytics products by Adobe Systems. It is a comprehensive marketing solution which enables marketers to measure, personalize and optimize marketing campaigns and digital experiences for optimal marketing performance.

### History

Adobe Marketing Cloud includes a set of analytics, social, advertising, media optimization, targeting, Web experience management and content management products aimed at the advertising industry and hosted on Amazon Web Services. Like other Adobe Cloud services (e.g., Adobe Creative Cloud), the Adobe Marketing Cloud allows users with valid subscriptions to download the entire collection and use it directly on their computers with open access to online updates.

The Adobe Marketing Cloud collection was introduced to the public in October 2012 as Adobe began retiring the Omniture name it acquired in October 2009. Products of the defunct company were then integrated step by step into the new Cloud service which includes the following eight applications: Adobe Analytics, Adobe Target, Adobe Social, Adobe Experience Manager, Adobe Media Optimizer, Adobe Campaign, Audience Manager and Primetime. In November 2013, Adobe Systems introduced mobile features to its Marketing Cloud, making smartphones and other mobile devices new targets for analytics.

On September 15, 2009, Omniture, Inc. and Adobe Systems announced that Adobe would be acquiring Omniture, an online marketing and web analytics business unit in Orem, Utah. The deal of $1.8 billion, was completed on October 23, 2009, and is now joined by other Adobe acquisitions such as Day Software and Efficient Frontier, as the main components of Adobe's Digital Marketing Business Unit. Around 2012, Adobe withdrew the Omniture brand while its products were being integrated into the Adobe Marketing Cloud.

### Reception

Adobe Marketing Cloud as a subscription model has made significant progress in terms of acceptance in the business world. In 2013, Gartner, an information technology research and advisory company, ranked the Adobe's solutions execution ability at the highest position on its Magic Quadrant for Web content management. This distinction is in line with the evolution of its preceding Cloud-based model suite Adobe Creative Cloud which met significant criticism in the beginning.

## Google Cloud Connect

Google Cloud Connect was a free cloud computing plug-in for Windows Microsoft Office 2003, 2007 and 2010 that can automatically store and synchronize any Microsoft Word document, PowerPoint presentation, or Excel spreadsheet to Google Docs in Google Docs or Microsoft Office formats. The Google Doc copy is automatically updated each time the Microsoft Office document is saved. Microsoft Office documents can be edited offline and synchronized later when online. Google Cloud Sync maintains previous Microsoft Office document versions and allows multiple users to collaborate, working on the same document at the same time. Google Cloud Connect was discontinued on April 30, 2013, as according to Google, all of Cloud Connect's features are available through Google Drive.

### Features

Google Cloud Connect could automatically or manually synchronize changes made to a Microsoft Office 2003, 2007, or 2010 document with Google Docs. Documents can be secured for private access by one user, shared with specific people for collaboration, or made public to anyone. Previous document versions can be retrieved.

- Backup: Microsoft Office documents could be manually or automatically backed up to Google Docs each time they are saved locally.

- Synchronize: Changes made to an Office document on one computer can sync when the file is opened on another computer.
- Protect: Microsoft Office documents synced to Google Docs can be made accessible to one person.
- Share: Microsoft Office documents synced to Google Docs can be made accessible only to selected people.
- Edit: A shared document can be set to only be viewed by others or edited as well.
- Publish: Documents synced to Google Docs can effectively be published by making them accessible to anyone.
- Collaborate: Multiple users can work on the same document at the same time.
- Notify: When one person edits a document, others sharing the document receive an email letting them know.
- Print: Use Google Cloud Print to print to local or remote network connected printers.
- Compare: Previous version are maintained allowing users to compare to older versions.
- Roll back: Users can return to a previous version of the document.
- Green: Green computing allows documents to be shared without printing or sending large files. Only links need be sent.
- Mobilize: Google Sync allows synced documents to be viewed and edited with most internet connected mobile devices.
- Storage: 5GB of Google Drive storage is included for free. Currently, additional storage costs per month are: 25GB-$2.49, 100GB-$4.99, etc. up to 16TB.

## Cloudike

Cloudike is a brandable file storage platform operated by Cloudike Inc., headquartered in San Jose, California. The platform provides cloud storage, file synchronization and contact synchronization, personal cloud, and client software.

The company's data storage approach is similar to that of Dropbox, Google Drive, and Apple iCloud that store user data and provide access to files from smartphones, laptops, tablets, etc. The main difference is that apart from functionality for end-users (Cloudike Personal), Cloudike offers customization for businesses (Cloudike Enterprise) under their own brands which is widely known as white-label.

## Overview

Cloudike started in 2013 as a SaaS-platform that grew into a multi-tier cloud solution used to build white-label enterprise data storages for OEMs, Mobile and Internet service providers. The platform has modules for enterprise data administration, storage API, and integration with billing systems. Cloudike enables building large-scale file storages based on OpenStack Swift or Amazon S3, or other storage systems compatible with Amazon S3 APIs.

## Technology

To synchronize user files with the server, Cloudike provides desktop clients for Windows and macOS. For Android and iOS devices, Cloudike offers mobile clients. Files and contact lists can be accessed via a web browser. Any data updates are synchronized between all computers and mobile devices that are associated with user accounts.

## API Back-end

Cloudike is based on a set of programmatic interfaces (APIs) written in Python; it uses Python frameworks Django and Tornado to create REST API, message broker software RabbitMQ, and MongoDB. To build a contact synchronization mechanism, Cloudike utilizes SabreDAV framework.

## Web Front-end

Web-frontend part is a single page application based on AngularJS.

## Features

### End-user Features

- File browsing, upload/download;
- Access to files and directories via WebDAV protocol;
- Content sharing, generation of public URLs and URL shortening functionality, multi-user collaboration;
- Clients for Windows (Windows XP, 7 and 8, 8.1), macOS (10.7 or higher);
- File versioning and restore;
- Address book (CardDAV);
- Thumbnails and previews for photo gallery;
- Video viewer;

- Events log;
- PDF viewer (using PDF.js);
- Viewer for Microsoft Office or OpenDocument formats (.odt, .odp, .ods, .doc, docx, .xls, etc.);

## Enterprise Modules

- User and group administration in Cloudike business accounts;
- Product usage statistics in the administrator panel;
- Billing settings for white-label storages.

## Critics

- Cloudike uses only MongoDB to store information about directories and files metadata and does not work with other databases;
- Cloudike doesn't offer an online text editor;
- So far, there is no such functionality as calendar synchronization (CalDAV).
- Connection with other file storages using ftp/sftp or Dropbox API is not supported.

## Competition

There are several other cloud platforms that provide white-label services similar to that of Cloudike. The list below contains some cloud storage platforms that might directly or indirectly compete with Cloudike.

- Synchronoss - a set of cloud solutions that allow users to connect, synchronize and activate connected devices.
- OwnCloud - an open-source software system for what is commonly termed file hosting.
- Funambol OneMediaHub - a white-label personal cloud solution that secures data and content on mobile devices and computers in the cloud, syncs it across diverse devices, and allows sharing with other people and systems.
- Storegate - file storage platform to secure, backup and synchronize personal files.
- SmartFile - a white-label onpremise/cloud solution to store and share files.

# CloudMe

CloudMe is a file storage service operated by *CloudMe AB* that offers cloud storage, file synchronization and client software. It features a blue folder that appears on all devices with the same content, all files are synchronized between devices. The CloudMe service is offered with a freemium business model and provides encrypted SSL connection with SSL Extended Validation Certificate. *CloudMe* provides client software for Microsoft Windows, macOS, Linux, Android, iOS, Google TV, Samsung Smart TV, WD TV, Windows Storage Server for NAS and web browsers.

As a cloud sync storage provider, CloudMe has a strong focus on the European market and differentiates itself from other storage providers with mobility and media features like Samsung SmartTV support.

Recently Novell announced support for the CloudMe service in their Dynamic File Services Suite. Novosoft Handy Backup version 7.3 also announced support for CloudMe. WinZip is also integrated with CloudMe. There are many third party mobile apps and software available for CloudMe, many using the WebDAV support of CloudMe.

## History

CloudMe was founded by Daniel Arthursson in 2012 and is mainly owned by Xcerion. The company runs its own servers and operates from Sweden, European Union. In 2012 CloudMe received the Red Herring Top 100 Global company, AlwaysON Global 250 award, White Bull 2012 Yearling Award and the White Bull 2014 Longhorn Award.

Previously CloudMe.com was called iCloud.com, but the service changed name after Apple acquired the domain and trademark for a rumoured 4.5 million dollars. For a while visitors to icloud.com were directed to cloudme.com. After the name change, the former iCloud.com service was split into two companies and services, CloudMe for file sync and storage, and CloudTop as the virtual cloud desktop that previously was the main attraction of the iCloud.com service and included file storage. Xcerion, the major owner of CloudMe and CloudTop initially gained an investment of $12 million to build the iCloud service.

Using a SaaS model, the CloudMe service is provided in a free version (3 GB storage up to 19 GB with referral program), a model often called freemium, and premium versions with either 10, 25, 100, 200, 500 GB storage for consumers, 2 TB and 5 TB for business. The closest competitor to CloudMe is Dropbox.

## Features

CloudMe features a Cloud storage and sync solution that allows the users to store, access and share their content, both with each other and with people outside the service. Sharing can be done by email, text messaging, Facebook and Google. Files can be stored in a blue folder, which is synchronized to all connected computers and devices. A web desktop and cloud OS service called CloudTop.com is available that uses CloudMe as its internet file system.

### Headquarters

CloudMe AB is located on Drottninggatan 23 in Linköping, Sweden.

## ownCloud

ownCloud is a suite of client-server software for creating file hosting services and using them. ownCloud is functionally very similar to the widely used Dropbox, with the primary functional difference being that ownCloud is free and open-source, and thereby allowing anyone to install and operate it without charge on a private server. It also supports extensions that allow it to work like Google Drive, with online document editing, calendar and contact synchronization, and more. Its openness eschews enforced quotas on storage space or the number of connected clients, instead having hard limits (like on storage space or number of users) defined only by the physical capabilities of the server.

### History

Frank Karlitschek, a KDE software developer, announced the development of ownCloud in January 2010, in order to provide a free software replacement to proprietary storage service providers. The company was founded in 2011.

OwnCloud Inc., the company founded by Karlitschek, has attracted funding from investors, including an injection of 6.3 million US$ in 2014.

In June 2016 Karlitschek and 12 contributors left OwnCloud Inc., resulting in the closure of ownCloud's U.S. operations. The departing developers forked the ownCloud code to start a new project called Nextcloud.

Attendees of the very first ownCloud Meetup meet at the Nextcloud Conf 2016

In July 2016 ownCloud GmbH, based in Nuremberg Germany, secured additional financing, with the investors taking a majority share, and expanded its management team.

## Overview

## Design

In order for desktop machines to synchronize files with their ownCloud server, desktop clients are available for PCs running Windows, macOS, FreeBSD or Linux. Mobile clients exist for iOS and Android devices. Files and other data (such as calendars, contacts or bookmarks) can also be accessed, managed, and uploaded using a web browser without any additional software. Any updates to the file system are pushed to all computers and mobile devices connected to a user's account.

Encryption of files may be enforced by the server administrator.

The ownCloud server is written in the PHP and JavaScript scripting languages. For remote access, it employs sabre/dav, an open-source WebDAV server. ownCloud is designed to work with several database management systems, including SQLite, MariaDB, MySQL, Oracle Database, and PostgreSQL.

## Features

ownCloud files are stored in conventional directory structures, and can be accessed via WebDAV if necessary. User files are encrypted both at rest and during transit. ownCloud can synchronise with local clients running Windows (Windows XP, Vista, 7 and 8), macOS (10.6 or later), or various Linux distributions.

ownCloud users can manage calendars (CalDAV), contacts (CardDAV) scheduled tasks and streaming media (Ampache) from within the platform.

From the administration perspective, ownCloud permits user and group administration (via OpenID or LDAP). Content can be shared by defining granular read/write permissions between users and/or groups. Alternatively, ownCloud users can create public URLs when sharing files. Logging of file-related actions is available in the Enterprise and Education service offerings.

Furthermore, users can interact with the browser-based ODF-format word processor, bookmarking service, URL shortening suite, gallery, RSS feed reader and document viewer tools from within ownCloud. For additional extensibility, ownCloud can be augmented with "one-click" applications and connection to Dropbox, Google Drive and Amazon S3.

## Distribution

ownCloud server and clients may be downloaded from the ownCloud website and from third-party repositories, such as Google Play and Apple iTunes, and repositories maintained by Linux distributions. In 2014, a dispute arose between ownCloud and Ubuntu regarding the latter allegedly neglecting maintenance of packages, resulting in the temporary removal of ownCloud from the Ubuntu repository.

ownCloud has been integrated with the GNOME desktop. Additional projects that use or link to ownCloud include a Raspberry Pi project to create a cloud storage system using the Raspberry Pi's small, low-energy form-factor.

In addition to the standard open-source packages, an Enterprise version of ownCloud is also sold, aimed at businesses which require advanced features and software support.

## References


- Sharma, Srinarayan; Vijayan Sugumaran; Balaji Rajagopalan (2002). "A framework for creating hybrid-open source software communities" (PDF). Info Systems Journal. 12: 7–25. doi:10.1046/j.1365-2575.2002.00116.x
- St. Laurent, Andrew M. (2008). Understanding Open Source and Free Software Licensing. O'Reilly Media. p. 4. ISBN 9780596553951
- Panker, Jon; Lewis, Mark; Fahey, Evan; Vasquez, Melvin Jafet (August 2007). "How do you pronounce IT?". TechTarget. Retrieved 24 May 2012
- Levine, Sheen S.; Prietula, Michael J. (2013-12-30). "Open Collaboration for Innovation: Principles and Performance". Organization Science. 25 (5): 1414–1433. ISSN 1047-7039. doi:10.1287/orsc.2013.0872
- Payne, Christian (February 2002). "On the Security of Open Source Software". Info Systems Journal. 12 (1): 61–78. doi:10.1046/j.1365-2575.2002.00118.x
- McHall, Tom (7 July 2011). "Gartner Says Worldwide Software as a Service Revenue Is Forecast to Grow 21 Percent in 2011". Gartner. Retrieved 28 July 2011
- Holtgrewe, Ursula (2004). "Articulating the Speed(s) of the Internet: The Case of Open Source/Free Software.". Time & Society. 13: 129–146. doi:10.1177/0961463X04040750
- Stamelos, Ioannis; Lefteris Angelis; Apostolos Oikonomou; Georgios L. Bleris (2002). "Code Quality Analysis in Open Source Software Development" (PDF). Info System Journal. 12: 43–60. doi:10.1109/MS.2007.2. Retrieved 2008-09-08
- Popp, Dr. Karl Michael (2015). Best Practices for commercial use of open source software. Norderstedt, Germany: Books on Demand. ISBN 978-3738619096
- Wilson, Deborah R; BonaPart, Alexa (7 August 2009). "Develop a Framework for SaaS Application Business Continuity Risk Mitigation". Gartner. Retrieved 24 April 2011
- Boulanger, A. (2005). Open-source versus proprietary software: Is one more reliable and secure than the other? IBM Systems Journal, 44(2), 239-248
- Tiemann, Michael. "History of the OSI". Open Source Initiative. Archived from the original on 24 September 2006. Retrieved 13 May 2014
- Landry, John; Rajiv Gupta (September 2000). "Profiting from Open Source". Harvard Business Review. doi:10.1225/F00503

- Michael J. Gallivan, "Striking a Balance Between Trust and Control in a Virtual Organization: A Content Analysis of Open Source Software Case Studies", Info Systems Journal 11 (2001): 277–304
- Nelson, Russell (2007-03-26). "Certification Mark". Open Source Initiative. Archived from the original on 2008-02-06. Retrieved 2007-07-22
- Popp, Dr. Karl Michael; Meyer, Ralf (2010). Profit from Software Ecosystems: Business Models, Ecosystems and Partnerships in the Software Industry. Norderstedt, Germany: Books on Demand. ISBN 9783839169834
- Reynolds, Carl; Jeremy Wyatt (February 2011). "Open Source, Open Standards, and Health Care Information Systems". JMIR. 13: e24. doi:10.2196/jmir.1521. Retrieved 2011-03-17
- Faraj, S., Jarvenpaa, S. L., & Majchrzak, Ann (2011). Knowledge Collaboration in Online Communities. Organization Science, 22(5), 1224-1239, doi:10.1287/orsc.1100.0614

5

# Technologies used in Cloud Computing

Cloud computing uses various technologies such as data centers, distributed file system for cloud, virtual private cloud, cloud communications and virtual appliance. Data centers house computers and storage systems and telecommunication networks. Cloud computing is best understood in confluence with the major topics listed in the following chapter.

## Cloud Database

A cloud database is a database that typically runs on a cloud computing platform, access to it is provided as a service.

Database services take care of scalability and high availability of the database. Database services make the underlying software-stack transparent to the user.

### Deployment Models

There are two primary methods to run a database in a cloud:

### Virtual Machine Image

Cloud platforms allow users to purchase virtual-machine instances for a limited time, and one can run a database on such virtual machines. Users can either upload their own machine image with a database installed on it, or use ready-made machine images that already include an optimized installation of a database. For example, Oracle provides a ready-made machine image with an installation of Oracle Database 11g Enterprise Edition on Amazon EC2and on Microsoft Azure.

### Database-as-a-service (DBaaS)

With a database as a service model, application owners do not have to install and maintain the database themselves. Instead, the database service provider takes responsibility for installing and maintaining the database, and application owners are charged according to their usage of the service. For example, Amazon Web Services provides three database as a service offerings as part of its cloud portfolio: SimpleDB, a NoSQL key-value store; Amazon RDS, a relational database service that includes support for MySQL, Oracle, and more; and

DynamoDB. Microsoft offers its Azure SQL Database service on its Azure cloud service platform. Cloud computing platform Rackspace offers database as a service for MySQL and MongoDB. Database as a service providers are not limited to cloud computing platforms. For example, MongoDB as a service provider mLab allows their customers to host their databases on AWS, Azure, or Google Cloud Platform. Database vendors have also launched their own services under this model. Oracle provides its own database as a service, allowing users to access Oracle Database 11g and 12c as cloud services. MongoDB recently launched its own hosted MongoDB as a service, MongoDB Atlas.

## Architecture and Common Characteristics

- Most database services offer web-based consoles, which the end user can use to provision and configure database instances. For example, the Amazon Web Services web-console enables users to launch database instances, create snapshots (similar to backups) of databases, and monitor database statistics.
- Database services consist of a database-manager component, which controls the underlying database instances using a service API. The service API is exposed to the end user, and permits users to perform maintenance and scaling operations on their database instances. For example, the Amazon Relational Database Service's service API enables creating a database instance, modifying the resources available to a database instance, deleting a database instance, creating a snapshot (similar to a backup) of a database, and restoring a database from a snapshot.
- Underlying software-stack stack typically includes the operating system, the database and third-party software used to manage the database. The service provider (e.g. MongoLab or ObjectRocket) is responsible for installing, patching and updating the underlying software stack and ensuring the overall health and performance of the database.
- Scalability features differ between vendors – some offer auto-scaling, others enable the user to scale up using an API, but do not scale automatically. There is typically a commitment for a certain level of high availability (e.g. 99.9% or 99.99%).

## Data Model

The design and development of typical systems utilize data management and relational databases as their key building blocks. Advanced queries expressed in SQL work well with the strict relationships that are imposed on information by relational databases. However, relational database technology was not initially designed or developed for use over distributed systems. This issue has been addressed with the addition of clustering enhancements to the relational databases, although some basic tasks require complex and expensive protocols, such as with data synchronization.

Modern relational databases have shown poor performance on data-intensive systems, therefore, the idea of NoSQL has been utilized within database management systems for cloud based systems. Within NoSQL implemented storage, there are no requirements for fixed table schemas, and the use of join operations is avoided. "The NoSQL databases have proven to provide efficient horizontal scalability, good performance, and ease of assembly into cloud applications."

It is also important to differentiate between cloud databases which are relational as opposed to non-relational or NoSQL:

### SQL Databases

Such as PostgreSQL, EDB Postgres Advanced Server, NuoDB, Oracle Database, Microsoft SQL Server, MariaDB and MySQL, are one type of database which can run in the cloud, either in a virtual machine or as a service, depending on the vendor. While SQL databases are easily vertically scalable, horizontal scalability poses a challenge, that cloud database services based on SQL have started to address.

### NoSQL Databases

Such as Apache Cassandra, CouchDB and MongoDB, are another type of database which can run in the cloud. NoSQL databases are built to service heavy read/write loads and can scale up and down easily, and therefore they are more natively suited to running in the cloud.: However, most contemporary applications are built around an SQL data model, so working with NoSQL databases often requires a complete rewrite of application code.

Some SQL databases have developed NoSQL capabilities including JSON, binary JSON (e.g. BSON or similar variants), and key-value store data types. These multi-model databases include PostgreSQL and EDB Postgres Advanced Server.

A multi-model database with relational and non-relational capabilities provides a standard SQL interface to users and applications and thus facilitates the usage of such databases for contemporary applications built around an SQL data model.

## Data Center

A data center is a facility used to house computer systems and associated components, such as telecommunications and storage systems. It generally includes redundant or backup power supplies, redundant data communications connections, environmental controls (e.g., air conditioning, fire suppression) and various security devices. Large data centers are industrial scale operations using as much electricity as a small town.

An operation engineer overseeing a network operations control room of a data center

## History

Indiana University Data Center. Bloomington, Indiana

Data centers have their roots in the huge computer rooms of the early ages of the computing industry. Early computer systems, complex to operate and maintain, required a special environment in which to operate. Many cables were necessary to connect all the components, and methods to accommodate and organize these were devised such as standard racks to mount equipment, raised floors, and cable trays (installed overhead or under the elevated floor). A single mainframe required a great deal of power, and had to be cooled to avoid overheating. Security became important – computers were expensive, and were often used for military purposes. Basic design-guidelines for controlling access to the computer room were therefore devised.

During the boom of the microcomputer industry, and especially during the 1980s, users started to deploy computers everywhere, in many cases with little or no care about operating requirements. However, as information technology (IT) operations started to grow in complexity, organizations grew aware of the need to control IT resources. The advent of Unix from the early 1970s led to the subsequent proliferation of freely available Linux-compatible PC operating-systems during the 1990s. These were called "servers", as timesharing operating systems like Unix rely heavily on the client-server model to facilitate sharing unique resources between multiple users. The availability of inexpensive networking equipment, coupled with new standards for network structured cabling, made it possible to use a hierarchical design that put the servers in a specific room inside the company. The use of the term "data center", as applied to specially designed computer rooms, started to gain popular recognition about this time.

The boom of data centers came during the dot-com bubble of 1997–2000. Companies needed fast Internet connectivity and non-stop operation to deploy systems and to establish a presence on the Internet. Installing such equipment was not viable for many smaller companies. Many companies started building very large facilities, called Internet data centers (IDCs), which provide commercial clients with a range of solutions for systems deployment and operation. New technologies and practices were designed to handle the scale and the operational requirements of such large-scale operations. These practices eventually migrated toward the private data centers, and were adopted largely because of their practical results. Data centers for cloud computing are called cloud data centers (CDCs). But nowadays, the division of these terms has almost disappeared and they are being integrated into a term "data center".

With an increase in the uptake of cloud computing, business and government organizations scrutinize data centers to a higher degree in areas such as security, availability, environmental impact and adherence to standards. Standards documents from accredited professional groups, such as the Telecommunications Industry Association, specify the requirements for data-center design. Well-known operational metrics for data-center availability can serve to evaluate the commercial impact of a disruption. Development continues in operational practice, and also in environmentally-friendly data-center design. Data centers typically cost a lot to build and to maintain.

## Requirements for Modern Data Centers

Racks of telecommunications equipment in part of a data center

IT operations are a crucial aspect of most organizational operations around the world. One of the main concerns is business continuity; companies rely on their information systems to run their operations. If a system becomes unavailable, company operations may be impaired or stopped completely. It is necessary to provide a reliable infrastructure for IT operations, in order to minimize any chance of disruption. Information security is also a concern, and for this reason a data center has to offer a secure environment which minimizes the chances of a security breach. A data center must therefore keep high standards for assuring the integrity and functionality of its hosted computer environment. This is accomplished through redundancy of mechanical cooling and power systems (including emergency backup power generators) serving the data center along with fiber optic cables.

The Telecommunications Industry Association's Telecommunications Infrastructure Standard for Data Centers specifies the minimum requirements for telecommunications infrastructure of data centers and computer rooms including single tenant enterprise data centers and multi-tenant Internet hosting data centers. The topology proposed in this document is intended to be applicable to any size data center.

Telcordia GR-3160, *NEBS Requirements for Telecommunications Data Center Equipment and Spaces*, provides guidelines for data center spaces within telecommunications networks, and environmental requirements for the equipment intended for installation in those spaces. These criteria were developed jointly by Telcordia and industry representatives. They may be applied to data center spaces housing data processing or Information Technology (IT) equipment. The equipment may be used to:

- Operate and manage a carrier's telecommunication network
- Provide data center based applications directly to the carrier's customers
- Provide hosted applications for a third party to provide services to their customers
- Provide a combination of these and similar data center applications

Effective data center operation requires a balanced investment in both the facility and the housed equipment. The first step is to establish a baseline facility environment suitable for equipment installation. Standardization and modularity can yield savings and efficiencies in the design and construction of telecommunications data centers.

Standardization means integrated building and equipment engineering. Modularity has the benefits of scalability and easier growth, even when planning forecasts are less than optimal. For these reasons, telecommunications data centers should be planned in repetitive building blocks of equipment, and associated power and support (conditioning) equipment when practical. The use of dedicated centralized systems requires more accurate forecasts of future needs to prevent expensive over construction, or perhaps worse — under construction that fails to meet future needs.

The "lights-out" data center, also known as a darkened or a dark data center, is a data center that, ideally, has all but eliminated the need for direct access by personnel, except under extraordinary circumstances. Because of the lack of need for staff to enter the data center, it can be operated without lighting. All of the devices are accessed and managed by remote systems, with automation programs used to perform unattended operations. In addition to the energy savings, reduction in staffing costs and the ability to locate the site further from population centers, implementing a lights-out data center reduces the threat of malicious attacks upon the infrastructure.

There is a trend to modernize data centers in order to take advantage of the performance and energy efficiency increases of newer IT equipment and capabilities, such as cloud computing. This process is also known as data center transformation.

Organizations are experiencing rapid IT growth but their data centers are aging. Industry research company International Data Corporation (IDC) puts the average age of a data center at nine years old. Gartner, another research company says data centers older than seven years are obsolete.

In May 2011, data center research organization Uptime Institute reported that 36 percent of the large companies it surveyed expect to exhaust IT capacity within the next 18 months.

Data center transformation takes a step-by-step approach through integrated projects carried out over time. This differs from a traditional method of data center upgrades that takes a serial and siloed approach. The typical projects within a data center transformation initiative include standardization/consolidation, virtualization, automation and security.

- Standardization/consolidation: The purpose of this project is to reduce the number of data centers a large organization may have. This project also helps to reduce the number of hardware, software platforms, tools and processes within a data center. Organizations replace aging data center equipment with newer ones that provide increased capacity and performance. Computing, networking and management platforms are standardized so they are easier to manage.

- Virtualize: There is a trend to use IT virtualization technologies to replace or consolidate multiple data center equipment, such as servers. Virtualization helps to lower capital and operational expenses, and reduce energy consumption. Virtualization technologies are also used to create virtual desktops, which can then be hosted in data centers and rented out on a subscription basis. Data released by investment bank Lazard Capital Markets reports that 48 percent of enterprise operations will be virtualized by 2012. Gartner views virtualization as a catalyst for modernization.

- Automating: Data center automation involves automating tasks such as provisioning, configuration, patching, release management and compliance. As enterprises suffer from few skilled IT workers, automating tasks make data centers run more efficiently.

- Securing: In modern data centers, the security of data on virtual systems is integrated with existing security of physical infrastructures. The security of a modern data center must take into account physical security, network security, and data and user security.

## Carrier Neutrality

Today many data centers are run by Internet service providers solely for the purpose of hosting their own and third party servers.

However traditionally data centers were either built for the sole use of one large company, or as carrier hotels or Network-neutral data centers.

These facilities enable interconnection of carriers and act as regional fiber hubs serving local business in addition to hosting content servers.

## Data Center Levels and Tiers

The Telecommunications Industry Association is a trade association accredited by ANSI (American National Standards Institute). In 2005 it published ANSI/TIA-942, Telecommunications Infrastructure Standard for Data Centers, which defined four levels of data centers in a thorough, quantifiable manner. TIA-942 was amended in 2008 and again in 2010 and 2014. *TIA-942:Data Center Standards Overview* describes the requirements for the data center infrastructure. The simplest is a Level 1 data center, which is basically a server room, following basic guidelines for the installation of computer systems. The most stringent level is a Level 4 data center, which is designed to host the most mission critical computer systems, with fully redundant subsystems, the ability to continuously operate for an indefinite period of time during primary power outages.

The Uptime Institute, a data center research and professional-services organization based in Seattle,WA defined what is commonly referred to today as "Tiers" or more accurately, the "Tier Standard". Uptime's Tier Standard levels describe the availability of data processing from the hardware at a location. The higher the Tier level, the greater the expected availability. The Uptime Institute Tier Standards are shown below.

For the 2014 TIA-942 revision, the TIA organization and Uptime Institute mutually agreed that TIA would remove any use of the word "Tier" from their published TIA-942 specifications, reserving that terminology to be solely used by Uptime Institute to describe it's system.

Other classifications exist as well. For instance the German Datacenter Star Audit program uses an auditing process to certify 5 levels of "gratification" that affect Data Center criticality.

Uptime Institute's Tier Standards:

| Tier Level | Requirements |
|---|---|
| I | • Single non-redundant distribution path serving the critical loads<br>• Non-redundant critical capacity components |

| | |
|---|---|
| II | • Meets all Tier I requirements, in addition to:<br>• Redundant critical capacity components<br>• Critical capacity components must be able to be isolated and removed from service while still providing N capacity to the critical loads. |
| III | • Meets all Tier II requirements in addition to:<br>• Multiple independent distinct distribution paths serving the IT equipment critical loads<br>• All IT equipment must be dual-powered provided with two redundant, distinct UPS feeders. Single corded IT devices must use a Point of Use Transfer Switch to allow the device to receive power from and select between the two UPS feeders.<br>• Each and every critical capacity component, distribution path, and component of any critical system must be able to be fully compatible with the topology of a site's architecture isolated for planned events (replacement, maintenance, or upgrade) while still providing N capacity to the critical loads.<br>• Onsite energy production systems (such as engine generator systems) must not have runtime limitations at the site conditions and design load. |
| IV | • Meets all Tier III requirements in addition to:<br>• Multiple independent distinct and active distribution paths serving the critical loads<br>• Compartmentalization of critical capacity components and distribution paths<br>• Critical systems must be able to autonomously provide N capacity to the critical loads after any single fault or failure<br>• Continuous Cooling is required for IT and UPS systems. |

While any of the industry's data center resiliency systems were proposed at a time when availability was expressed as a theory, and a certain number of 'Nines" on the right side of the decimal point, it has generally been agreed that this approach was somewhat deceptive or too simplistic, so vendors today usually discuss availability in details that they can actually affect, and in much more specific terms. Hence, the leveling systems available today no longer define their results in percentages of uptime.

Note: The Uptime Institute also classifies the Tiers for each of the three phases of a data center, its design documents, the constructed facility, its ongoing operational sustainability

## Design Considerations

A data center can occupy one room of a building, one or more floors, or an entire building. Most of the equipment is often in the form of servers mounted in 19 inch rack cabinets, which are usually placed in single rows forming corridors (so-called aisles) between them. This allows people access to the front and rear of each cabinet. Servers differ greatly in size from 1U servers to large freestanding storage silos which occupy many square feet of floor space. Some equipment such as mainframe computers and storage devices are often as big as the racks themselves, and are placed alongside them. Very large data centers may use shipping containers packed with 1,000 or more servers each; when repairs or upgrades are needed, whole containers are replaced (rather than repairing individual servers).

Local building codes may govern the minimum ceiling heights.

A typical server rack, commonly seen in colocation

## Design Programming

Design programming, also known as architectural programming, is the process of researching and making decisions to identify the scope of a design project. Other than the architecture of the building itself there are three elements to design programming for data centers: facility topology design (space planning), engineering infrastructure design (mechanical systems such as cooling and electrical systems including power) and technology infrastructure design (cable plant). Each will be influenced by performance assessments and modelling to identify gaps pertaining to the owner's performance wishes of the facility over time.

Various vendors who provide data center design services define the steps of data center design slightly differently, but all address the same basic aspects as given below.

## Modeling Criteria

Modeling criteria are used to develop future-state scenarios for space, power, cooling, and costs in the data center. The aim is to create a master plan with parameters such as number, size, location, topology, IT floor system layouts, and power and cooling technology and configurations. The purpose of this is to allow for efficient use of the existing mechanical and electrical systems and also growth in the existing data center without the need for developing new buildings and further upgrading of incoming power supply.

## Design Recommendations

Design recommendations/plans generally follow the modelling criteria phase. The optimal technology infrastructure is identified and planning criteria are developed, such as critical power capacities, overall data center power requirements using an agreed upon PUE (power utilization efficiency), mechanical cooling capacities, kilowatts per cabinet, raised floor space, and the resiliency level for the facility.

## Conceptual Design

Conceptual designs embody the design recommendations or plans and should take into account "what-if" scenarios to ensure all operational outcomes are met in order to future-proof the facility. Conceptual floor layouts should be driven by IT performance requirements as well as lifecycle costs associated with IT demand, energy efficiency, cost efficiency and availability. Future-proofing will also include expansion capabilities, often provided in modern data centers through modular designs. These allow for more raised floor space to be fitted out in the data center whilst utilising the existing major electrical plant of the facility.

## Detailed Design

Detailed design is undertaken once the appropriate conceptual design is determined, typically including a proof of concept. The detailed design phase should include the detailed architectural, structural, mechanical and electrical information and specification of the facility. At this stage development of facility schematics and construction documents as well as schematics and performance specification and specific detailing of all technology infrastructure, detailed IT infrastructure design and IT infrastructure documentation are produced.

## Mechanical Engineering Infrastructure Designs

CRAC Air Handler

Mechanical engineering infrastructure design addresses mechanical systems involved in maintaining the interior environment of a data center, such as heating, ventilation and air conditioning (HVAC); humidification and dehumidification equipment; pressurization; and so on. This stage of the design process should be aimed at saving space and costs, while ensuring business and reliability objectives are met as well as achieving PUE and green requirements. Modern designs include modularizing and scaling IT loads, and making sure capital spending on the building construction is optimized.

## Electrical Engineering Infrastructure Design

Electrical Engineering infrastructure design is focused on designing electrical configurations that accommodate various reliability requirements and data center sizes. Aspects may include utility service planning; distribution, switching and bypass from power sources; uninterruptable power source (UPS) systems; and more.

These designs should dovetail to energy standards and best practices while also meeting business objectives. Electrical configurations should be optimized and operationally compatible with the data center user's capabilities. Modern electrical design is modular and scalable, and is available for low and medium voltage requirements as well as DC (direct current).

## Technology Infrastructure Design

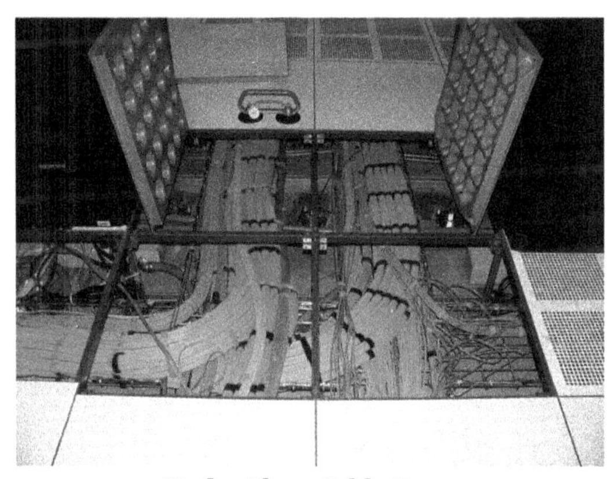

Under Floor Cable Runs

Technology infrastructure design addresses the telecommunications cabling systems that run throughout data centers. There are cabling systems for all data center environments, including horizontal cabling, voice, modem, and facsimile telecommunications services, premises switching equipment, computer and telecommunications management connections, keyboard/video/mouse connections and data communications. Wide area, local area, and storage area networks should link with other building signaling systems (e.g. fire, security, power, HVAC, EMS).

## Availability Expectations

The higher the availability needs of a data center, the higher the capital and operational costs of building and managing it. Business needs should dictate the level of availability required and should be evaluated based on characterization of the criticality of IT systems estimated cost analyses from modeled scenarios. In other words, how can an appropriate level of availability best be met by design criteria to avoid financial and operational risks as a result of downtime? If the estimated cost of downtime within a specified time unit exceeds the amortized capital costs and operational expenses, a higher level of availability should be factored into the data center design. If the cost of avoiding downtime greatly exceeds the cost of downtime itself, a lower level of availability should be factored into the design.

## Site Selection

Aspects such as proximity to available power grids, telecommunications infrastructure, networking services, transportation lines and emergency services can affect costs, risk, security and other factors to be taken into consideration for data center design. Whilst a wide array of location factors are taken into account (e.g. flight paths, neighbouring uses, geological risks) access to suitable available power is often the longest lead time item. Location affects data center design also because the climatic conditions dictate what cooling technologies should be deployed. In turn this impacts uptime and the costs associated with cooling. For example, the topology and the cost of managing a data center in a warm, humid climate will vary greatly from managing one in a cool, dry climate.

## Modularity and Flexibility

Cabinet aisle in a data center

Modularity and flexibility are key elements in allowing for a data center to grow and change over time. Data center modules are pre-engineered, standardized building blocks that can be easily configured and moved as needed.

A modular data center may consist of data center equipment contained within shipping containers or similar portable containers. But it can also be described as a design style in which components of the data center are prefabricated and standardized so that they can be constructed, moved or added to quickly as needs change.

## Environmental Control

The physical environment of a data center is rigorously controlled. Air conditioning is used to control the temperature and humidity in the data center. ASHRAE's "Thermal Guidelines for Data Processing Environments" recommends a temperature range of 18–27 °C (64–81 °F), a dew point range of −9 to 15 °C (16 to 59 °F), and ideal relative humidity of 60%, with an allowable range of 40% to 60% for data center environments. The temperature in a data center will naturally rise because the electrical power used heats the air. Unless the heat is removed, the ambient temperature will rise, resulting in electronic equipment malfunction. By controlling the air temperature, the server components at the board level are kept within the manufacturer's specified temperature/ humidity range. Air conditioning systems help control humidity by cooling the return space air below the dew point. Too much humidity, and water may begin to condense on internal components. In case of a dry atmosphere, ancillary humidification systems may add water vapor if the humidity is too low, which can result in static electricity discharge problems which may damage components. Subterranean data centers may keep computer equipment cool while expending less energy than conventional designs.

Modern data centers try to use economizer cooling, where they use outside air to keep the data center cool. At least one data center (located in Upstate New York) will cool servers using outside air during the winter. They do not use chillers/air conditioners, which creates potential energy savings in the millions. Increasingly indirect air cooling is being deployed in data centers globally which has the advantage of more efficient cooling which lowers power consumption costs in the data center. Many newly constructed data centers are also using Indirect Evaporative Cooling (IDEC) units as well as other environmental features such as sea water to minimize the amount of energy needed to cool the space.

Telcordia GR-2930, *NEBS: Raised Floor Generic Requirements for Network and Data Centers*, presents generic engineering requirements for raised floors that fall within the strict NEBS guidelines.

There are many types of commercially available floors that offer a wide range of structural strength and loading capabilities, depending on component construction and the materials used. The general types of raised floors include stringer, stringerless, and structural platforms, all of which are discussed in detail in GR-2930 and summarized below.

- *Stringered raised floors* - This type of raised floor generally consists of a vertical array of steel pedestal assemblies (each assembly is made up of a steel base plate, tubular upright, and a head) uniformly spaced on two-foot centers and mechanically fastened to the concrete floor. The steel pedestal head has a stud that is inserted into the pedestal upright and the overall height is adjustable with a leveling nut on the welded stud of the pedestal head.

- *Stringerless raised floors* - One non-earthquake type of raised floor generally consists of an array of pedestals that provide the necessary height for routing cables and also serve to support each corner of the floor panels. With this type of floor, there may or may not be provisioning to mechanically fasten the floor panels to the pedestals. This stringerless type of system (having no mechanical attachments between the pedestal heads) provides maximum accessibility to the space under the floor. However, stringerless floors are significantly weaker than stringered raised floors in supporting lateral loads and are not recommended.
- *Structural platforms* - One type of structural platform consists of members constructed of steel angles or channels that are welded or bolted together to form an integrated platform for supporting equipment. This design permits equipment to be fastened directly to the platform without the need for toggle bars or supplemental bracing. Structural platforms may or may not contain panels or stringers.

Data centers typically have raised flooring made up of 60 cm (2 ft) removable square tiles. The trend is towards 80–100 cm (31–39 in) void to cater for better and uniform air distribution. These provide a plenum for air to circulate below the floor, as part of the air conditioning system, as well as providing space for power cabling.

## Metal Whiskers

Raised floors and other metal structures such as cable trays and ventilation ducts have caused many problems with zinc whiskers in the past, and likely are still present in many data centers. This happens when microscopic metallic filaments form on metals such as zinc or tin that protect many metal structures and electronic components from corrosion. Maintenance on a raised floor or installing of cable etc. can dislodge the whiskers, which enter the airflow and may short circuit server components or power supplies, sometimes through a high current metal vapor plasma arc. This phenomenon is not unique to data centers, and has also caused catastrophic failures of satellites and military hardware.

## Electrical Power

Backup power consists of one or more uninterruptible power supplies, battery banks, and/or diesel / gas turbine generators.

To prevent single points of failure, all elements of the electrical systems, including backup systems, are typically fully duplicated, and critical servers are connected to both the “A-side” and “B-side” power feeds. This arrangement is often made to achieve N+1 redundancy in the systems. Static transfer switches are sometimes used to ensure instantaneous switchover from one supply to the other in the event of a power failure.

A bank of batteries in a large data center, used to provide power until diesel generators can start

## Low-voltage Cable Routing

Data cabling is typically routed through overhead cable trays in modern data centers. But some are still recommending under raised floor cabling for security reasons and to consider the addition of cooling systems above the racks in case this enhancement is necessary. Smaller/less expensive data centers without raised flooring may use anti-static tiles for a flooring surface. Computer cabinets are often organized into a hot aisle arrangement to maximize airflow efficiency.

## Fire Protection

FM200 Fire Suppression Tanks

Data centers feature fire protection systems, including passive and Active Design elements, as well as implementation of fire prevention programs in operations. Smoke detectors are usually installed to provide early warning of a fire at its incipient stage. This allows investigation, interruption of power, and manual fire suppression using hand held fire extinguishers before the fire grows to a large size. An active fire protection system, such as a fire sprinkler system or a clean agent fire suppression gaseous system, is often provided to control a full scale fire if it develops. High sensitivity smoke detectors, such as aspirating smoke detectors, activating clean agent fire suppression gaseous systems activate earlier than fire sprinklers.

- Sprinklers = structure protection and building life safety.
- Clean agents = business continuity and asset protection.
- No water = no collateral damage or clean up.

Passive fire protection elements include the installation of fire walls around the data center, so a fire can be restricted to a portion of the facility for a limited time in the event of the failure of the active fire protection systems. Fire wall penetrations into the server room, such as cable penetrations, coolant line penetrations and air ducts, must be provided with fire rated penetration assemblies, such as fire stopping.

## Security

Physical security also plays a large role with data centers. Physical access to the site is usually restricted to selected personnel, with controls including a layered security system often starting with fencing, bollards and mantraps. Video camera surveillance and permanent security guards are almost always present if the data center is large or contains sensitive information on any of the systems within. The use of finger print recognition mantraps is starting to be commonplace.

## Energy use

Google Data Center, The Dalles, Oregon

Energy use is a central issue for data centers. Power draw for data centers ranges from a few kW for a rack of servers in a closet to several tens of MW for large facilities. Some facilities have power densities more than 100 times that of a typical office building. For higher power density facilities, electricity costs are a dominant operating expense and account for over 10% of the total cost of ownership (TCO) of a data center. By 2012 the cost of power for the data center is expected to exceed the cost of the original capital investment.

## Greenhouse Gas Emissions

In 2007 the entire information and communication technologies or ICT sector was estimated to be responsible for roughly 2% of global carbon emissions with data centers accounting for 14% of the ICT footprint. The US EPA estimates that servers and data centers are responsible for up to 1.5% of the total US electricity consumption, or roughly.5% of US GHG emissions, for 2007. Given a business as usual scenario greenhouse gas emissions from data centers is projected to more than double from 2007 levels by 2020.

Siting is one of the factors that affect the energy consumption and environmental effects of a datacenter. In areas where climate favors cooling and lots of renewable electricity is available the environmental effects will be more moderate. Thus countries with favorable conditions, such as: Canada, Finland, Sweden, Norway and Switzerland, are trying to attract cloud computing data centers.

In an 18-month investigation by scholars at Rice University's Baker Institute for Public Policy in Houston and the Institute for Sustainable and Applied Infodynamics in Singapore, data center-related emissions will more than triple by 2020.

## Energy Efficiency

The most commonly used metric to determine the energy efficiency of a data center is power usage effectiveness, or PUE. This simple ratio is the total power entering the data center divided by the power used by the IT equipment.

$$\text{PUE} = \frac{\text{Total Facility Power}}{\text{IT Equipment Power}}$$

Total facility power consists of power used by IT equipment plus any overhead power consumed by anything that is not considered a computing or data communication device (i.e. cooling, lighting, etc.). An ideal PUE is 1.0 for the hypothetical situation of zero overhead power. The average data center in the US has a PUE of 2.0, meaning that the facility uses two watts of total power (overhead + IT equipment) for every watt delivered to IT equipment. State-of-the-art data center energy efficiency is estimated to be roughly 1.2. Some large data center operators like Microsoft and Yahoo! have published projections of PUE for facilities in development; Google publishes quarterly actual efficiency performance from data centers in operation.

The U.S. Environmental Protection Agency has an Energy Star rating for standalone or large data centers. To qualify for the ecolabel, a data center must be within the top quartile of energy efficiency of all reported facilities.

European Union also has a similar initiative: EU Code of Conduct for Data Centres

## Energy use Analysis

Often, the first step toward curbing energy use in a data center is to understand how energy is being used in the data center. Multiple types of analysis exist to measure data center energy use. Aspects measured include not just energy used by IT equipment itself, but also by the data center facility equipment, such as chillers and fans.

## Power and Cooling Analysis

Power is the largest recurring cost to the user of a data center. A power and cooling analysis, also referred to as a thermal assessment, measures the relative temperatures in specific areas as well as the capacity of the cooling systems to handle specific ambient temperatures. A power and cooling analysis can help to identify hot spots, over-cooled areas that can handle greater power use density, the breakpoint of equipment loading, the effectiveness of a raised-floor strategy, and optimal equipment positioning (such as AC units) to balance temperatures across the data center. Power cooling density is a measure of how much square footage the center can cool at maximum capacity.

## Energy Efficiency Analysis

An energy efficiency analysis measures the energy use of data center IT and facilities equipment. A typical energy efficiency analysis measures factors such as a data center's power use effectiveness (PUE) against industry standards, identifies mechanical and electrical sources of inefficiency, and identifies air-management metrics.

## Computational Fluid Dynamics (CFD) Analysis

This type of analysis uses sophisticated tools and techniques to understand the unique thermal conditions present in each data center—predicting the temperature, airflow, and pressure behavior of a data center to assess performance and energy consumption, using numerical modeling. By predicting the effects of these environmental conditions, CFD analysis in the data center can be used to predict the impact of high-density racks mixed with low-density racks and the onward impact on cooling resources, poor infrastructure management practices and AC failure of AC shutdown for scheduled maintenance.

## Thermal Zone Mapping

Thermal zone mapping uses sensors and computer modeling to create a three-dimensional image of the hot and cool zones in a data center.

This information can help to identify optimal positioning of data center equipment. For example, critical servers might be placed in a cool zone that is serviced by redundant AC units.

## Green Data Centers

This water-cooled data center in the Port of Strasbourg, France claims the attribute *green*.

Data centers use a lot of power, consumed by two main usages: the power required to run the actual equipment and then the power required to cool the equipment. The first category is addressed by designing computers and storage systems that are increasingly power-efficient. To bring down cooling costs data center designers try to use natural ways to cool the equipment. Many data centers are located near good fiber connectivity, power grid connections and also people-concentrations to manage the equipment, but there are also circumstances where the data center can be miles away from the users and don't need a lot of local management. Examples of this are the 'mass' data centers like Google or Facebook: these DC's are built around many standardized servers and storage-arrays and the actual users of the systems are located all around the world. After the initial build of a data center staff numbers required to keep it running are often relatively low: especially data centers that provide mass-storage or computing power which don't need to be near population centers.Data centers in arctic locations where outside air provides all cooling are getting more popular as cooling and electricity are the two main variable cost components.

## Network Infrastructure

An example of "rack mounted" servers

Communications in data centers today are most often based on networks running the IP protocol suite. Data centers contain a set of routers and switches that transport traffic between the servers and to the outside world. Redundancy of the Internet connection is often provided by using two or more upstream service providers.

Some of the servers at the data center are used for running the basic Internet and intranet services needed by internal users in the organization, e.g., e-mail servers, proxy servers, and DNS servers.

Network security elements are also usually deployed: firewalls, VPN gateways, intrusion detection systems, etc. Also common are monitoring systems for the network and some of the applications. Additional off site monitoring systems are also typical, in case of a failure of communications inside the data center.

## Data Center Infrastructure Management

Data center infrastructure management (DCIM) is the integration of information technology (IT) and facility management disciplines to centralize monitoring, management and intelligent capacity planning of a data center's critical systems. Achieved through the implementation of specialized software, hardware and sensors, DCIM enables common, real-time monitoring and management platform for all interdependent systems across IT and facility infrastructures.

Depending on the type of implementation, DCIM products can help data center managers identify and eliminate sources of risk to increase availability of critical IT systems. DCIM products also can be used to identify interdependencies between facility and IT infrastructures to alert the facility manager to gaps in system redundancy, and provide dynamic, holistic benchmarks on power consumption and efficiency to measure the effectiveness of "green IT" initiatives.

It's important to measure and understand data center efficiency metrics. A lot of the discussion in this area has focused on energy issues, but other metrics beyond the PUE can give a more detailed picture of the data center operations. Server, storage, and staff utilization metrics can contribute to a more complete view of an enterprise data center. In many cases, disc capacity goes unused and in many instances the organizations run their servers at 20% utilization or less. More effective automation tools can also improve the number of servers or virtual machines that a single admin can handle.

DCIM providers are increasingly linking with computational fluid dynamics providers to predict complex airflow patterns in the data center. The CFD component is necessary to quantify the impact of planned future changes on cooling resilience, capacity and efficiency.

## Managing the Capacity of a Data Center

Several parameters may limit the capacity of a data center. For long term usage, the main limitations will be available area, then available power. In the first stage of its life cycle, a data center will see its occupied space growing more rapidly than consumed energy. With constant densification of new IT technologies, the need in energy is going to become dominant, equaling then overcoming the need in area (second then third phase of cycle). The development and multiplication of connected objects, the needs in storage and data treatment lead to the necessity of data centers to grow more and more rapidly. It is therefore important to define a data center strategy before being cornered. The decision, conception and building cycle lasts several years. Therefore, it is imperative to initiate this strategic consideration when the data center reaches about 50% of its power capacity. Maximum occupation of a data center needs to be stabilized around 85%, be it in power or occupied area. Resources thus managed will allow a rotation zone for managing hardware replacement and will allow temporary cohabitation of old and new generations. In the case where this limit would be overcrossed durably, it would not be possible to proceed to material replacements, which would invariably lead to smothering the information system. The data center is a resource in its own right of the information system, with its own constraints of time and management (life span of 25 years), it therefore needs to be taken into consideration in the framework of the SI midterm planning (between 3 and 5 years).

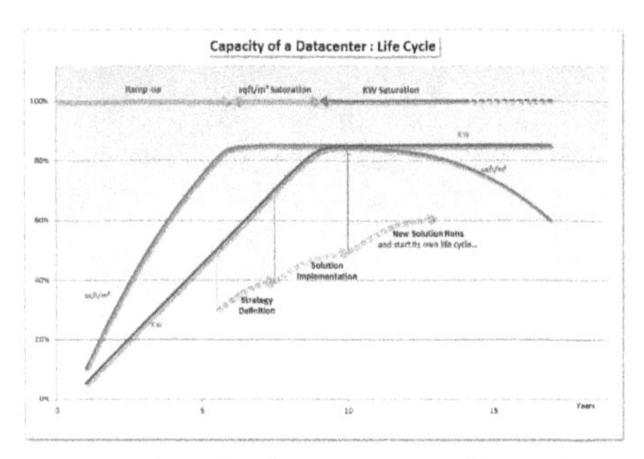


Capacity of a datacenter - Life Cycle

## Applications

A 40-foot Portable Modular Data Center

The main purpose of a data center is running the IT systems applications that handle the core business and operational data of the organization. Such systems may be proprietary and developed internally by the organization, or bought from enterprise software vendors. Such common applications are ERP and CRM systems.

A data center may be concerned with just operations architecture or it may provide other services as well.

Often these applications will be composed of multiple hosts, each running a single component. Common components of such applications are databases, file servers, application servers, middleware, and various others.

Data centers are also used for off site backups. Companies may subscribe to backup services provided by a data center. This is often used in conjunction with backup tapes. Backups can be taken off servers locally on to tapes. However, tapes stored on site pose a security threat and are also susceptible to fire and flooding. Larger companies may also send their backups off site for added security. This can be done by backing up to a data center. Encrypted backups can be sent over the Internet to another data center where they can be stored securely.

For quick deployment or disaster recovery, several large hardware vendors have developed mobile/modular solutions that can be installed and made operational in very short time. Companies such as:

A modular data center connected to the power grid at a utility substation

- Cisco Systems,
- Sun Microsystems (Sun Modular Datacenter),
- Bull (mobull),
- IBM (Portable Modular Data Center),
- Schneider-Electric (Portable Modular Data Center),
- HP (Performance Optimized Datacenter),
- ZTE Corporation,
- Huawei (Container Data Center Solution), and
- Google (Google Modular Data Center) have developed systems that could be used for this purpose.
- BASELAYER has a patent on the software defined modular data center.

## US Wholesale and Retail Colocation Providers

According to data provided in the third quarter of 2013 by Synergy Research Group, "the scale of the wholesale colocation market in the United States is very significant relative to the retail market, with Q3 wholesale revenues reaching almost $700 million. Digital Realty Trust is the wholesale market leader, followed at a distance by DuPont Fabros." Synergy Research also described the US colocation market as the most mature and well-developed in the world, based on revenue and the continued adoption of cloud infrastructure services.

Estimates from Synergy Research Group's Q3 2013 data.

| Rank | Company name | US market share |
|---|---|---|
| 1 | Various providers | 34% |
| 2 | Equinix | 18% |
| 3 | CenturyLink-Savvis | 8% |
| 4 | SunGard | 5% |
| 5 | AT&T | 5% |
| 6 | Verizon | 5% |
| 7 | Telx | 4% |
| 8 | CyrusOne | 4% |
| 9 | Level 3 Communications | 3% |
| 10 | Internap | 2% |

# Distributed File System for Cloud

A distributed file system for cloud is a file system that allows many clients to have access to data and supports operations (create, delete, modify, read, write) on that data. Each data file may be partitioned into several parts called chunks. Each chunk may be stored on different remote machines, facilitating the parallel execution of applications. Typically, data is stored in files in a hierarchical tree, where the nodes represent directories. There are several ways to share files in a distributed architecture: each solution must be suitable for a certain type of application, depending on how complex the application is. Meanwhile, the security of the system must be ensured. Confidentiality, availability and integrity are the main keys for a secure system.

Users can share computing resources through the Internet thanks to cloud computing which is typically characterized by scalable and elastic resources – such as physical servers, applications and any services that are virtualized and allocated dynamically. Synchronization is required to make sure that all devices are up-to-date.

Distributed file systems enable many big, medium, and small enterprises to store and access their remote data as they do local data, facilitating the use of variable resources.

## Overview

### History

Today, there are many implementations of distributed file systems. The first file servers were developed by researchers in the 1970s. Sun Microsystem's Network File System became available in the 1980s. Before that, people who wanted to share files used the sneakernet method, physically transporting files on storage media from place to place. Once computer networks started to proliferate, it became obvious that the existing file systems had many limitations and were unsuitable for multi-user environments. Users initially used FTP to share files. FTP first ran on the PDP-10 at the end of 1973. Even with FTP, files needed to be copied from the source computer onto a server and then from the server onto the destination computer. Users were required to know the physical addresses of all computers involved with the file sharing.

### Supporting Techniques

Modern data centers must support large, heterogenous environments, consisting of large numbers of computers of varying capacities. Cloud computing coordinates the operation of all such systems, with techniques such as data center networking (DCN), the MapReduce framework, which supports data-intensive computing applications in parallel and distributed systems, and virtualization techniques that provide dynamic resource allocation, allowing multiple operating systems to coexist on the same physical server.

### Applications

Cloud computing provides large-scale computing thanks to its ability to provide the needed CPU and storage resources to the user with complete transparency. This makes cloud computing particularly suited to support different types of applications that require large-scale distributed processing. This data-intensive computing needs a high performance file system that can share data between virtual machines (VM).

Cloud computing dynamically allocates the needed resources, releasing them once a task is finished, requiring users to pay only for needed services, often via a service-level agreement. Cloud computing and cluster computing paradigms are becoming increasingly important to industrial data processing and scientific applications such as astronomy and physics, which frequently require the availability of large numbers of computers to carry out experiments.

## Architectures

Most distributed file systems are built on the client-server architecture, but other, decentralized, solutions exist as well.

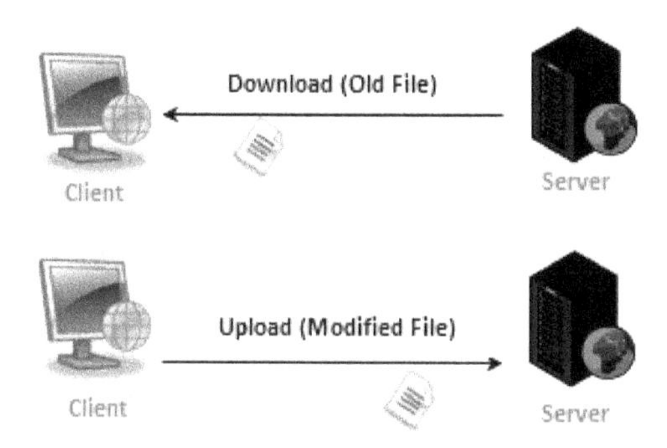


upload and download model

## Client-server Architecture

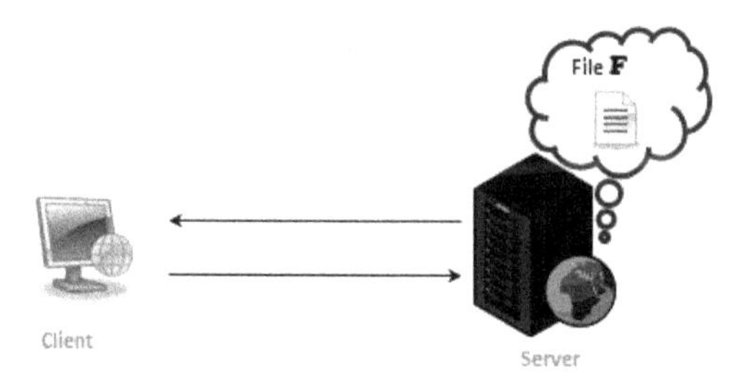


Remote access model

Network File System (NFS) uses a client-server architecture, which allows sharing files between a number of machines on a network as if they were located locally, providing a standardized view. The NFS protocol allows heterogeneous clients' processes, probably running on different machines and under different operating systems, to access files on a distant server, ignoring the actual location of files. Relying on a single server results in the NFS protocol suffering from potentially low availability and poor scalability. Using multiple servers does not solve the availability problem since each server is working independently. The model of NFS is a remote file service. This model is also called the remote access model, which is in contrast with the upload/download model:

- Remote access model: Provides transparency, the client has access to a file. He send requests to the remote file (while the file remains on the server).
- Upload/download model: The client can access the file only locally. It means that the client has to download the file, make modifications, and upload it again, to be used by others' clients.

The file system used by NFS is almost the same as the one used by Unix systems. Files are hierarchically organized into a naming graph in which directories and files are represented by nodes.

## Cluster-based Architectures

A cluster-based architecture ameliorates some of the issues in client-server architectures, improving the execution of applications in parallel. The technique used here is file-striping: a file is split into multiple chunks, which are "striped" across several storage servers. The goal is to allow access to different parts of a file in parallel. If the application does not benefit from this technique, then it would be more convenient to store different files on different servers. However, when it comes to organizing a distributed file system for large data centers, such as Amazon and Google, that offer services to web clients allowing multiple operations (reading, updating, deleting,...) to a large number of files distributed among a large number of computers, then cluster-based solutions become more beneficial. Note that having a large number of computers may mean more hardware failures. Two of the most widely used distributed file systems (DFS) of this type are the Google File System (GFS) and the Hadoop Distributed File System (HDFS). The file systems of both are implemented by user level processes running on top of a standard operating system (Linux in the case of GFS).

## Design Principles

### Goals

Google File System (GFS) and Hadoop Distributed File System (HDFS) are specifically built for handling batch processing on very large data sets. For that, the following hypotheses must be taken into account:

- High availability: the cluster can contain thousands of file servers and some of them can be down at any time.
- A server belongs to a rack, a room, a data center, a country, and a continent, in order to precisely identify its geographical location.
- The size of a file can vary from many gigabytes to many terabytes. The file system should be able to support a massive number of files.
- The need to support append operations and allow file contents to be visible even while a file is being written.
- Communication is reliable among working machines: TCP/IP is used with a remote procedure call RPC communication abstraction. TCP allows the client to know almost immediately when there is a problem and a need to make a new connection.

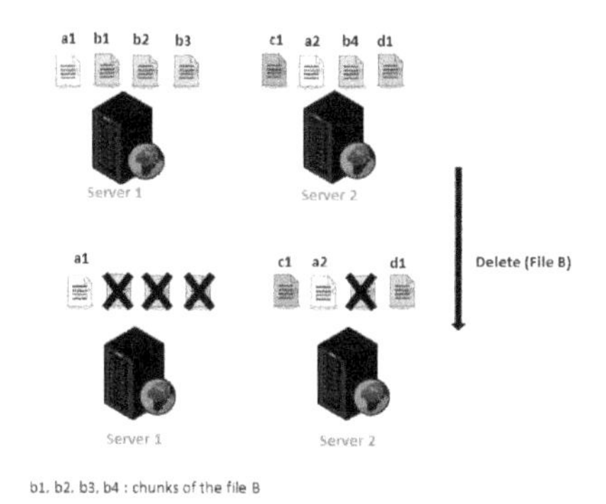


load balancing and rebalancing: Delete file

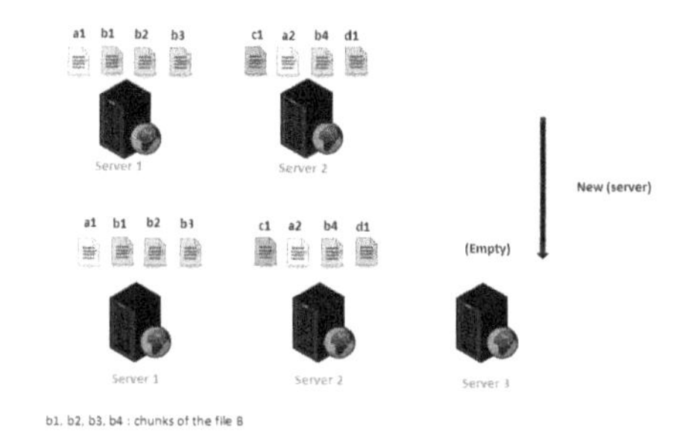


load balancing and rebalancing: New server

## Load Balancing

Load balancing is essential for efficient operation in distributed environments. It means distributing work among different servers, fairly, in order to get more work done in the same amount of time and to serve clients faster. In a system containing N chunkservers in a cloud (N being 1000, 10000, or more), where a certain number of files are stored, each file is split into several parts or chunks of fixed size (for example, 64 megabytes), the load of each chunkserver being proportional to the number of chunks hosted by the server. In a load-balanced cloud, resources can be efficiently used while maximizing the performance of MapReduce-based applications.

## Load Rebalancing

In a cloud computing environment, failure is the norm, and chunkservers may be upgraded, replaced, and added to the system. Files can also be dynamically created, deleted, and appended. That leads to load imbalance in a distributed file system, meaning that the file chunks are not distributed equitably between the servers.

Distributed file systems in clouds such as GFS and HDFS rely on central or master servers or nodes (Master for GFS and NameNode for HDFS) to manage the metadata and the load balancing. The master rebalances replicas periodically: data must be moved from one DataNode/chunkserver to another if free space on the first server falls below a certain threshold. However, this centralized approach can become a bottleneck for those master servers, if they become unable to manage a large number of file accesses, as it increases their already heavy loads. The load rebalance problem is NP-hard.

In order to get large number of chunkservers to work in collaboration, and to solve the problem of load balancing in distributed file systems, several approaches have been proposed, such as reallocating file chunks so that the chunks can be distributed as uniformly as possible while reducing the movement cost as much as possible.

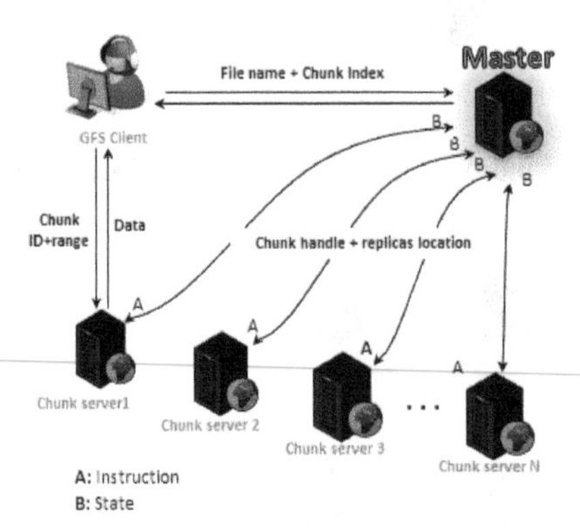


Google file system architecture

## Google File System

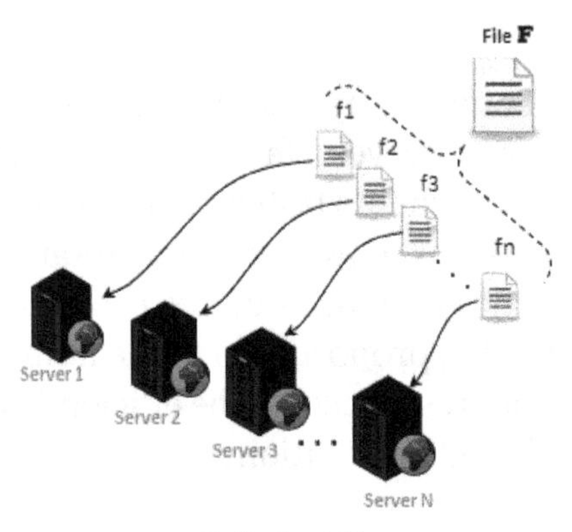


Splitting File

### Description

Google, one of the biggest internet companies, has created its own distributed file system, named Google File System (GFS), to meet the rapidly growing demands of Google's data processing needs, and it is used for all cloud services. GFS is a scalable distributed file system for data-intensive applications. It provides fault-tolerant, high-performance data storage a large number of clients accessing it simultaneously.

GFS uses MapReduce, which allows users to create programs and run them on multiple machines without thinking about parallelization and load-balancing issues. GFS architecture is based on having a single master server for multiple chunkservers and multiple clients.

The master server running in dedicated node is responsible for coordinating storage resources and managing files's metadata (the equivalent of, for example, inodes in classical file systems). Each file is split to multiple chunks of 64 megabytes. Each chunk is stored in a chunk server. A chunk is identified by a chunk handle, which is a globally unique 64-bit number that is assigned by the master when the chunk is first created.

The master maintains all of the files's metadata, including file names, directories, and the mapping of files to the list of chunks that contain each file's data. The metadata is kept in the master server's main memory, along with the mapping of files to chunks. Updates to this data are logged to an operation log on disk. This operation log is replicated onto remote machines. When the log become too large, a checkpoint is made and the main-memory data is stored in a B-tree structure to facilitate mapping back into main memory.

## Fault Tolerance

To facilitate fault tolerance, each chunk is replicated onto multiple (default, three) chunk servers. A chunk is available on at least one chunk server. The advantage of this scheme is simplicity. The master is responsible for allocating the chunk servers for each chunk and is contacted only for metadata information. For all other data, the client has to interact with the chunk servers.

The master keeps track of where a chunk is located. However, it does not attempt to maintain the chunk locations precisely but only occasionally contacts the chunk servers to see which chunks they have stored. This allows for scalability, and helps prevent bottlenecks due to increased workload.

In GFS, most files are modified by appending new data and not overwriting existing data. Once written, the files are usually only read sequentially rather than randomly, and that makes this DFS the most suitable for scenarios in which many large files are created once but read many times.

## File Processing

When a client wants to write-to/update a file, the master will assign a replica, which will be the primary replica if it is the first modification. The process of writing is composed of two steps:

- Sending: First, and by far the most important, the client contacts the master to find out which chunk servers hold the data. The client is given a list of replicas identifying the primary and secondary chunk servers. The client then contacts the nearest replica chunk server, and sends the data to it. This server will send the data to the next closest one, which then forwards it to yet another replica, and so on. The data is then propagated and cached in memory but not yet written to a file.

- Writing: When all the replicas have received the data, the client sends a write request to the primary chunk server, identifying the data that was sent in the sending phase. The primary server will then assign a sequence number to the write operations that it has received, apply the writes to the file in serial-number order, and forward the write requests in that order to the secondaries. Meanwhile, the master is kept out of the loop.

Consequently, we can differentiate two types of flows: the data flow and the control flow. Data flow is associated with the sending phase and control flow is associated to the writing phase. This assures that the primary chunk server takes control of the write order. Note that when the master assigns the write operation to a replica, it increments the chunk version number and informs all of the replicas containing that chunk of the new version number. Chunk version numbers allow for update error-detection, if a replica wasn't updated because its chunk server was down.

Some new Google applications did not work well with the 64-megabyte chunk size. To solve that problem, GFS started, in 2004, to implement the BigTable approach.

## Hadoop Distributed File System

HDFS, developed by the Apache Software Foundation, is a distributed file system designed to hold very large amounts of data (terabytes or even petabytes). Its architecture is similar to GFS, i.e. a master/slave architecture. The HDFS is normally installed on a cluster of computers. The design concept of Hadoop is informed by Google's, with Google File System, Google MapReduce and BigTable, being implemented by Hadoop Distributed File System (HDFS), Hadoop MapReduce, and Hadoop Base (HBase) respectively. Like GFS, HDFS is suited for scenarios with write-once-read-many file access, and supports file appends and truncates in lieu of random reads and writes to simplify data coherency issues.

An HDFS cluster consists of a single NameNode and several DataNode machines. The NameNode, a master server, manages and maintains the metadata of storage DataNodes in its RAM. DataNodes manage storage attached to the nodes that they run on. NameNode and DataNode are software designed to run on everyday-use machines, which typically run under a GNU/Linux OS. HDFS can be run on any machine that supports Java and therefore can run either a NameNode or the Datanode software.

On an HDFS cluster, a file is split into one or more equal-size blocks, except for the possibility of the last block being smaller. Each block is stored on multiple DataNodes, and each may be replicated on multiple DataNodes to guarantee availability. By default, each block is replicated three times, a process called "Block Level Replication".

The NameNode manages the file system namespace operations such as opening, closing, and renaming files and directories, and regulates file access. It also determines the mapping of blocks to DataNodes. The DataNodes are responsible for servicing read and write requests from the file system's clients, managing the block allocation or deletion, and replicating blocks.

When a client wants to read or write data, it contacts the NameNode and the NameNode checks where the data should be read from or written to. After that, the client has the location of the DataNode and can send read or write requests to it.

The HDFS is typically characterized by its compatibility with data rebalancing schemes. In general, managing the free space on a DataNode is very important. Data must be moved from one DataNode to another, if free space is not adequate; and in the case of creating additional replicas, data should be moved to assure system balance.

## Other Examples

Distributed file systems can be optimized for different purposes. Some, such as those designed for internet services, including GFS, are optimized for scalability. Other designs for distributed file systems support performance-ointensive applications usually executed in parallel. Some examples include: MapR File System (MapR-FS), Ceph-FS, Fraunhofer File System (BeeGFS), Lustre File System, IBM General Parallel File System (GPFS), and Parallel Virtual File System.

MapR-FS is a distributed file system that is the basis of the MapR Converged Platform, with capabilities for distributed file storage, a NoSQL database with multiple APIs, and an integrated message streaming system. MapR-FS is optimized for scalability, performance, reliability, and availability. Its file storage capability is compatible with the Apache Hadoop Distributed File System (HDFS) API but with several design characteristics that distinguish it from HDFS. Among the most notable differences are that MapR-FS is a fully read/write filesystem with metadata for files and directories distributed across the namespace, so there is no NameNode.

Ceph-FS is a distributed file system that provides excellent performance and reliability. It answers the challenges of dealing with huge files and directories, coordinating the activity of thousands of disks, providing parallel access to metadata on a massive scale, manipulating both scientific and general-purpose workloads, authenticating and encrypting on a large scale, and increasing or decreasing dynamically due to frequent device decommissioning, device failures, and cluster expansions.

BeeGFS is the high-performance parallel file system from the Fraunhofer Competence Centre for High Performance Computing. The distributed metadata architecture of BeeGFS has been designed to provide the scalability and flexibility needed to run HPC and similar applications with high I/O demands.

Lustre File System has been designed and implemented to deal with the issue of bottlenecks traditionally found in distributed systems. Lustre is characterized by its efficiency, scalability, and redundancy. GPFS was also designed with the goal of removing such bottlenecks.

## Communication

High performance of distributed file systems requires efficient communication between computing nodes and fast access to the storage systems. Operations such as open, close, read, write, send, and receive need to be fast, to ensure that performance. For example, each read or write request accesses disk storage, which introduces seek, rotational, and network latencies.

The data communication (send/receive) operations transfer data from the application buffer to the machine kernel, TCP controlling the process and being implemented in the kernel. However, in case of network congestion or errors, TCP may not send the data directly. While transferring data from a buffer in the kernel to the application, the machine does not read the byte stream from the remote machine. In fact, TCP is responsible for buffering the data for the application.

Choosing the buffer-size, for file reading and writing, or file sending and receiving, is done at the application level. The buffer is maintained using a circular linked list. It consists of a set of BufferNodes. Each BufferNode has a DataField. The DataField contains the data and a pointer called NextBufferNode that points to the next BufferNode. To find the current position, two pointers are used: CurrentBufferNode and EndBufferNode, that represent the position in the BufferNode for the last write and read positions. If the BufferNode has no free space, it will send a wait signal to the client to wait until there is available space.

## Cloud-based Synchronization of Distributed File System

More and more users have multiple devices with ad hoc connectivity. The data sets replicated on these devices need to be synchronized among an arbitrary number of servers. This is useful for backups and also for offline operation. Indeed, when user network conditions are not good, then the user device will selectively replicate a part of data that will be modified later and off-line. Once the network conditions become good, the device is synchronized. Two approaches exist to tackle the distributed synchronization issue: user-controlled peer-to-peer synchronization and cloud master-replica synchronization.

- user-controlled peer-to-peer: software such as rsync must be installed in all users' computers that contain their data. The files are synchronized by peer-to-peer synchronization where users must specify network addresses and synchronization parameters, and is thus a manual process.

- cloud master-replica synchronization: widely used by cloud services, in which a master replica is maintained in the cloud, and all updates and synchronization operations are to this master copy, offering a high level of availability and reliability in case of failures.

## Security Keys

In cloud computing, the most important security concepts are confidentiality, integrity, and availability ("CIA"). Confidentiality becomes indispensable in order to keep private data from being disclosed. Integrity ensures that data is not corrupted.

## Confidentiality

Confidentiality means that data and computation tasks are confidential: neither cloud provider nor other clients can access the client's data. Much research has been done about confidentiality, because it is one of the crucial points that still presents challenges for cloud computing. A lack of trust in the cloud providers is also a related issue. The infrastructure of the cloud must ensure that customers' data will not be accessed by unauthorized parties.

The environment becomes insecure if the service provider can do all of the following:

- locate the consumer's data in the cloud
- access and retrieve consumer's data
- understand the meaning of the data (types of data, functionalities and interfaces of the application and format of the data).

The geographic location of data helps determine privacy and confidentiality. The location of clients should be taken into account. For example, clients in Europe won't be interested in using datacenters located in United States, because that affects the guarantee of the confidentiality of data. In order to deal with that problem, some cloud computing vendors have included the geographic location of the host as a parameter of the service-level agreement made with the customer, allowing users to choose themselves the locations of the servers that will host their data.

Another approach to confidentiality involves data encryption. Otherwise, there will be serious risk of unauthorized use. A variety of solutions exists, such as encrypting only sensitive data, and supporting only some operations, in order to simplify computation. Furthermore, cryptographic techniques and tools as FHE, are used to preserve privacy in the cloud.

## Integrity

Integrity in cloud computing implies data integrity as well as computing integrity. Such integrity means that data has to be stored correctly on cloud servers and, in case of failures or incorrect computing, that problems have to be detected.

Data integrity can be affected by malicious events or from administration errors (e.g. during backup and restore, data migration, or changing memberships in P2P systems).

Integrity is easy to achieve using cryptography (typically through message-authentication code, or MACs, on data blocks).

There exist checking mechanisms that effect data integrity. For instance:

- HAIL (High-Availability and Integrity Layer) is a distributed cryptographic system that allows a set of servers to prove to a client that a stored file is intact and retrievable.
- Hach PORs (proofs of retrievability for large files) is based on a symmetric cryptographic system, where there is only one verification key that must be stored in a file to improve its integrity. This method serves to encrypt a file F and then generate a random string named "sentinel" that must be added at the end of the encrypted file. The server cannot locate the sentinel, which is impossible differentiate from other blocks, so a small change would indicate whether the file has been changed or not.
- PDP (provable data possession) checking is a class of efficient and practical methods that provide an efficient way to check data integrity on untrusted servers:
    - PDP: Before storing the data on a server, the client must store, locally, some meta-data. At a later time, and without downloading data, the client is able to ask the server to check that the data has not been falsified. This approach is used for static data.
    - Scalable PDP: This approach is premised upon a symmetric-key, which is more efficient than public-key encryption. It supports some dynamic operations (modification, deletion, and append) but it cannot be used for public verification.
    - Dynamic PDP: This approach extends the PDP model to support several update operations such as append, insert, modify, and delete, which is well suited for intensive computation.

### Availability

Availability is generally effected by replication. Meanwhile, consistency must be guaranteed. However, consistency and availability cannot be achieved at the same time; each is prioritized at some sacrifice of the other. A balance must be struck.

Data must have an identity to be accessible. For instance, Skute is a mechanism based on key/value storage that allows dynamic data allocation in an efficient way. Each server must be identified by a label in the form continent-country-datacenter-room-rack-server. The server can reference multiple virtual nodes, with each node having a selection of data (or multiple partitions of multiple data). Each piece of data is identified by a key space which is generated by a one-way cryptographic hash function (e.g. MD5) and is localised by the hash function value of this key. The key space may be partitioned into multiple partitions with each partition referring to a piece of data. To perform replication, virtual nodes must be replicated and referenced by other servers. To maximize data durability and data availability, the replicas must be placed on different servers and every server should be in a different geographical location, because data availability increases with geographical diversity. The process of replication includes an evaluation of space availability, which must be above a certain minimum thresh-hold on each chunk server. Otherwise, data are replicated to another chunk server. Each partition, i, has an availability value represented by the following formula:

$$\mathrm{avail}_i = \sum_{i=0}^{|s_i|} \sum_{j=i+1}^{|s_i|} \mathrm{conf}_i.\mathrm{conf}_j.\mathrm{diversity}(s_i, s_j)$$

where $s_i$ are the servers hosting the replicas, $\mathrm{conf}_i$ and $\mathrm{conf}_j$ are the confidence of servers $i$ and $j$ (relying on technical factors such as hardware components and non-technical ones like the economic and political situation of a country) and the diversity is the geographical distance between $s_i$ and $s_j$.

Replication is a great solution to ensure data availability, but it costs too much in terms of memory space. DiskReduce is a modified version of HDFS that's based on RAID technology (RAID-5 and RAID-6) and allows asynchronous encoding of replicated data. Indeed, there is a background process which looks for widely replicated data and deletes extra copies after encoding it. Another approach is to replace replication with erasure coding. In addition, to ensure data availability there are many approaches that allow for data recovery. In fact, data must be coded, and if it is lost, it can be recovered from fragments which were constructed during the coding phase. Some other approaches that apply different mechanisms to guarantee availability are: Reed-Solomon code of Microsoft Azure and RaidNode for HDFS. Also Google is still working on a new approach based on an erasure-coding mechanism.

There is no RAID implementation for cloud storage.

## Economic Aspects

The cloud computing economy is growing rapidly. The US government has decided to spend 40% of its compound annual growth rate (CAGR), expected to be 7 billion dollars by 2015.

More and more companies have been utilizing cloud computing to manage the massive amount of data and to overcome the lack of storage capacity, and because it enables them to use such resources as a service, ensuring that their computing needs will be met without having to invest in infrastructure (Pay-as-you-go model).

Every application provider has to periodically pay the cost of each server where replicas of data are stored. The cost of a server is determined by the quality of the hardware, the storage capacities, and its query-processing and communication overhead. Cloud computing allows providers to scale their services according to client demands.

The pay-as-you-go model has also eased the burden on startup companies that wish to benefit from compute-intensive business. Cloud computing also offers an opportunity to many third-world countries that wouldn't have such computing resources otherwise. Cloud computing can lower IT barriers to innovation.

Despite the wide utilization of cloud computing, efficient sharing of large volumes of data in an untrusted cloud is still a challenge.

## Virtual Appliance

A virtual appliance is a pre-configured virtual machine image, ready to run on a hypervisor; virtual appliances are a subset of the broader class of software appliances. Installation of a software appliance on a virtual machine and packaging that into an image creates a virtual appliance. Like software appliances, virtual appliances are intended to eliminate the installation, configuration and maintenance costs associated with running complex stacks of software.

A virtual appliance is not a complete virtual machine platform, but rather a software image containing a software stack designed to run on a virtual machine platform which may be a Type 1 or Type 2 hypervisor. Like a physical computer, a hypervisor is merely a platform for running an operating system environment and does not provide application software itself.

Many virtual appliances provide a Web page user interface to permit their configuration. A virtual appliance is usually built to host a single application; it therefore represents a new way to deploy applications on a network.

### File Formats

Virtual appliances are provided to the user or customer as files, via either electronic downloads or physical distribution. The file format most commonly used is the Open Virtualization Format (OVF). The Distributed Management Task Force (DMTF) publishes the OVF specification documentation. Most virtualization vendors, including VMware, Microsoft, Oracle, and Citrix, support OVF for virtual appliances.

## Grid Computing

Virtualization solves a key problem in the grid computing arena – namely, the reality that any sufficiently large grid will inevitably consist of a wide variety of heterogeneous hardware and operating system configurations. Adding virtual appliances into the picture allows for extremely rapid provisioning of grid nodes and importantly, cleanly decouples the grid operator from the grid consumer by encapsulating all knowledge of the application within the virtual appliance.

## Infrastructure as a Service

Virtual appliances are critical resources in infrastructure as a service cloud computing. The file format of the virtual appliance is the concern of the cloud provider and usually not relevant to the cloud user even though the cloud user may be the owner of the virtual appliance. However, challenges may arise with the transfer of virtual appliance ownership or transfer of virtual appliances between cloud data centers. In this case, virtual appliance copy or export/import features can be used to overcome this problem.

## Software as a Service

With the rise of virtualization as a platform for hosted services provision, virtual appliances have come to provide a direct route for traditional on-premises applications to be rapidly redeployed in a software as a service (SaaS) mode – without requiring major application re-architecture for multi-tenancy. By decoupling the hardware and operating system infrastructure provider from the application stack provider, virtual appliances allow economies of scale on the one side to be leveraged by the economy of simplicity on the other. Traditional approaches to SaaS, such as that touted by Salesforce.com, leverage shared infrastructure by forcing massive change and increased complexity on the software stack.

A concrete example of the virtual appliances approach to delivering SaaS is the Amazon Elastic Compute Cloud (EC2) – a grid of Xen hypervisor nodes coupled with the availability of pre-packaged virtual appliances in the Amazon Machine Image format. Amazon EC2 reduces the cost-barrier to the point where it becomes feasible to have each customer of a hosted SaaS solution provisioned with their own virtual appliance instance(s) rather than forcing them to share common instances. Prior to EC2, single-tenant hosted models were too expensive, leading to the failure of many early ASP offerings.

Furthermore, in contrast to the multi-tenancy approaches to SaaS, a virtual appliance can also be deployed on-premises for customers that need local network access to the running application, or have security requirements that a third-party hosting model does not meet. The underlying virtualization technology also allows for rapid movement of virtual appliances instances between physical execution environments. Traditional approaches to SaaS fix the application in place on the hosted infrastructure.

## Virtual Private Cloud

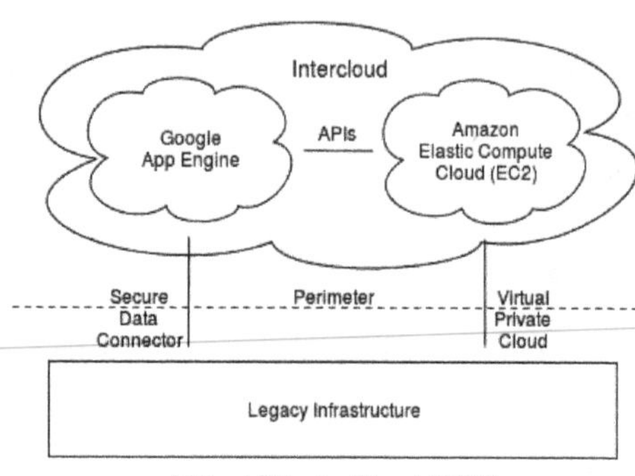


Virtual Private Cloud (VPC)

A virtual private cloud (VPC) is an on-demand configurable pool of shared computing resources allocated within a public cloud environment, providing a certain level of isolation between the different organizations (denoted as *users* hereafter) using the resources. The isolation between one VPC user and all other users of the same cloud (other VPC users as well as other public cloud users) is achieved normally through allocation of a private IP subnet and a virtual communication construct (such as a VLAN or a set of encrypted communication channels) per user. In a VPC, the previously described mechanism, providing isolation within the cloud, is accompanied with a VPN function (again, allocated per VPC user) that secures, by means of authentication and encryption, the remote access of the organization to its VPC cloud resources. With the introduction of the described isolation levels, an organization using this service is in effect working on a 'virtually private' cloud (that is, as if the cloud infrastructure is not shared with other users), and hence the name VPC.

VPC is most commonly used in the context of cloud infrastructure as a service. In this context, the infrastructure provider, providing the underlying public cloud infrastructure, and the provider realizing the VPC service over this infrastructure, may be different vendors.

### Implementations

Amazon Web Services launched Amazon Virtual Private Cloud on 26 August 2009, which allows the Amazon Elastic Compute Cloud service to be connected to legacy infrastructure over an IPsec virtual private network connection.

In AWS, VPC is free to use, however users will be charged for any virtual private networks (VPN) they use. EC2 and RDS instances running in a VPC can also be purchased using Reserved Instances, however will have a limitation on resources being guaranteed.

Google App Engine supported similar functionality via their *Secure Data Connector* product which was launched on 7 April 2009. Google deprecated this service on 14 March 2013 and no longer accepts new signups. The service is expected to continue running for existing users until (at least) 20 April 2015.

Microsoft Azure offers the possibility of setting up a VPC using Virtual Networks.

## Cloud Communications

Cloud communications are Internet-based voice and data communications where telecommunications applications, switching and storage are hosted by a third-party outside of the organization using them, and they are accessed over the public Internet. Cloud services is a broad term, referring primarily to data-center-hosted services that are run and accessed over an Internet infrastructure. Until recently, these services have been data-centric, but with the evolution of VoIP (voice over Internet protocol), voice has become part of the cloud phenomenon. Cloud telephony (also known as hosted telephony) refers specifically to voice services and more specifically the replacement of conventional business telephone equipment, such as a Private branch exchange (PBX), with third-party VoIP service.

Cloud communications providers deliver voice and data communications applications and services, hosting them on servers that the providers own and maintain, giving their customers access to the "cloud." Because they only pay for services or applications they use, customers have a more cost-effective, reliable and secure communications environment, without the headaches associated with more conventional PBX system deployment.

Companies can cut costs with cloud communications services without sacrificing features. The success of Google and others as cloud-based providers has demonstrated that a cloud-based platform can be just as effective as a software-based platform, but at a much lower cost. Voice services delivered from the cloud increases the value of hosted telephony, as users can equally well turn to a cloud-based offering instead of relying on a facilities-based service provider for hosted VoIP. This expands their options beyond local or regional carriers.

In the past, businesses have been able to do this for IT services, but not telecommunication. Cloud communications is attractive because the cloud can now become a platform for voice, data and video. Most hosted services have been built around voice, and are usually referred to as hosted VoIP. The cloud communications environment serves as a platform upon which all these modes can seamlessly work as well as integrate.

There are three trends in enterprise communications pushing users to access the cloud and allowing them to do it from any device they choose, a development traditional IT communications infrastructure was not designed to handle. The first trend is increasingly distributed company operations in branches and home offices, making wide area networks cumbersome, inefficient and costly. Second, more communications devices need access to enterprise networks – iPhones, printers and VoIP handsets, for example. Third, data centers housing enterprise IT assets and applications are consolidating and are often being located and managed remotely.

## Applications

Cloud telephony services were predominantly used for business processes, such as advertising, e-commerce, human resources, and payments processing. Services include distributed call centers and economical teleworking. The scale of services, features and functionality is expected to evolve even further in the coming years, to embrace mobilisation, facilitate more direct collaboration and streamline communications.

## Potential Advantages

For a small or medium-sized business, the capital investment to set up VoIP infrastructure in-house could be too high compared to the potential return, but cloud telephony could offer the same services on a lower-cost subscription basis. The cloud telephony provider is also an expert in the technology, whereas a small business is unlikely to have an employee with the same level of expertise, or cannot justify the expense of a full-time telecommunication infrastructure position. Traditional telephony applications required on-premises maintenance, PBX, and a great deal of wiring through a Main Distribution Frame (MDF).

Cloud communications are promoted to help businesses with collaboration, scalability and supporting access via multiple locations and devices.

## Risks

Cloud technology still must exist on physical servers, and the physical location of those servers is important under many nation's laws.

## Products

Cloud telephony companies can provide "hosted" (off-site) software versions of services that were previously constructed on-site in hardware. These can also allow the users to be more geographically distributed, since the voice traffic moves over the Internet. Examples include:

- Private branch exchange
- SIP Trunking

- Call center
- Fax services
- Interactive voice response
- Text messaging
- Voice broadcast
- Call-tracking software
- Contact center telephony

## References


- Kasacavage, Victor (2002). Complete book of remote access: connectivity and security. The Auerbach Best Practices Series. CRC Press. p. 227. ISBN 0-8493-1253-1
- "Walking the talk: Microsoft builds first major container-based data center". Archived from the original on 2008-06-12. Retrieved 2008-09-22
- Agrawal, Rakesh; et al. (2008). "The Claremont report on database research" (PDF). SIGMOD Record. ACM. 37 (3): 9–19. ISSN 0163-5808. doi:10.1145/1462571.1462573
- Burkey, Roxanne E.; Breakfield, Charles V. (2000). Designing a total data solution: technology, implementation and deployment. Auerbach Best Practices. CRC Press. p. 24. ISBN 0-8493-0893-3
- Hansen, Per Brinch (April 1970). "The nucleus of a Multiprogramming System". Communications of the ACM. 13 (4): 238–241. ISSN 0001-0782. doi:10.1145/362258.362278
- Strobl, Marius (2013). Virtualization for Reliable Embedded Systems. Munich: GRIN Publishing GmbH. p. 54,63. ISBN 978-3-656-49071-5
- Denning, Peter J. (December 1976). "Fault tolerant operating systems". ACM Computing Surveys. 8 (4): 359–389. ISSN 0360-0300. doi:10.1145/356678.356680
- Tanenbaum, Andrew S. (1979). Structured Computer Organization. Englewood Cliffs, New Jersey: Prentice-Hall. ISBN 0-13-148521-0
- Borden, T.L. et al.; Multiple Operating Systems on One Processor Complex. IBM Systems Journal, vol.28, no.1, pp. 104-123, 1989
- Kraemer, Brian (June 11, 2008). "IBM's Project Big Green Takes Second Step". ChannelWeb. Archived from the original on 2008-06-11. Retrieved 2008-05-11
- Baiardi, F.; A. Tomasi; M. Vanneschi (1988). Architettura dei Sistemi di Elaborazione, volume 1 (in Italian). Franco Angeli. ISBN 88-204-2746-X
- Roch, Benjamin (2004). "Monolithic kernel vs. Microkernel" (PDF). Archived from the original (PDF) on 2006-11-01. Retrieved 2006-10-12
- "Improving the reliability of commodity operating systems". Doi.acm.org. doi:10.1002/spe.4380201404. Retrieved 2010-06-19

# Permissions

All chapters in this book are published with permission under the Creative Commons Attribution Share Alike License or equivalent. Every chapter published in this book has been scrutinized by our experts. Their significance has been extensively debated. The topics covered herein carry significant information for a comprehensive understanding. They may even be implemented as practical applications or may be referred to as a beginning point for further studies.

We would like to thank the editorial team for lending their expertise to make the book truly unique. They have played a crucial role in the development of this book. Without their invaluable contributions this book wouldn't have been possible. They have made vital efforts to compile up to date information on the varied aspects of this subject to make this book a valuable addition to the collection of many professionals and students.

This book was conceptualized with the vision of imparting up-to-date and integrated information in this field. To ensure the same, a matchless editorial board was set up. Every individual on the board went through rigorous rounds of assessment to prove their worth. After which they invested a large part of their time researching and compiling the most relevant data for our readers.

The editorial board has been involved in producing this book since its inception. They have spent rigorous hours researching and exploring the diverse topics which have resulted in the successful publishing of this book. They have passed on their knowledge of decades through this book. To expedite this challenging task, the publisher supported the team at every step. A small team of assistant editors was also appointed to further simplify the editing procedure and attain best results for the readers.

Apart from the editorial board, the designing team has also invested a significant amount of their time in understanding the subject and creating the most relevant covers. They scrutinized every image to scout for the most suitable representation of the subject and create an appropriate cover for the book.

The publishing team has been an ardent support to the editorial, designing and production team. Their endless efforts to recruit the best for this project, has resulted in the accomplishment of this book. They are a veteran in the field of academics and their pool of knowledge is as vast as their experience in printing. Their expertise and guidance has proved useful at every step. Their uncompromising quality standards have made this book an exceptional effort. Their encouragement from time to time has been an inspiration for everyone.

The publisher and the editorial board hope that this book will prove to be a valuable piece of knowledge for students, practitioners and scholars across the globe.

# Index

**A**

Access Controllability, 38

Adoption Drivers, 141

Application Programming Interface, 49, 120, 125

Archive Storage, 56

Attack Surface Area, 51

**B**

Big Data, 158, 160

**C**

Carrier Neutrality, 179

Ciphertext-policy, 39

Cloud Clients, 11-12, 41-42

Cloud Collaboration, 17-21

Cloud Database, 129, 172, 174

Cloud Engineering, 16, 105-106, 135

Cloud Manufacturing Resources, 23

Cloud Printing, 21-22, 34

Cloud Security Controls, 36

Cloud Storage Gateway, 49, 65

Cluster-based Architectures, 198

Community Cloud, 13-14, 41

Consumer End Storage, 34

Content Caching, 61

Cooling Analysis, 190

Copyright Infringement, 53, 62, 64

Corrective Controls, 37

**D**

Data Center, 3, 13-14, 26, 33, 36, 40, 43, 46, 63, 78-79, 101, 109, 126, 128, 132, 161, 174-185, 187-194, 196, 198, 213

Data Encryption, 64, 100, 205

Data Escrow, 144

Data Recovery, 29, 40, 51, 207

Data Security, 14, 34, 38, 40, 48, 65, 142

Deployment Models, 12, 35, 109, 172

Design Programming, 181

Detective Controls, 37

Deterrent Controls, 36

Disaster Recovery, 7, 51, 78, 115, 194

Distributed Cloud, 14

Distributed File System, 94, 98, 158-160, 172, 198-200, 202-203

**E**

Effective Encryption, 39

Energy Efficiency, 33, 178, 182, 189-190

Enterprise Modules, 166

Environmental Control, 185

**F**

Fault Tolerance, 93, 201

Fibre Channel Host Bus Adapters, 94

Fibre Channel Storage Area Networks, 93

Fibre Channel Switches, 87, 93

File Hosting Service, 49, 61-62, 64

File Processing, 201

File Sync, 61, 167

Fully Homomorphic Encryption, 48

**H**

Hard Resources, 24

Hardware Virtualization, 2

Hybrid Cloud, 13-15, 23, 30, 41, 44-46, 133

Hybrid Storage, 57

**I**

Identity Management, 37

Intercloud, 15, 41, 44

**L**

Load Balancing, 75, 102, 199-200

Load Rebalancing, 199

Logical Network

Isolation, 82

Logical Unit Number, 80

Low-voltage Cable Routing, 187

**M**

Message Format, 65, 70

Message Sender, 68

Mobile Backend, 117, 137
Multicloud, 15

**N**
Network Booting, 80
Network File System, 94, 196-197
Network Infrastructure, 3, 77
Noisy Neighbors, 34

**O**
Object Storage, 9, 49-51, 53-58, 103, 131
Open Integration Protocols, 141
Open Source Initiative, 146-149, 156, 170-171
Open Standards, 127, 171
Operating Systems, 9-10, 47, 66, 78-79, 83, 95-97, 122, 127-128, 143, 147, 160, 175, 196-197, 213

**P**
Performance Interference, 34
Personal File Storage, 61
Personnel Security, 38
Physical Security, 37, 178, 188
Preventive Controls, 36
Privacy Policy, 27
Privacy Solutions, 28
Private Cloud, 7, 12-14, 16-17, 23, 32, 41, 44-45, 172, 210
Programming Languages, 9, 47, 60, 160
Proprietary Software, 120, 147, 152, 154-156, 170
Public Cloud, 5, 13-17, 19, 22-23, 26, 35-36, 41, 43, 45-46, 107-111, 210

**R**
Representational State Transfer, 72, 123
Resource Limits, 112
Rich Custom Metadata, 55

**S**
Searchable Encryption, 28, 37, 39
Security Keys, 205
Server Message Block, 96-97
Serverless Computing, 12, 110-112
Serverless Frameworks, 113
Service Models, 8-9, 25
Soft Resources, 24
Software Applications, 24, 137
Software Development Kit, 119
Software Target, 79
Storage Array, 79, 83
Storage Charges, 61
Storage Consolidation, 78
Storage Device
Standards, 59

**T**
Thermal Zone Mapping, 190
Tree Structure, 201

**U**
Unstructured Data, 54

**V**
Vendor Lock-in, 20, 30-31
Virtual Machine Image, 51, 172, 208

www.ingramcontent.com/pod-product-compliance
Lightning Source LLC
Jackson TN
JSHW052202130125
77033JS00004B/203

* 9 7 8 1 6 3 5 4 9 6 7 6 5 *